ARMED WITH
RIGHTEOUSNESS

Winning Your Battles with Satan

This is an updated version of Steven's previous
book, *Putting on the Armor of God*, with the
addition of an important new chapter.

Steven A. Cramer
Best-Selling Author

Donald Curtis

CFI
AN IMPRINT OF CEDAR FORT, INC.
SPRINGVILLE, UTAH

ISBN 978-1-4621-2170-0

Published by CFI, an imprint of Cedar Fort, Inc.
2373 W. 700 S., Springville, UT 84663
Distributed by Cedar Fort, Inc. www.cedarfort.com

Previously published as *Putting on the Armor of God*

LIBRARY OF CONGRESS CATALOGING-IN-PUBLICATION DATA

Names: Cramer, Steven A., author.
Title: Armed with righteousness : winning your battles with Satan / Steven A.
  Cramer.
Description: Springville, Utah : CFI, an imprint of Cedar Fort, Inc., [2017]
  | Includes index.
Identifiers: LCCN 2017051370 (print) | LCCN 2017052514 (ebook) | ISBN
  9781462128822 (epub, pdf, mobi) | ISBN 9781462121700 (perfect bound : alk.
  paper)
Subjects: LCSH: Christian life--Mormon authors. | Devil. | Mormons--Conduct
  of life. | Spiritual warfare.
Classification: LCC BX8656 (ebook) | LCC BX8656 .C725 2017 (print) | DDC
  248.4/89332--dc23
LC record available at https://lccn.loc.gov/2017051370

Cover design by Jeff Harvey
Cover design © 2018 Cedar Fort, Inc.
Edited and typeset by Grant S. White, Nicole Terry, and Kaitlin Barwick

Printed in the United States of America

10 9 8 7 6 5 4 3 2 1

Printed on acid-free paper

Also by

STEVEN A. CRAMER

—•—

Contents

Acknowledgments xi
Note from the Author xii
Revelations Forming This Book's Foundation xiii
Scriptural Names for Satan or the Devil xv
Preface xvii

Part One: Know Your Enemy

1: It All Began with Ego 2
Lucifer's Premortal Glory and Status 2
"Worship Me"—Lucifer's Attack on Elohim and Jehovah 4
"Worship Me"—Lucifer's Ego Led to His Fall 6
"Worship Me"—Lucifer's Attack on Our First Ancestors 7
"Worship Me"—Lucifer's Attack on Moses 8
"Worship Me"—Lucifer's Attack on Christ 10

2: War 12

3: Surrounded 18
Estimating the Size of Our Enemy's Army 18
Surrounded by the Enemy's Army 19
Joined by Mortal Traitors and Conspiring Men 21
Supported by the Lord's Army 23

4: Satanic Subliminals 26
How Satan Puts Thoughts into Our Minds 26
Scriptural Examples of Satanic Whisperings 28
Latter-day Examples of Satanic Whisperings 30
Examples of Divine Whisperings 34
The Lord Guarantees a Balance 36

5: Enemy Propaganda 40
"There Is No Devil" 40
"How to Sin and Get Away with It" 42
Counterfeits and Detours 44

6: Enemy Ridicule 47

Part Two: Determine Your Strategy

7: The Battleground of Thought 52
   A Theatrical Stage 54
   A Temple 57
   An Electromagnet 59

8: The Battleground of Prayer 62
   Satan Says "Don't Pray" 63
   Openness and Honesty 65
   Are We Worthy to Pray? 68
   The Need for Persistence 70
   Why Are Answers Delayed? 71

9: The Battleground of Temptation 75
   Everyone Is Tempted 76
   Temptations Are Necessary 77
   It Is Not a Sin to be Tempted 78
   "It Is Safe to Sin in Secret" 79
   Disguised Temptations 82
   Gradual Temptations 84
   Exploiting Our Weak Points 85
   A Protective Breastplate 86
   The Savior Understands Our Temptations 88
   Don't Battle Temptation Alone 90

10: Prisoner of War 92
   Demon Possession 93
   Prisoners to Addiction 97
   Satan Cannot Take You Prisoner by Force 100

11: The Battleground of Immorality 103
   Satan's Weapons of Necking and Petting 108
   Satan's Weapon of Pornography 111
   Satan's Weapon of Masturbation 117
   Satan's Weapon of Fornication 122
   Satan's Weapon of Adultery 125
   Satan's Weapon of Homosexuality 129
   You Are Wanted 138
   Clean Again 140

12: Strategies of Defense 142
   Don't Create Unnecessary Temptations 142
   Deciding Ahead of Time 144
   Separate Yourself from the Temptation 146

It's Not Worth It 146
Send the Devil Away 148
Defending Ourselves with the Shield of Faith 149
Deflector #1: Use Light as a Shield 150
Deflector #2: Use Prayer as a Shield 151
Deflector #3: Use Music as a Shield 152
Deflector #4: Use Scripture as a Shield 153
Deflector #5: Use Commitment to Christ as a Shield 154
Deflector #6: Use Love for God as a Shield 155
Deflector #7: Allow the Savior to Be Your Shield 156
Keeping Score 158

13: The Battleground of Repentance 162
Repentance Applies to Everyone 163
Blessed Are the Repentant 164
The Best Motivation for Repentance 165
Repentance—Stopping or Going? 166
Total Abandonment 167
Do It Now 168
Repentance Is Incomplete without Confession 170
Your Repentance Will Be Accepted 173

14: The Battleground of Change 175
Control versus Change 176
The Starting Point 178
Change Takes Time 180
It Is Never Too Late to Change 182
The Choice Is Ours 183

15: The Battleground of Memory 184

16: The Battleground of Perfectionism 189
1. "You Have to Be Perfect Right Now" 189
2. "Nothing Less Than Perfection Is Acceptable to God" 192
3. "God Cannot Love You Because You Are Imperfect" 194

Part Three: Victory through Christ

17: A Strong Foundation 200
Self-Centered or Christ-Centered? 200
Substitutes 203
Partnership with Christ 205
Risks and Guarantees 208

18: Rescued 211

19: The Power to Win 216

  God Has All Power 216

  God Is Able 217

  Beyond Any Circumstance 218

  A Modern Miracle 220

20: Putting on the Armor 222

  Spiritual Formulas 225

  The Sword of the Spirit 227

  Personalizing the Promises 229

21: Trusting the Promises 232

Part Four: Temple and Family History

22: Armed with Righteousness 240

  I. Temple Worship 240

    1. We Are Perfected 241

    2. We Are Protected 243

    3. We Are Piloted 250

    4. We Are Given Power 253

    5. We Are Given a Place 255

  II. Family History 256

  III. Conclusion 261

Epilogue 263

Part Five: Resource Materials

Appendix A 268

  Breaking the Cycle of Masturbation 268

Appendix B 273

  A Recommended Method for Making Your

    Armor Invincible 273

  Start Your 3 x 5 Arsenal with These Verses 282

Index 287

Acknowledgments

I GRATEFULLY ACKNOWLEDGE AND DEDICATE THIS BOOK TO THE hundreds of people who have helped me understand Satan's cunning and vicious devices by sharing the details of their battles with him. The similarity of their heartaches and defeats made me want to expose the enemy and help others recognize his diabolical conspiracy.

I am also indebted to the following:

To George Pace, who was responsible for putting me on the path toward Christ and making it possible to receive the grace and power to win battles I had lost for most of my life.

To Charles Beckett, for helping me let go of my bondage to past mistakes so that I could receive Christ's healing of my present ones and discover his incredible, stubborn love for us.

To Michael Ballam, who helped me visualize the enemy and strengthened my resolve to expose his tactics.

To Pay Ray, who willingly spent many, many hours in the ward library collecting the reference materials I requested, long before such things were so readily available on the Internet.

To Lyle Mortimer, who suggested this project and made it possible to share it with the readers.

To Dr. Fran Smeath, whose invaluable editorial suggestions corrected so many flaws and made the manuscript far more accessible to the reader.

Note from the Author

OF ALL THE WONDERFUL THINGS WE HAVE HEARD FROM THE Brethren since this book was first published, I found the following words from Elder Jeffrey R. Holland to be astonishingly nurturing and encouraging. I am most grateful for the opportunity to share them with you before you begin your reading of this revised edition.

First was this delightful insight, " . . . that surely the thing God enjoys most about being God is the thrill of being merciful, especially to those who don't expect it and often feel they don't deserve it."

He said: [Please note that I have separated his comments into individual lines for emphasis.]

"I do not know who in this vast audience today may need to hear the message of forgiveness . . .

"but however late you think you are,

"however many chances you think you have missed,

"however many mistakes you feel you have made or talents you think you don't have,

"or however far from home and family and God you feel you have traveled,

"I testify that you have not traveled beyond the reach of divine love.

"It is not possible for you to sink lower than the infinite light of Christ's Atonement shines.

He also said:

". . . there is nothing . . . that you have done that cannot be undone.

"There is no problem which you cannot overcome.

"There is no dream that in the unfolding of time and eternity cannot yet be realized."

(Jeffrey R. Holland, "The Laborers in the Vineyard," *Ensign*, May 2012)

Revelations Forming This Book's Foundation

Ephesians 6:10–18

FINALLY, MY BRETHREN, BE STRONG IN THE LORD, AND IN THE power of his might.

Put on the whole armour of God, that ye may be able to stand against the wiles of the devil.

For we wrestle not against flesh and blood, but against principalities, against powers, against the rulers of the darkness of this world, against spiritual wickedness in high places.

Wherefore take unto you the whole armour of God, that ye may be able to withstand in the evil day, and having done all, to stand.

Stand therefore, having your loins girt about with truth, and having on the breastplate of righteousness;

And your feet shod with the preparation of the gospel of peace;

Above all, taking the shield of faith, wherewith ye shall be able to quench all the fiery darts of the wicked.

And take the helmet of salvation, and the sword of the Spirit, which is the word of God:

Praying always with all prayer and supplication in the Spirit, and watching thereunto with all perseverance and supplication for all saints.

D&C 27:15–18

WHEREFORE, LIFT UP YOUR HEARTS AND REJOICE, AND GIRD UP your loins, and take upon you my whole armor, that ye may be able to withstand the evil day, having done all, that ye may be able to stand.

Stand, therefore, having your loins girt about with truth, having on the breastplate of righteousness, and your feet shod with the preparation of the gospel of peace, which I have sent mine angels to commit unto you;

Taking the shield of faith wherewith ye shall be able to quench all the fiery darts of the wicked;

And take the helmet of salvation, and the sword of my Spirit, which I will pour out upon you, and my word which I reveal unto you, and be agreed as touching all things whatsoever ye ask of me, and be faithful until I come, and ye shall be caught up, that where I am ye shall be also. Amen.

Scriptural Names for Satan or the Devil

Accuser	Revelation 12:10
Adversary	1 Samuel 1:6; 1 Peter 5:8
Author of all sin	Helaman 6:30
Awful monster	2 Nephi 9:19
Beelzebub	Mark 3:22
Deceiver	2 John 1 7
Demon	Bible Dictionary, p. 656
Destroyer	D&C 101:54
Devourer	1 Peter 5:8
Enemy	Matthew 13:39
Enemy to all righteousness	Mosiah 4:14; Alma 34:23
Enemy unto God	Moroni 7:12
Evil one	2 Nephi 9:23; Helaman 8:28
Evil spirit	Mosiah 2:32; 4:14
Father of contention	3 Nephi 11:29
Father of lies	2 Nephi 9:9; Moses 4:4
God of this world	2 Corinthians 4:4
Great dragon	Revelation 12:9; 20:2
Liar	D&C 93:25
Lucifer	Isaiah 14:12; D&C 76:26
Man of sin	2 Thessalonians 2:3
Master of sin	Mosiah 4:14
Murderer	John 8:44
Perdition	D&C 76:26
Prince of the devils	Mark 3:22
Prince of the power of the air	Ephesians 2:3

Prince of this world	John 12:31; 14:30
Roaring lion	1 Peter 5:8
Serpent	Revelation 12:9; Moses 4:19
Slanderer (Greek for devil)	Bible Dictionary, p. 656
Son of perdition	2 Thessalonians 2:3
Son of the morning	Isaiah 14:12; D&C 76:26
Spoiler (Hebrew for devil)	Bible Dictionary, p. 656
Tempter	Matthew 4:3
Wicked one	Matthew 13:19; D&C 93:25.

Preface

Suppose you are in a foreign country. Not being familiar with the customs, you unintentionally offend someone. You are told that you must satisfy the offense in combat with a powerful opponent. You are then ushered into a room where you face a menacing giant with bulging muscles. The contest is not fair. You are also told that the combat will be in karate. You are terrified. Not only does your opponent have the advantage physically, but you don't know the first thing about karate. Incredibly, you are then told that you will not even be allowed to see your opponent during the combat. The battle will take place only after you are blindfolded. This example suggests something of the odds between us and our powerful enemy, Satan, for as Elder M. Russell Ballard said, "The devil is a dirty fighter, and we must be aware of his tactics" (*Ensign*, November 1990, 36).

The devil has many advantages in the battle for our souls. For example, he and the evil spirits who follow him can watch us and see everything we do while they remain invisible, hidden just on the other side of the veil. Unless we learn to discern their presence and attacks, it is as though we are fighting blindfolded. You and I passed through a veil of forgetfulness when we came here. Satan did not. He remembers everything and knows each of us from the premortal existence.

> Satan drew a third of the hosts of heaven with him, and when they were cast out, that third of the hosts of heaven brought with them the knowledge that they had in the spirit world, while our knowledge was temporarily taken from us through our birth into mortality. (LeGrand Richards, *Ensign*, May 1981, 32–33)

Unlike this example, however, our battles are not with Satan alone, but also with the multitudes of spirits that support him and aid his efforts to deceive and defeat us. We are vastly outnumbered. Satan has the additional advantage of experience. We are new to this mortal experience. We are only brief visitors from another world, merely "strangers and pilgrims on the earth" (Hebrews 11:13). We are beginners in the tactics of spiritual warfare while Satan is a professional warrior. He and his army of evil spirits have been here on earth developing their combat skills for thousands of years.

Finally, our battle with Satan is not a single match but must be fought every day of our lives, for he and his demons never leave our sides. They are constantly working for our destruction day by day, night by night, around the clock and through the years. Our battles with Satan's forces will continue until the day we finish our probations. We must realize in soberness that we are engaged in a war that will determine our eternal destinies, a war that deserves every awareness and caution we can muster. It is unfortunate that many people are so preoccupied with the daily affairs and pleasures of this temporary world that they go through life as if earth were a playground instead of the battleground it really is.

President Kimball emphasized that it is important to have "an awareness of the existence, the power, and the plans of Satan" (As quoted by Elder ElRay L. Christiansen, *Ensign*, November 1974, 24). Elder Melvin J. Ballard said, "It is well to know the forces and the powers that are arrayed against us, and their purposes, that we may close our ranks and fortify ourselves" (*New Era,* March 1984, 38). And N. Eldon Tanner of the First Presidency stressed the need for parents to teach their children the reality of Satan's power:

> They must be taught that Satan is real and that he will use all agencies at his disposal to tempt them to do wrong, to lead them astray, make them his captives, and keep them from the supreme happiness and exaltation they could otherwise enjoy. (*Ensign,* July 1973, 8)

President Benson counseled that "A study of Satan's methods can alert us to his seductions" (*Ensign*, December 1971, 55). And President Marion G. Romney, in conjunction with a lengthy address on Satan's cunning devices, commented:

> I am not calling attention to these things to frighten, stampede, or discourage anyone. I refer to them because I know they are

true and I am persuaded that if we are to "conquer Satan and . . . escape the hands of the servants of Satan that do uphold his work" (D&C 10:5), we must understand and recognize the situation as it is. This is no time for Latter-day Saints to equivocate. (*Ensign*, June 1971, 36)

Even though Satan has a well-planned agenda, many people feel that if they ignore the reality of the devil and avoid thinking of him, they will somehow be protected from his influence. Precisely the opposite is true. It is difficult, if not impossible, to conquer an enemy we do not recognize, understand, or respect. The less we believe in Satan, and the less we recognize his "cunning devices," the more power he will have over us. Jesus said that *knowledge* of gospel truths can make us free (see John 8:32). In the same way, *ignorance* of Satan and his powers can make us slaves, captives, and prisoners of war, bound in his very chains of hell. "My people are gone into captivity, because they have no knowledge" (2 Nephi 15:13).

This book is intended to reveal the strategies and techniques used by Satan to deceive and defeat the disciples of Christ. Like peeling an onion, it will expose Satan's devices layer by layer until we are fully equipped to recognize the veil of darkness and deceit, the pretense and camouflage with which he cloaks his unceasing attacks on mankind. Each chapter will peel away another layer until we reach the core and recognize him in all his cunning and vicious hatred for God and those who seek to live the gospel and worship Christ.

We will also learn that Jesus Christ has infinite power and resources with which to make us free—once we understand and apply the principles that make this possible. As we study the various aspects of Satan's strategies, we will also study Christ's countermeasures, the principles of spiritual warfare which he has revealed. We will learn how to utilize the armor of God in defending and shielding ourselves from Lucifer's attacks. As we learn to use the spiritual weapons Christ has provided to take the offensive in our battles, we will be able to crush the opposition of Satan's forces and drive them away before they can harm us. After all, "for this purpose the Son of God was manifested, that he might destroy the works of the devil" (1 John 3:8).

Jesus Christ loves us and will do whatever it takes to balance the odds, rescue us from our defeats, teach us how to fight our battles with Satan, and return us to our heavenly home. Satan hates us and is determined to defeat us and destroy our chances of obtaining the celestial kingdom. The Savior's goal is to cleanse and perfect us so that we can share in the perfect joys of eternity. The devil's goal is to keep us in sin and defeat so that he can rule over us in spiritual captivity for eternity. You and I stand between these two opposing powers and cast the deciding vote.

Some things revealed about Satan and his powers may be alarming, but they are not presented to frighten. Satan can have no advantage over us once we recognize and understand his techniques and strategies (see 2 Corinthians 2:11). As Elder James E. Faust explained, "We need not become paralyzed with fear of Satan's power. He can have no power over us unless we permit it" (*Ensign*, November 1987, 35). At this very moment the Lord is aware of our past and present struggles and has already planned the path to victory. It is the author's hope that this book will identify that path, "for we have a labor to perform whilst in this tabernacle of clay, that we may conquer the enemy of all righteousness, and rest our souls in the kingdom of God" (Moroni 9:6).

Note: All italics throughout the book are the author's emphasis unless otherwise noted in the citation.

PART ONE

———— ◆ ————

Know Your Enemy

1

It All Began with Ego

DURING THE PREMORTAL COUNCIL IN HEAVEN, WITH WELL OVER 100 billion spirit children in attendance (see Chapter 3), Heavenly Father explained his plans for a mortal probation, including the need for a Savior to come to earth and redeem us from the physical death of our bodies and the spiritual death resulting from our sins. The Father then asked his assembled children, "Whom shall I send?" Ever anxious to further the Father's work, Jesus immediately answered the call: "Here am I, send me" (Abraham 3:27). But there quickly followed a second volunteer. "And another answered and said: Here am I, send me. And the Lord said: I will send the first. And the second was angry, and kept not his first estate; and, at that day, many followed after him" (Abraham 3:27–28). Who was this second volunteer? Do not say it was Satan because it was not. It was Lucifer. Before the war that followed Lucifer's rebellion there was no Satan. God did not *create* the devil. Lucifer deliberately chose to *become* our enemy. It was only after the war in heaven that "he *became* Satan, yea, even the devil" (Moses 4:4; See also 2 Nephi 2:17).

LUCIFER'S PREMORTAL GLORY AND STATUS

The background of our enemy is worthy of consideration. In the premortal world Lucifer was a high-ranking servant of the Father and was known, not only to the family of spirit children appointed to come to this earth, but also throughout the entire heavens as an "angel of

God who was in authority in the presence of God" (D&C 76:25). Elder ElRay L. Christiansen described Lucifer as "a brilliant, influential character who had considerable authority in the premortal world" (*New Era*, July 1975, 48–49). "Both Jesus and Lucifer were strong leaders with great knowledge and influence" (Jess L. Christensen, *Ensign*, June 1986, 25). Like Jesus, Lucifer was also with the Father "from the beginning," but Jesus was Lucifer's older brother (see Moses 4:1; 5:24; Colossians 1:15; D&C 93:21). Elder Bruce R. McConkie explained that Satan's high status in the premortal existence is implied by the title of Lucifer.

> This name of Satan means literally *lightbearer* or *shining one*. It is thus intended to convey a realization of his high status of prominence and authority in pre-existence before his rebellion and fall (see D&C 76:25–27; Isa. 14:12–20; Luke 10:18; 2 Ne. 2:17–18.). (*Mormon Doctrine*, Salt Lake City, Utah: Bookcraft, 1966, 461; emphasis in original)

Explaining Satan's premortal title "Son of the Morning," Elder McConkie also said:

> This name-title of Satan indicates he was one of the early born spirit children of the Father. Always used in association with the name *Lucifer, son of the morning* also apparently signifies *son of light* or *son of prominence*, meaning that Satan held a position of power and authority in pre-existence. (see D&C 76:25–27; Isa. 14:12–20). (*Mormon Doctrine,* Salt Lake City, Utah: Bookcraft, 1966, 744; emphasis in original)

Elder ElRay L. Christiansen described Lucifer's failure to apply the wisdom he should have gained by his high status and authority:

> We must have witnessed that tragic scene when Lucifer—brilliant but lacking in intelligence to properly apply his knowledge . . . rose in hateful rebellion against God. (*Ensign*, November 1974, 22)

When the rebellion required Satan's expulsion from the heavenly realms above, celestial kingdoms throughout "the heavens wept over him—he was Lucifer, a son of the morning" (D&C 76:26). Realizing the extent of Lucifer's high position helps us comprehend how this heavenly being could start a war of opinion that would divide Father's children and result in the rebellion of one third of his family.

"WORSHIP ME"—LUCIFER'S ATTACK ON ELOHIM AND JEHOVAH

When Heavenly Father explained the need for a Savior to come to earth as his Only Begotten Son, to atone for our sins, it was not necessarily a sin for Lucifer to volunteer. Someone had to fulfill that assignment and it could just as well have been Lucifer as Jesus. But Heavenly Father recognized the ulterior motives in Lucifer's offer. Even with the powerful influence and status he already held in that premortal hierarchy, Lucifer wasn't satisfied. It would appear that merely serving for the development of mankind in the earthly school Father was planning was not enough for Lucifer, and that the reason he volunteered was to feed his hunger for the glory of public acclaim.

Having observed countless millions of Father's children leave the safety of their heavenly home to experience mortality on worlds that preceded ours, Lucifer knew there was always a failure rate. On world after world he had observed that there were always those who chose rebellion and disobedience over the principles that would have prepared and qualified them to return to Father's presence. In this knowledge he thought he had found the perfect opportunity to fill his vain ambition for greater glory and acclaim than he already had. Concern for the loss of those who failed mortal probation would have been commendable, except that Lucifer's offer, unlike Christ's, was not based upon love of his brothers and sisters, but on the selfish desire to feed his feelings of self-importance and ego. "Was it not through pride that the devil became the devil?" asked President Ezra Taft Benson. "Christ wanted to serve. The devil wanted to rule. Christ wanted to bring men to where he was. The devil wanted to be above men" (*Ensign*, May 1986, 6).

By offering a plan that supposedly eliminated risk of failure and offered a one hundred percent success rate, Lucifer was asking the family to reject Heavenly Father and Christ and to put himself in charge. We might well have heard him say: I can do better than they can. With my plan you will not face risk or failure. Trust me. I know a better way. I guarantee to bring every person back. And thus were sown the seeds of doubt that led to mass rebellion. Lucifer's offer had nothing to do with executing the Father's sacred plan of individual agency. His intention was to substitute his own plan of compulsion and to elevate himself above his elder brother, Jesus. He was so convincing that he persuaded one third of all Father's children appointed to come to this world to choose him over Christ and then tried to force that choice on the other two thirds.

Here is the scriptural description of the premortal debate. Christ's respectful offer was, "Father, thy will be done, and the glory be thine forever" (Moses 4:2). In pitiful contrast, Lucifer's arrogant proposal was "Behold, here am I, send me, I will be thy son, and I will redeem all mankind, that one soul shall not be lost, and surely I will do it; wherefore give me thine honor" (Moses 4:1).

There would not have been a war in heaven if the only problem was a difference of opinion. But when Lucifer volunteered to come as our Savior, enforcing his own plan of compulsion, it was really a plot to overthrow Heavenly Father, take possession of his throne and position of authority, and exercise total dominion over all the spirits destined to come to this earth. It was mutiny. It was bold rebellion. *"Satan rebelled against me,"* the Father said, "and sought to destroy the agency of man, which I, the Lord God, had given him, and also, that I should give unto him mine own power" (Moses 4:3). In open vision, Joseph Smith "beheld Satan, that old serpent, even the devil, *who rebelled against God,* and sought to take the kingdom of our God and his Christ" (D&C 76:28). Both then and now, Satan actually "seeketh the throne of him who sitteth upon the throne, even the Lamb" (D&C 88:115).

We see the supreme importance of the agency Heavenly Father had granted to his children when he allowed Lucifer to use that very agency to sell his idea of removing it. Father was so committed to protecting our agency that he paid the awful, unthinkable price of losing one third of all his children before their earthly probation even began.

> For, behold, the devil . . . rebelled against me, saying, "Give me thine honor," which is my power; and also a third part of the hosts of heaven turned he away from me because of their agency; And they were thrust down, and thus came the devil and his angels. (D&C 29:36–37)

"Worship Me"—Lucifer's Ego Led to His Fall

"I will ascend into heaven," Lucifer boasted. "I will exalt my throne above the stars of God . . . I will ascend above the heights of the clouds; I will be like the most high" (Isaiah 14:13–14). Critics of Mormonism use this description of Lucifer's vain ambition to suggest that our doctrine and goal of becoming like Heavenly Father is blasphemous and satanic. But Jesus carefully taught that exaltation is the Father's goal for each of his children (see Matthew 5:48; 10:24–25; D&C 132). Lucifer's sin was not the desire to be like Father. It was his selfish, greedy desire to *replace* Heavenly Father. He was unwilling to come to earth and prove himself worthy of exaltation and glory. He wanted the glory right then, with no price, no sacrifice, no risk, no testing or proving of his obedience. Like a spoiled child, Lucifer was demanding immediate promotion at the cost of removing Heavenly Father from his rightful position of authority over his own family. He wanted to surpass Jesus and Father in glory, power, and dominion without even passing through a mortal probation.

I want it and I want it now. I don't care how many millions of worlds Elohim has peopled, he always loses some of the spirits who won't obey. I have a better plan. I can save every soul. Put me in charge. Let me be master. Not one soul will be lost under my leadership because I will remove the test and the agency. It was this arrogant rebellion and scheming aspiration which caused Lucifer's fall. Lehi explained it this way:

> And I, Lehi, according to the things which I have read, must needs suppose that an angel of God, according to that which is written, had fallen from heaven; wherefore, he became a devil, having sought that which was evil before God. (2 Nephi 2:17)

The Prophet Joseph Smith explained it this way:

> The contention in heaven was—Jesus said there would be certain souls that would not be saved; and the devil said he could save them all, and laid his plans before the grand council, who gave their vote in favor of Jesus Christ. So the devil rose up in rebellion against God, and was cast down, with all who put up their heads for him. (*Teachings of the Prophet Joseph Smith,* Salt Lake City, Utah: Deseret Book, 1968, 357)

And Heavenly Father described it this way:

By the power of mine Only Begotten, I caused that he should be cast down; And he became Satan, yea, even the devil, the father of all lies, to deceive and to blind men, and to lead them captive at his will, even as many as would not hearken unto my voice. (Moses 4:3–4)

Isaiah was astonished when he was shown this in vision and lamented, "How art thou fallen from heaven, O Lucifer, son of the morning!" (Isaiah 14:12). Lucifer's fall was truly an unprecedented catastrophe which caused heavenly beings throughout the universe to weep for him and those he had already destroyed (see D&C 76:25–27).

"Worship Me"—Lucifer's Attack on Our First Ancestors

Exiled to the earth without a physical body, Satan continues in the lost cause of feeding his wounded ego. Even though his diabolical scheme failed in the premortal world, Satan has not abandoned his plan and still "opposeth and exalteth himself above all that is called God, or that is worshipped; so that he as God sitteth in the temple of God, shewing himself that he is God" (2 Thessalonians 2:4). Not only does he seek to lead his brothers and sisters into sinful rebellion, but he seeks equally to win our devotion and adoration. "Behold Satan hath come among the children of men, and tempteth them to worship him" (Moses 6:49). We see this from the beginning of history. For example, when Adam and Eve taught the gospel to their children, Satan countered the commands to worship God with his own command to worship him, the substitute god. It would appear that several generations passed after their expulsion from the Garden of Eden before Adam and Eve were taught the full gospel message. They were grandparents before they were taught the principle of animal sacrifice (see Moses 5:1–5). Finally the voice of the Lord was heard, coming from the Garden nearby, teaching them to worship the Lord by offering up the firstlings of their flocks, though the symbolism was not revealed at that time. One can imagine what a strange ritual this must have seemed to Adam's children, especially considering that Adam could offer no explanation of its purpose. After a time of probation, an angel appeared and taught them that the animal sacrifice was instituted in symbolism of the coming sacrifice of the Son of God for their sins. Other things were taught, and Adam was filled with the Holy Ghost and made many prophecies.

At last Adam and Eve could see the wisdom and purpose in the fall, the necessity of opposition and testing, and the forgiveness and mercy made possible by the coming of the Son of God in the flesh. What wonderful news. After decades of doubt and wondering, they now knew, by revelation, much of the plan of salvation (see Moses 5:5–11). Eagerly they called a conference with their children and grandchildren to explain the revelations they had received (Moses 5:12). But their children were skeptical. If all this were really so, why hadn't God explained it to them before? And furthermore, if these doctrines were so important, why hadn't God explained it to *everyone* instead of expecting them to believe Adam, the man who had no answers for decades? Why would it come second hand?

Sensing a glorious opportunity to deceive the doubting posterity of Adam and win devotees to himself, Satan stepped through the veil and appeared to the assembly. "And Satan came among them, saying: "I am also a son of God;" and he commanded them, saying: "Believe it not" (Moses 5:13). The response of Adam's posterity to Satan's appearance must have been gratifying to him, for "they believed it not" (Moses 5:13). They believed Satan rather than their own parents. We are surprised, but how would we have responded? For the first time in the history of the world, here was a glorious, radiant being giving (false) revelation to a group of inexperienced people. They had to choose between the second-hand information from their parent's alleged revelation, and the direct revelation from the radiant being before their very eyes. "And they loved Satan more than God. And men began from that time forth to be carnal, sensual, and devilish" (Moses 5:13).

"WORSHIP ME"—LUCIFER'S ATTACK ON MOSES

Throughout the centuries Satan has continued to counter divine revelations and win souls by his deceptions. Yet, no matter how many followers pledge allegiance to his leadership, his sick ego is never satisfied. We see yet another example of this insatiable need for the praise of men in his attempt to deceive Moses. The first time Jehovah, the premortal Christ, appeared to Moses face to face, Moses was astonished, not only by the revelations he received, but also by the majesty and glory of this heavenly being.

> Now mine own eyes have beheld God; but not my natural, but my spiritual eyes, for my natural eyes could not have beheld; for I should have withered and died in his presence; but his glory was upon me; and I beheld his face, for I was transfigured before him (Moses 1:11).

Satan was aware of all this. Shortly after the Savior left Moses alone on the mountain, Lucifer stepped through the veil disguised as an angel of light, attempting to steal the adoration he knew Moses felt for the Lord. His goal was simple: to persuade Moses to worship *him* instead of Jehovah. Lucifer's request that Moses feed his hungry ego was direct and clear: "Moses, son of man, worship me" (Moses 1:12). While Satan's dazzling imitation of glory successfully deceived Adam's descendants, Moses was not fooled. The contrast between Jehovah's beautiful, shining glory and the devil's paltry imitation was so great that Moses said to Satan:

> Where is thy glory, that I should worship thee? For behold, I could not look upon God, except his glory should come upon me, and I were transfigured before him. But I can look upon thee in the natural man. Is it not so, surely? Where is thy glory, for it is darkness unto me? And I can judge between thee and God. (Moses 1:13–15)

One might expect a normal person to be dissuaded by such an unequivocal testimony, but not Satan. If nothing else, he is persistent, even to the point of helpless compulsion. His overwhelming need to have men worship him and feed his ego is dramatically revealed in the events which followed Moses' first rejection and dismissal of the would-be deceiver. When Moses told him to leave, Satan "cried with a loud voice, and ranted upon the earth, and commanded, saying: I am the Only Begotten, worship me" (Moses 1:19). So powerful and compelling was this tantrum-like demand for worship that "Moses began to fear exceedingly. Nevertheless, calling upon God, he received strength, and he commanded, saying: Depart from me, Satan, for this one God only will I worship, which is the God of glory" (Moses 1:20).

Threatened by the priesthood power of this noble prophet, "Satan began to tremble" (Moses 1:21). However, it would appear that the overpowering need to feed his ego by superseding the Savior, who had just visited this new prophet, compelled Satan to continue resisting the command to leave. Moses repeated the command, this time using his priesthood authority more directly: "In the name of the Only Begotten, depart hence, Satan" (Moses 1:21). Satan cannot disobey a direct command given through the authority of Jesus Christ. He knew he must leave the presence of Moses, but, oh, how bitter was defeat for this arrogant rebel. In terrible frustration "Satan cried with a loud voice, with weeping, and wailing, and gnashing of teeth; and he departed hence, even from the presence of Moses, that he beheld him not" (Moses 1:22). Moses passed a frightening, difficult test, and in reward was immediately "filled with the Holy Ghost" and received further revelations from his loving elder brother (see Moses 1:24–42). We must be careful to recognize the Lord's spirit so we are not misled by Satanic imitations.

"Worship Me"—Lucifer's Attack on Christ

One would expect that Satan would be afraid to risk his inflated ego by asking the Son of God to worship him, but he was not. Apparently his demented arrogance has no limitations. Elder Melvin J. Ballard helps us understand Satan's delusions: "I want to say to you that he is vain enough to think, and he believes it confidently, that in the end he will be victorious and become king of this world" (*New Era*, March 1984, 35). When the glorious Son of God finally came to earth for his own mortal probation, Satan was at his side, attempting to lead him into sin (see Matthew 4:1–7). When the first two temptations failed to divert the Savior from his assigned path, Satan cast aside all pretense and revealed the depth of his insatiable aspiration as he attempted to bribe the Son of God, the very creator of the earth.

> And the devil . . . shewed unto him all the kingdoms of the world in a moment of time. And the devil said unto him, "All this

power will I give thee, and the glory of them: for that is delivered unto me; and to whomsoever I will I give it." (Luke 4:5–6)

It is difficult to imagine a more preposterous situation: an unembodied outcast who had lost his high position in heaven, daring to offer Jesus Christ possession and control of the very things that he, the Lord, had created. We can understand the devil deceiving the descendants of Adam. We can understand his gall at attempting to deceive Moses. Compared to the Savior, they were but inexperienced amateurs. But to attempt the same deception on the Son of God seems insane. Casting aside all pride and revealing the agony of his unfulfilled, sick ego, Satan pleads, he begs, "All these things will I give thee, *if thou wilt fall down and worship me*" (Matthew 4:9). Or as Luke recorded it, "if thou therefore wilt worship me, all shall be thine" (Luke 4:7).

> The tempter offered to Jesus all these honors and privileges on easy terms, merely to fall down and worship the evil one. And, said he, "I will give them all unto you. No need of dying on Calvary; just worship me. They are mine, and they shall be yours."
>
> It is true that he who offered the kingdoms of this world was temporarily, at least, ruling over them but his was a squatter's right. His title was not valid. Jesus Christ, had he accepted such a title, would have been defrauded and presently would have found that the title was worthless. (Melvin J. Ballard, *New Era*, March 1984, 34)

The Savior's noble reply set the enemy in retreat. "Get thee hence, Satan: for it is written, Thou shalt worship the Lord thy God, and him only shalt thou serve. Then the devil leaveth him, and, behold, angels came and ministered unto him" (Matthew 4:10–11). I would not be surprised to learn that Jesus joined those angels in weeping over the pitiful creature the once noble Lucifer had become, a desperate, scheming enemy.

2

War

IN 1990, THE POWERFUL, MECHANIZED COUNTRY OF IRAQ INVADED the comparatively tiny, unarmed country of Kuwait and started a war that soon involved much of the world. For many suspenseful months Saddam Hussein held mankind captive to newspapers and televisions as the world marshaled its resources against him and anxiously awaited the outcome. How sad that an even greater war is being waged daily for the souls of men, and hardly anyone pays attention. When Lucifer's alternative plan of compulsion was rejected by the premortal council, he rose in rebellion and sought to persuade the rest of Father's children to join him in imposing their will on the Father. The scriptures describe the resulting conflict as war.

> And there was war in heaven: Michael and his angels fought against the dragon; and the dragon fought and his angels, And prevailed not; neither was their place found any more in heaven. And the great dragon was cast out, that old serpent, called the Devil, and Satan, which deceiveth the whole world: he was cast out into the earth, and his angels were cast out with him. (Revelation 12:7–9)

It is crucial to realize that the war which began so long ago has never ended, but continues in ever-increasing intensity here on earth. The issues are the same. Only the battleground has changed.

> That war, so bitter, so intense, has gone on, and it has never ceased. It is the war between truth and error, between agency and compulsion, between the followers of Christ and those who

have denied Him. His enemies have used every stratagem in that conflict. They've indulged in lying and deceit. They've employed money and wealth. They've tricked the minds of men. They've murdered and destroyed and engaged in every other unholy and impure practice to thwart the work of Christ. (Gordon B. Hinckley, *Ensign*, November 1986, 42)

This is not a war for territory or wealth; it is a contest for the eternal souls of men and women, boys and girls, the literal off-spring of God, our Heavenly Father. But how many of us realize how serious this conflict is? Do we understand what the devil is trying to do to us? In a very real sense it is a war—a hot war—between right and wrong, between the powers of heaven and the forces of Lucifer. The scriptures warn that the devil will make war with the Saints of God. He will attack them with all the wicked devices his pornographic mind can devise, but he never will stop God's work. (Mark E. Petersen, *Ensign*, May 1980, 69)

Satan has the authority and the power to cause our spiritual destruction *if* we allow it, for "*it was given unto him* to make war with the saints, and to overcome them; and power was given him over all kindreds, and tongues, and nations" (Revelation 13:7).

"And we beheld, and lo, he is fallen! is fallen, even a son of the morning . . . for we beheld Satan, that old serpent, even the devil, who rebelled against God, and sought to take the king-dom of our God and His Christ—Wherefore, *he maketh war with the saints of God*, and encompasseth them round about." (D&C 76:27–29)

Unfortunately, many Latter-day Saints are easy targets because they are not familiar with their enemy and are untutored in the techniques of spiritual warfare. It is the author's hope that this will no longer be true by the end of this book. Many have wondered why the Old Testament and the Book of Mormon are filled with hundreds of pages recounting the wars between God's people and evil nations who sought to force them into captivity. Endless details are presented of battles, armaments, attacks, and counterattacks. Curious about this, Sister Kathleen S. McConkie asked:

Why? Why did Mormon include so much detail about the wars? With all the wonderful spiritual events that must have taken place, why would he use so much valuable space on the plates to record military intrigue and battle strategy? (*Ensign*, January 1992, 19)

These scriptural accounts reveal a *pattern*. When God's people are delivered, it is the result of their righteousness, faith, courage, determination, and masterful military strategy that enables them to defeat an enemy which most often outnumbers them. These accounts are included in scripture to draw attention to the parallels in the *spiritual* war each of us must fight with Satan in today's modern battlegrounds, to teach the need of strategy, fortifying our weaknesses and vulnerabilities, protecting ourselves with the armor of God, and other principles of spiritual warfare needed to win our battles with Satan. (All of this will be discussed in coming chapters.) Sister McConkie described how she felt when she discovered this.

> Then it hit me. That was it! *This* was the war that applied to me—not a war of swords and spears, but the eternal war for my soul and those of my family. Satan is waging an all-out war against truth and righteousness. His forces are everywhere, and we are involved in that war whether we like it or not. The danger is real, and the stakes are high. All around us we see the battle casualties, their lives ruined and their souls scarred. If we expect to avoid becoming casualties ourselves, we desperately need the Lord's guidance—and there is no better place to find it than in the book of scripture prepared specifically for our day: The Book of Mormon! (*Ensign*, January 1992, 19, emphasis in original)

As opposing armies face each other across the front line, each side seeks to use its most effective weapons. It is not with bullets that Satan attacks us, but with fiery darts of temptation, discouragement, and falsehood. Aflame with the poison of darkness and evil desires, these spiritual weapons penetrate, blinding us to the truth and creating desires and appetites for evils we would not otherwise even consider (see 1 Nephi 15:24). This we will study in Chapter 9, "The Battleground of Temptation."

President N. Eldon Tanner warned, "We must never forget that Satan is real and determined to destroy us" (*New Era,* June 1978, 9). We would not look on the war with Satan so casually if we really grasped the intensity of his hatred and desire to lure us into spiritual captivity. Peter likened Lucifer's vicious hatred and determination to the prowling of a ferocious, wild lion. "Be sober, be vigilant," he warned, "because your adversary the devil, as a roaring lion, walketh about, seeking whom he may devour" (1 Peter 5:8). His imagery is compelling. We would be very cautious, indeed, if we knew such a dangerous threat was loose in the neighborhood. Well, he is. Satan is a violent, cruel and merciless adversary. "Woe to the inhibitors of the earth and of the sea! for the devil is come down unto you, *having great wrath*, because he knoweth that he hath but a short time" (Revelation 12:12).

> There is no crime he would not commit, no debauchery he would not set up, no plague he would not send, no heart he would not break, no life he would not take, no soul he would not destroy. He comes as a thief in the night; he is a wolf in sheep's clothing. (*Messages of the First Presidency*, comp. James R. Clark, 6 vols., Salt Lake City, Utah: Bookcraft, 1965–75, 6:179)

The problem with the example of a "roaring lion" is that Satan is not so obvious in his attacks. Working secretly, behind the veil and in darkness, he is unseen and, therefore, if undetected by one's spiritual sensitivity, of far greater danger than a mere lion. "True Christians know that invisible forces are waging war against God and his people who are striving to do his will" (ElRay L. Christiansen, *Ensign*, July 1975, 49). A lion stops hunting once his belly is full and he feels satisfied, but Satan is never satisfied no matter how many victims he captures, his war is relentless and unceasing.

> We must remember that Satan is *always* on the job, determined to destroy the work of the Lord and to destroy mankind, and as soon as we deviate from the path of righteousness, we are in great danger of being destroyed. (N. Eldon Tanner, *Ensign*, December 1971, 34)
>
> When God has had a people on the earth, it matters not in what age. Lucifer, the son of the morning, and the millions of fallen spirits that were cast out of heaven have warred against God, against Christ, against the work of God. And they are not backward in doing it in our day and generation. Whenever the Lord set his hand to perform any work, those powers labored to overthrow it. (Wilford Woodruff, as quoted in *Ensign*, November 1986, 43)

As the Savior's second coming draws nearer, Satan is fighting more intensely than ever before in the history of mankind. "We know that as the second coming of the Savior approaches, the tempo of Satan's campaign for the souls of men is being and will continue to be accelerated" (Marion G. Romney, *Ensign*, June 1971, 36). Elder ElRay L. Christiansen observed, "There was never a time when the adversary has provided more enticements, more subtle temptations, and more false justifications for wrongdoing than now" (*New Era*, September 1975, 4). During a talk in the Seattle Temple on 1 June, 1987, Elder Vaughn J. Featherstone said:

> The season of the world before us will be like no other in the history of mankind. Satan has unleashed every evil, every scheme, every blatant, vile Perversion ever known to man in any generation. Just as this is the dispensation of the fullness of times, so it is also the dispensation of the fullness of evil.

To understand this war with Satan it is important to realize that this world is unique and different from all the other worlds God has created and peopled. Out of the countless millions of worlds created by Heavenly Father, it was to *this* world alone that Jehovah, the premortal Christ, came to obtain his mortal body and enact the Atonement. His long-awaited mortal birth was announced to a waiting universe of watchful worlds by the sudden appearance of a new star (see Helaman 14:4–5). And it was to this world that Lucifer was exiled. Because of Lucifer's presence here, this world has become the most wicked of all the worlds Heavenly Father has created (see Moses 7:35–37). Is it any wonder that all of Father's children who have passed into glory now watch the war Lucifer is waging here on earth and await the final battle when he will be conquered forever, and Jehovah and his followers will achieve final victory? As Elder Melvin J. Ballard explained:

> The prophets of old foretold the time to come when this question would be settled. Some of them called the conflict Armageddon. Whatever the name is, there is coming a time when the question as to who has the right to rule and reign will be settled. Every righteous man, living and dead, will be interested and engaged in that conflict, and so will every wicked man, living and dead.
>
> What will the end of the matter be? How soon it will come I do not know, but this I know: that evidences of the approaching

conflict are speeding on, and come it will, and the days are being employed in preparation for it by such activity on both sides that we would be astonished if we knew that *we are going to be the center of great interest in the universe,* because we are approaching great and important and critical days in the history of this world. (*New Era,* March 1984, 35)

There can be no neutrality for Latter-day Saints. We chose the Lord's way in the premortal phase of the war and we must make that choice again here, in the midst of all the darkness, evil, and hatred the devil can conjure up. The Lord has called us to take upon ourselves the armor of God, join in the war against Satan, and wield every possible influence to expose and defeat his efforts.

> The Prince of Darkness has dragged out the heavy artillery. He is no longer limited to arrows and swords and BB guns. Now he is Darth Vader, with laser guns, light speeds, and the death star. We are near the end of a fight to the finish, and no holds are barred. (Bruce C. Hafen, *Ensign,* October 1982, 66)

3

Surrounded

No general would commit his soldiers to fight an enemy without first estimating the size and strength of the opposing army. We mortals are vastly outnumbered by the billions of evil soldiers in the devil's army, and if we would win our battles with Satan, we must first understand that the battle is not with him alone. Except for when we enter the temple, "we are surrounded by demons, yea, we are encircled about by the angels of him who hath sought to destroy our souls" (Helaman 13:37). These demons, these soldiers in the devil's army of evil spirits, are the angels of the devil who were expelled from heaven at the conclusion of the premortal phase of the war between Lucifer and God (see Revelation 12:9; D&C 29:36–37). That same war continues today, and Elder Melvin J. Ballard warned that when Father sent us into mortality, we were to be placed "in the presence of the enemy who was now a majority" (*New Era*, March 1984, 33).

ESTIMATING THE SIZE OF OUR ENEMY'S ARMY

It is helpful to estimate the number of evil spirits who are attempting our destruction so that we might properly respect the overwhelming odds arrayed against us, and know how important it is to rely upon Christ as we defend ourselves with the armor of God. We can calculate the approximate number of spirits in Satan's army because we know he brought with him one third of Father's family who had been selected to come to this earth (see D&C 29:36; Revelation 12:4). One cannot divide by a third unless there is a specific total to be divided.

> Do you suppose that one-third part of all beings that existed in eternity came with him? No, but one third of the spirits that were begotten and organized and brought forth to become tenants of fleshly bodies to dwell upon this earth. (*Discourses of Brigham Young,* Salt Lake City, Utah: Deseret Book, 1951, 68)

It has been estimated that the disembodied population of the spirit world is approximately seventy billion spirits—those people who have previously lived on this world. (see Elder Neal A. Maxwell, *Notwithstanding My Weaknesses,* Salt Lake City, Utah: Deseret Book, 1981, 55.) Seventy billion spirits who have already passed through mortality, plus approximately five billion mortals alive on earth today equals seventy-five billion people. If we ignore the unborn spirits yet to come to earth before the millennium and assume that seventy-five billion represents the two thirds of God's children who were to come to earth in mortal bodies, then we could easily estimate the number of spirits who follow Satan. If two thirds equals seventy-five billion, then half of that would equal one third, which is over thirty-seven billion. I am not offering that number as an official census; it is merely an estimate which illustrates that whatever the exact number may be, Satan and the remaining third of God's spirit children who now war against us would number in the tens of billions.

SURROUNDED BY THE ENEMY'S ARMY

Thirty-seven billion spirits in Satan's army would mean that he has at his command at least seven evil spirits to tempt and war against each mortal alive on the earth today, (thirty-seven billion evil spirits divided by five billion mortals equals seven each.) However, the odds against the righteous are much greater than that, for that is not the way Satan assigns his manpower. Because he is not allowed to tempt little children, Satan's forces must be reserved to war against only those who are accountable (see D&C 29:47). When we subtract all the children under eight years old and all those who cannot be held accountable for other reasons, we're left with a lot more spirits to work on the adults. There is, however, an even more compelling reason to conclude that Satan could have hundreds or thousands of his demons assigned to defeat each member of the Church. President George Albert Smith said, "The devil has the world so perfectly at his disposal that it requires few devils to keep it in subjection," and that "the whole legion of devils *has nothing to do but look after the 'Mormons'* and stir up the hearts of the children of men to destroy them" (as quoted by Carlos E. Asay in *Ensign*, November 1981, 67). President Smith illustrated this insight with the following parable:

> A man traveling through the country came to a large city, very rich and splendid: he looked at it and said to his guide, "This must be a very righteous people, for I can only see but one little devil in this great city."
>
> The guide replied, "You do not understand, sir. This city is so perfectly given up to wickedness . . . that it requires but one devil to keep them all in subjection."
>
> Traveling on a little farther, he came to a rugged path and saw an old man trying to get up the hill side, surrounded by seven great, big, coarse-looking devils.
>
> "Why," says the traveler, "this must be a tremendously wicked old man! See how many devils there are around him!"
>
> "This," replied the guide, "is the only righteous man in the country; and there are seven of the biggest devils trying to turn him out of his path, and they all cannot do it." (*Journal of Discourses,* vol. 5:363–64)

President Wilford Woodruff said, "Look at the number of devils we have around us. We have, I should say, one hundred to every man, woman and child." (*Journal of Discourses,* vol. 21:125–126) Elder Gene R. Cook also taught that it is primarily the Latter-day Saints the devil focuses his efforts upon. "Satan especially desires to deceive the Latter-day Saints, those who know the truth about him, those who can particularly influence others in their teaching and living of the gospel" (*Ensign*, May 1982, 26). To accomplish this military objective Satan has organized his followers into a powerful, trained army. "And the devil shall gather together his armies; even the hosts of hell." (D&C 88:113). Like any army, they have specialists, cunning strategies and well-organized plans of attack which have been developed and perfected over thousands of years of combat experience.

Mormon wrote that "the devil is an enemy unto God, and fighteth against him *continually*, and inviteth and enticeth to sin, and to do that which is evil *continually* (Moroni 7:12). "Continually" means that Satan's forces are working against us twenty-four hours a day, around the clock, around the calendar, throughout the centuries, until the Lord decrees that the battle is over. President Brigham Young said of this ever-present attack:

> It requires all the care and faithfulness which we can exercise in order to keep the faith of the Lord Jesus for there are invisible agencies around us in sufficient numbers to encourage the slightest disposition they may discover in us to forsake the true way, *and fan into a flame the slightest spark of discontent and unbelief.* [These] spirits are watching us continually for an opportunity to influence us to do evil or to make us decline in the performance of our duties. (*Journal of Discourses,* vol. 12:128)

It must be emphasized that in spite of this massive opposition, all the combined power of Satan's billions of evil spirits cannot move us from our chosen courses when we protect ourselves with the armor of God, center our lives on Christ, and rely moment by moment on the gift of the Holy Ghost. We could apply the Lord's assurance to ancient Israel to our own battles today: "When thou goest out to battle against thine enemies, and seest . . . a people more than thou, be not afraid of them: for the Lord thy God is with thee" (Deuteronomy 20:1).

JOINED BY MORTAL TRAITORS AND CONSPIRING MEN

In the first temptation, Lucifer hid behind the cloak of the veil and spoke to Eve through the serpent. Today he also speaks and influences mankind through the hosts of conspiring men who are willing to manipulate and harm their brothers and sisters for the wealth and power that can be had through partnership with the devil. Thus, not all our enemies hide behind the invisibility of the veil. Many of Satan's most effective representatives live among us in bodies of flesh. They look like us but they are traitors who have gone over to the side of the enemy and wield great influence in advancing his goals. President Spencer W. Kimball indicated that "Satan [has] reached forth with his wicked, evil hand to pull into his forces the people of this earth" (*Ensign*, May 1975, 109). "We must be aware that one of the most powerful forces Satan uses to destroy our purity of life is the deceit of conspiring men" (*Ensign*, November 1977, 5). It is to these traitors the Lord referred when he warned of the "evils and designs which do and will exist in the hearts of conspiring men in the last days" (D&C 89:4).

> Satan . . . presents his principles and arguments in the most approved style, with great charm and grace. He is very careful to integrate himself into the favor of the powerful and influential among mankind. He unites with popular movements and programs, only to use them as a means of doing that which ultimately oppresses and takes away God-given freedoms. (Brigham Young, as quoted in *New Era,* September 1975, 5)

Thus the world is filled with modern Korihors who are given constant access to radio, television, and the printed media to espouse the "new morality" and other doctrines which make Satan laugh and dance in triumph. These antichrists are powerful and persuasive. They are applauded for their views and supported by the masses who resent any restraint on their right to do whatever gives them pleasure.

> Using his superior knowledge, his unique powers of persuasion, half-truths, and complete lies, the evil one uses the spirit children who followed him, plus mortal beings who have yielded to his evil ways, to wage his war against the Saints. (ElRay L. Christiansen, *New Era,* September 1975, 5)
>
> I declare to you that he has his recruiting stations everywhere in the world and that they are armed. He has soldiers, and he has plenty of them. He is enlisting men and women on his side in preparation for the great conflict in the vain hope that when the struggle ensues he will have a majority and thereby be successful. (Melvin J. Ballard, *New Era,* March 1984, 35)

We must conclude, then, that we are behind enemy lines, outnumbered and surrounded by deadly opponents, both seen and unseen. "If our eyes were only opened to see the powers that are about us, that seek to influence us, we could not have the courage to walk alone and unassisted" (Melvin J. Ballard, *New Era,* March 1984, 33–34). Because of this overwhelming army, President Brigham Young marveled that we do not have more casualties than we do.

> Thousands of temptations assail, and you make a miss here and a slip there, and say that you have not lived up to all the knowledge you have. True; but often it is a marvel to me that you have lived up to so much as you have, considering the power of the enemy upon this earth. Few that have ever lived have fully understood that power. I do not fully comprehend that awful power and influence Satan has upon the earth, but I understand enough to know that it is a marvel that the Latter-day Saints are as good as they are. (*Discourses of Brigham Young,* Salt Lake City, Utah: Deseret Book, 1951, 80)

Yet with all this understanding, let us not fear. What we have learned is sobering, indeed, and should make us acutely aware of the dangers of compromise. It should also make us aware of the need to live worthy of the companionship of the Holy Spirit. But "though an host should encamp against me, my heart shall not fear" (Psalms 27:3). "No matter how many he shall gather on his side nor how bitter the conflict, he shall be defeated and banished from the earth and cast out of his own place" (Melvin J. Ballard, *New Era,* March 1984, 35).

SUPPORTED BY THE LORD'S ARMY

The Lord also has multitudes of servants on the other side of the veil, "ministering spirits, sent forth to minister for them who shall be heirs of salvation" (Hebrews 1:14; also Psalms 104:4; Moroni 10:14; D&C 76:88). These valiant spirits move unseen among us to inspire and encourage progress, just as Satan's spirits work to discourage, deceive and pull us down.

Ancient Syria was warring against Israel. That is to say, they were *trying* to war against Israel, but every move was discerned and reported to the king by the prophet Elisha. In anger, the Syrian king sent a large army to the little town of Dothan where Elisha was known to be. During the night the army surrounded the village with horses, chariots, and a great army. The next morning Elisha's young servant awoke and discovered the threatening force. He knew why they were there. And he also knew, or at least he *thought* he knew, that there was no chance of escape. "Alas, my master," he cried, "how shall we do?" (2 Kings 6:15) How confused he must have been when Elisha replied, "Fear not: for they that be with us are more than they that be with them" (2 Kings 6:16). What could he possibly be talking about? No one was with them. They were defenseless, helpless. Who was with them? The servant didn't understand that Elisha was referring to the spiritual army of the Lord.

> And Elisha prayed, and said, Lord, I pray thee, open his eyes, that he may see. And the Lord opened the eyes of the young man; and he saw: and, behold, the mountain was full of horses and chariots of fire round about Elisha. (2 Kings 6:17)

Lucifer has great power and comparatively unlimited men and women in his army. But so does the Lord.

> In the gospel of Jesus Christ you have help from both sides of the veil and you must never forget that. When disappointment and discouragement strike, you remember and never forget that if our eyes could be opened we would see horses and chariots of fire as far as the eye can see, riding at reckless speed to come to our protection. They will always be there, these armies of heaven, in defense of Abraham's seed. (Jeffrey R. Holland, *New Era*, October 1980, 15)
>
> For I will go before your face. I will be on your right hand and on your left, and my Spirit shall be in your hearts, and mine angels round about you, to bear you up. (D&C 84:88)

If we wear the armor of God, walk in obedience to the commandments, stay close to the scriptures, and in tune with the Holy Spirit, it is totally irrelevant how many evil spirits Satan surrounds us with. We can walk tall; we can walk fearlessly, even while surrounded by the enemy, for "thus saith the Lord unto you, Be not afraid nor dismayed by reason of this great multitude; for the battle is not yours, but God's" (2 Chronicles 20:15). And "the angel of the Lord encampeth round about them that fear him, and delivereth them" (Psalms 34:7).

God loves us. He is watching us. He wants us to succeed. We

will know some day that he has not left one thing undone for the eternal welfare of each of us. If we only knew it, heavenly hosts are pulling for us—friends in heaven that we cannot remember who yearn for our victory. (Ezra Taft Benson, *Speeches of the Year,* 1974, Provo: BYU Press, 1975, 313)

4

Satanic Subliminals

To properly defend ourselves against an enemy, we must know what kinds of weapons he has and how he can use them to harm or destroy us. For this reason it is important to learn exactly *how* Satan presents his temptations, *how* he communicates his evil invitations, and causes discouragement, depression, doubt, and confusion. All messages, impressions, suggestions, urges, encouragements or discouragements, feelings, temptations, and warnings sent from the other side of the veil, whether from deity or Satan, are communicated directly to the spirit, which then relays the information to our mortal, conscious minds as thoughts, impressions, and feelings. If we are ever to conquer the devil and break free of our weaknesses and sinful habits, it is vital to understand Satan's ability to tempt and deceive us by direct, personal, and individual communication between our spirits and him, or the evil spirits which follow him. When we understand the *mechanics* of this communication, we will be better prepared to recognize and resist Satanic deceptions and to respond to the whisperings of the Spirit sent from the Lord.

How Satan Puts Thoughts into Our Minds

We can see the mechanics of this information-transfer from the spiritual realm to the physical in the account of Brigham Smoot, a missionary who served in the Samoan islands in the 1800s. Elder Smoot did not know how to swim, but the day after he arrived in Samoa, the other missionaries persuaded him to go wading in the ocean, the only way they had of bathing. Unknown to the elders, there was a deep hole in the reef where they were wading that day. Elder Smoot had the misfortune to step into this hole and immediately disappeared from view. The other elders went into panic, trying to figure out what had happened to him. It was quite some time before they found him at the bottom of the deep hole and dragged his body to the beach. Blood flowed from his eyes, nose and mouth. There was no pulse and no breathing. He was dead. Frantically they tried to revive him but with no success.

As they were about to give up in despair, his companion, Elder Wood, told the other missionaries that *he felt inspired* that the only way the elder's spirit could re-enter his body would be to administer to him. They took his body back to their house, dressed him in clean garments and a suit, and then administered a priesthood blessing. As they sealed the anointing, Elder Smoot's spirit did return to the body and they all felt his life return. Elder Smoot then sat up, quite well and normal, and proceeded to tell them everything that had happened while his body was dead. He told them how, as a disembodied spirit, he had stood on the beach and watched them search for his body. He told of watching them work to revive him. And then, realizing they weren't going to be successful, he went to his companion, Elder Wood, touched him on the shoulder and spoke to him, telling him that the only way to bring life back into the body was to use the priesthood. Of course Elder Wood was not aware of the touch, because a mortal body of flesh cannot feel a spiritual body. Nor was he consciously aware of hearing his dead companion speak to him. But the dead elder wasn't speaking to Elder Wood's conscious mind, he was speaking spirit to spirit. When Elder Wood's spirit heard the message from the dead elder, it transferred the information into his conscious mind and this was when Elder Wood suddenly felt *impressed,* or *inspired,* to use the priesthood. (Related by Duane S. Crowther in *Life Everlasting,* Salt Lake City, Utah: Bookcraft, 47–48, original sources cited therein.)

This experience demonstrates that a spiritual being can speak to a mortal man and cause thoughts to occur in his conscious mind, even though the individual is not consciously aware of the communication or the source of the ideas. Unless we are on guard, Satan can talk to our spirits without us even being aware of it. "And behold, others he flattereth away and telleth them there is no hell; and he saith unto them: I am no devil, for there is none—*and thus he whispereth in their ears,* until he grasps them with his awful chains" (2 Nephi 28:22).

> We should be on guard always to resist Satan's advances. *He has power to place thoughts in our minds* and to whisper to us in unspoken . . . impressions to entice us to satisfy our appetites or desires and in various other ways he plays upon our weaknesses and desires. (*Answers To Gospel Questions,* comp. Joseph Fielding Smith Jr., 5 vols, Salt Lake City, Utah: Deseret Book, 1957–66, vol. 3:81)

Satan and his evil spirits skillfully use this ability to talk directly to our spirits. They continually whisper discouraging and harmful suggestions which then appear in our minds as if they were our own undesirable thoughts and evil impulses. Failing to recognize Satan's influence, most of us assume that all our thoughts originated within ourselves. We cringe at the idea that Satan could manipulate our minds and toy with our thoughts. But have you ever had the experience of evil thoughts suddenly appearing in your mind, which had no possible origin in your previous train of thought? Poof! Suddenly the thoughts and desires are there, seemingly out of nowhere. Well, they didn't come from "nowhere." They came from your enemy, Satan. As Lawrence R. Peterson Jr. explained, "The temptations we are all subject to often take the form of whisperings and promptings to our minds and hearts" (*Ensign,* My 1984, 31).

> Now there is not a person alive who has not, at some point in his life, had an inappropriate thought enter into his mind, *primarily because Satan has the power to put it there.* (Ronald A. Dalley, *New Era,* August 1984, 45)

SCRIPTURAL EXAMPLES OF SATANIC WHISPERINGS

The Book of Mormon emphasizes the role that Satan's whisperings had in the wicked escapades of many generations.

> Now behold, those secret oaths and covenants . . . *were put into the heart of Gadianton* by that same being who did entice our first

parents to partake of the forbidden fruit—Yea, that same being who did plot with Cain, that if he would murder his brother Abel it should not be known unto the world. And he did plot with Cain and his followers from that time forth.

Yea, it is that same being who *put it into the heart of Gadianton* to still carry on the work of darkness, and of secret murder; and he has brought it forth from the beginning of man even down to this time. (Helaman 6:26–27, 29)

We see another example of Satan's subliminal messages in the crazy idea of building a tower to get to heaven without obeying the commandments. This idea came from the whisperings of Satan for he has always tried to persuade man to rely upon their own skills and works instead of the Lord and his gospel.

And also it is that same being *who put it into the hearts of the people* to build a tower sufficiently high that they might get to heaven. And it was that same being who led on the people who came from that tower into this land; who spread the works of darkness and abominations over all the face of the land, until he dragged the people down to an entire destruction, and to an everlasting hell. (Helaman 6:28)

One of the most famous whispered penetrations of the heart is seen in Judas Iscariot's betrayal of the Christ. Some have thought this was simply the result of his own dissatisfaction or confusion, but John testified that it was "the devil [who] put into the heart of Judas Iscariot, Simon's son, to betray him" (John 13:2).

During the restoration of the Gospel, Satan attempted to manipulate well-meaning Christians to interrupt the translation of the Book of Mormon. When Martin Harris lost the first hundred and sixteen pages of the initial translation, Satan whispered suggestions to those in possession of the manuscript as to how they could alter the words and discredit the prophet if he retranslated the same pages. "And, behold, *Satan hath put it into their hearts* to alter the words which you have caused to be written, or which you have translated, which have gone out of your hands" (D&C 10:10). But the Lord was prepared to counter these Satanic whisperings:

Verily, I say unto you, that I will not suffer that Satan shall accomplish his evil design in this thing.

For behold, *he has put it into their hearts* to get thee to tempt the Lord thy God, in asking to translate it over again. (D&C 10:14–15)

LATTER-DAY EXAMPLES OF SATANIC WHISPERINGS

Many General Authorities have reported experiencing intense opposition to the work of their callings. President Heber J. Grant revealed Satan's behind-the-scene "whisperings" by giving the following testimony in general conference in April 1941:

> There are two spirits striving with us always, one telling us to continue our labor for good, and one telling us that with the faults and failings of our nature we are unworthy.
>
> I can truthfully say that from October 1882 until February 1883, that spirit followed me *day and night* telling me that I was unworthy to be an Apostle of the Church and I ought to resign.
>
> When I would testify of my knowledge that Jesus is the Christ, the Son of the Living God, the Redeemer of mankind, *it seemed as though a voice would say to me:* "You lie! You lie! You have never seen him." (Quoted in *Faith Precedes The Miracle*, Spencer W. Kimball, Salt Lake City, Utah: Deseret Book, 1972, 37)

The scriptures refer to these vile, Satanic whisperings as "the fiery darts of the adversary" (see 1 Nephi 15:24; D&C 3:8). The mental and emotional taunts fired at us through the devil's whispered suggestions are like darts of fiery, burning poison. They strike deep, penetrating the mind and inflaming the heart with strong mental and emotional responses. Emotions are powerful motivators and often have a greater influence on our chosen actions than do our thoughts. Satan is a master at manipulating emotions through the vicious whisperings he has perfected with practice on billions of our predecessors. He knows how to create worry and doubt, fear, hatred, resentment and jealousy, stress, anger, lust, depression, feelings of emptiness and loneliness, and so on. Have you felt angry in the last week? Have you felt lonely, alone or misunderstood? Have you felt anxiety or fear, doubt, resentment, depression, rebellion, or the desire to retreat from life's challenges? No such feelings come from above. You have been under the influence of powerful demonic spirits who know how to trigger your self-defeating emotions and thought patterns and then laugh and rejoice at your misery.

I have a friend who has fought a valiant fight to conquer life-long addictions and build her faith in Christ's promises. Because of the spiritual war she was fighting to conquer and escape a wicked past, she was targeted by Satan with a campaign of whispered discouragements and lies. Unfortunately, she compromised her defenses by forsaking frequent prayer, scripture study, and church attendance. This cracked her armor and enabled Satan to penetrate her defenses with vicious lies and suggestions designed to defeat her. She was temporarily deceived into believing that the lies he had whispered actually represented her own true feelings. As you read her statements written at that time of vulnerability, you will easily recognize that Satanic origins, though at the time she did not.

> I have felt totally lost, hopeless, and helpless. I have been seriously debating requesting excommunication because there is no way I can overcome my habits and evil desires.
>
> I don't feel like going to church anymore. I feel the church would be better off without me. Some people just aren't meant for such, and I'm one of them. I just don't belong.
>
> No matter how hard I try to build the type of faith I should, it is useless. You can't change the spots on a leopard. I am trapped in cycles I can't get out of.
>
> I'm not denying Christ or his Atonement, it's just not for me. My nature is carnal and fallen and I am trapped and hopeless. (Personal correspondence)

Truly those are words right out of the mouth of the great deceiver. He would love to have everyone believing these powerfully defeating lies. While these hopeless expressions really did represent her feelings at the time, they did not represent her true, innermost desires for righteousness and victory. Thankfully this good sister confided these feelings to her priesthood leader (a wonderful thing to do when we feel overwhelmed). He recognized that such feelings never come from the Lord, but always from Satan, and explained, "Satan always hits us the hardest when we're at our lowest, and *he deceived you.*" Under the influence of the Holy Spirit, she realized it was true. Like a joyful prisoner escaping the deepest, darkest dungeon, she later acknowledged, "I feel very ashamed for what I wrote and my feelings at the time. *I was totally deceived by Satan.*"

We can see another illustration of the deadly power of Satan's whisperings in the experience of a lonely seminary teacher who felt he was losing the girl he deeply loved. When he received a call informing him that she had died, he was heartbroken. He said:

> I began gasping for air. I couldn't breath. I said, "Oh God, I feel like I'm going to die now, help me to not die." Oh, my heart was heavy. Then one week of hell came upon me, as Satan moved in for the kill as he saw a seminary teacher down.

He then described Satan's cunning cruelty as he gleefully took advantage of this time of vulnerability and whispered lies in ever-increasing intensity. Even though this good man knew the source of the diabolical suggestions, they caused him great difficulty in the time of his deep sorrow. He said:

> The next day I woke up and I had the strong feeling that came over me. "You're still in pain? What kind of a God would do that to you? Why don't you go out and take alcohol into your body and numb the hurt?" I overcame that temptation.
>
> The next day was a little different. "You're still in pain? Why don't you take some of the drugs that you've received from the boys and girls you counsel, and use them yourself. They'll be very effective in removing the sorrow." I overcame that one.
>
> The next day it came a little differently. "Who would want you now? At your age, what woman in the world would want you to hold [her] hand or place your lips against hers? There is no one!" A great depression came to me.
>
> The following day: "You've saved your virtue and God did this to you? Find a woman to lay with and show him." I overcame that temptation. And I remember the fifth one. "You're still in sorrow? Well, it doesn't really matter anyway, because you're not worth anything. Why don't you just take the gun, and load it, and do it?" And I overcame that temptation. (Don J. Black, cassette recording, *Hand To Hand Combat With Satan*, American Fork, Utah: Covenant Communications, 1984)

A mission president made a difficult decision after much prayer and pondering. Many of his zone leaders and others disagreed with the decision. He began to worry. He awoke one morning with terrible feelings of gloomy darkness. A voice whispered in his mind, You have made a terrible mistake. As he pondered that possibility, he felt fear and uncertainty. Then the voice whispered, Your leadership is destroyed. How will you ever be able to trust yourself to make another decision? As he gave way to these whisperings he was engulfed in suffocating darkness. He felt as if he were spiraling downward through a drain. Finally recognizing the source of these suggestions, he got out of bed and knelt in prayer. Soon he was able to drive the evil spirits away and receive the whispered guidance of the Holy Spirit: "Never doubt the decisions you make after praying and receiving inspiration."

> All inspiration does not come from God (see D&C 46:7). The evil one has the power to tap into those channels of revelation and send conflicting signals which can mislead and confuse us. There are promptings from evil sources which are so carefully counterfeited as to deceive even the very elect, (see Matthew 24:4) *Nevertheless, we can learn to discern these spirits.* (Boyd K. Packer, *Ensign*, November 1989, 14)

The whisperings in all these examples seem obvious as we read them, but they are not so obvious in real life. Unless we recognize their source, they are subtle, deceptive, and persuasive. Sooner or later we will fall victim unless we learn to recognize and reject the cunning whisperings of our deadly enemies.

> Yea, ye ought to marvel because ye are given away that the devil has got so great hold upon your hearts. Yea, how could you have given way to the enticing of him who is seeking to hurl away your souls down to everlasting misery and endless wo? (Helaman 7:15–16)

If the devil finds that his whisperings are not enticing us away from our commitments to gospel covenants, he will attempt to distract and confuse our efforts, perhaps by prompting us to substitute a *lesser* good for a greater good. Consider the scheming distortion of truth which he whispered to Tohru Hotta, a Japanese convert, as was later related in a letter to the missionary who taught him the gospel. He said:

When I joined the Church, I didn't fully understand the deep significance of the law of tithing. However, I knew and trusted you, Elder Dan Hawkley, and I made a promise to you to pay tithing. I could tell you were anxious that I should keep that promise. I could not forget the challenge I had been given.

However, to be honest, I must admit that I was anxious to buy a beautiful and glittering Japanese Bible like the one you had. I wanted it to help me remember what I had been taught, as well as to remember the Elder who had helped to teach me. But it was too expensive for me to buy one. (*New Era,* December 1979, 13)

So far, no sin had been committed. It was certainly a righteous desire for this new convert to Christianity to have his own personal Bible. He continued: "I reasoned that if I didn't pay my tithing, I could obtain the Bible." Now the door has been opened to Satan, and immediately he was there. *"Satan spoke in a whisper:* 'Buy it. It's your money. Don't worry.'" (Ibid., 13) Fortunately, Brother Hotta recognized the source of the suggestion that followed his momentary consideration of neglecting tithing. Because he recognized his enemy, Brother Hotta successfully resisted the temptation. Many do not.

While the ability of Satan's army to surround us and whisper lies is alarming, we should rejoice in the knowledge that through the influence of the Holy Ghost, we can discern and reject all their encroachments. Satan cannot force us to listen to his lies. He can have absolutely no power over our minds and hearts except as we allow.

EXAMPLES OF DIVINE WHISPERINGS

Perhaps we feel angered to learn how Satan can prompt us to do things we don't want to do by the influence of his undetected whisperings. Throughout this book we will expose his pattern of lies and cunning enticements. But we must always remember that the Holy Ghost uses the same power of "whispering" to guide, inspire and encourage us.

Thoughts originate from three sources—from within us, from the promptings of the Holy Spirit, and from the evil sources around us provided by Satan and his hosts as they "whisper in our ears." We must, therefore, learn to recognize the source of our thoughts and control them accordingly. (Ronald A. Dalley, *New Era,* August 1984, 44)

As Sister Ardeth G. Kapp said, "The Holy Ghost communicates with us through 'whisperings' just as Satan and other spirit beings do" (*Ensign,* November 1990, 94).

One day, as Julie Allen was having her morning prayer, she heard her little child call out from its crib, "Mama, Mama." She said that she felt so full of joy and appreciation for her child at that moment that she asked, in her prayer, "Heavenly Father, can You hear her? Isn't she precious? Do You know how I feel when she calls, 'Mamma?'" Immediately the whispered answer formed in her mind, "Yes! That is how I feel when you call 'Father.'" (*Ensign,* January 1985, 67)

After two years in prison, a lonely inmate received a whispered assurance of the Lord's love for him. He said:

> I fell to my knees on the concrete floor and opened my heart to the Christ. I wept and begged him to forgive me for what I had been doing. I pleaded to be acceptable and to find the path back to him. As I talked with him, I felt the terrible burden I had been carrying for so long gently lifted from my shoulders. I felt a warm comforting spirit around me. It was so strong that I felt I could have reached out and touched my Lord.
>
> I was allowed to know that I had never been alone here, that even Christ had been called names as I had, that I was forgiven and loved by him and that I could yet be counted a member of his Church and attain heights greater than I could imagine, (see Steven A. Cramer, *Conquering Your Own Goliaths,* Salt Lake City, Utah: Deseret Book, 1988, 3–4)

We now understand that all messages from the other side of the veil, whether they come from Satan and his army, from the Holy Ghost, or other righteous messengers, all whisperings are communicated directly to our spirits, and then relayed into our conscious minds as thoughts, impressions, and suggestions. "I will tell you in your mind and in your heart, by the Holy Ghost, which shall come upon you and which shall dwell in your heart. Now, behold, this is the spirit of revelation." (D&C 8:2–3) Mormon related the influence of the Spirit's "whisperings" in guiding his condensing of centuries of sacred records into the Book of Mormon we have today.

I do this for a wise purpose; *for thus it whispereth me*, according to the workings of the Spirit of the Lord which is in me. And now, I do not know all things; but the Lord knoweth all things which are to come; wherefore, he worketh in me to do according to his will. (Words of Mormon 1:7)

THE LORD GUARANTEES A BALANCE

Between the extremes of Satan's power to captivate and of his utter powerlessness stretches the spectrum of his ability to entice or tempt.

> As a being of spirit, he works in the realm of spirit, *counterbalanced* by the Spirit of God. In this way, free agency is preserved, giving us a choice between good and evil. As Lehi taught, "Man could not act for himself save it should be that he was enticed by the one or the other." (2 Nephi 2:16)
>
> If Satan entices us to do evil, so the Holy Spirit "entices" us to virtue (see Mosiah 3:19). *Free agency demands that neither the Holy Spirit nor the evil spirit have power to control the person against his will.* (Lawrence R. Peterson Jr., *Ensign*, July 1984, 31)

We see this balance illustrated in the experience of Vickie Soule, who was prompted by the evil one to surrender her son to death by suffocation, while the Holy Spirit whispered instructions on how to save him. Five-year-old Kristopher suddenly passed out and she had no idea why until one of the other children told her he had swallowed some pennies. She could see they were lodged in his throat but she couldn't open his mouth. She watched in helpless panic as her son went completely limp and turned black and blue. Vickie related that she was engulfed by an evil, dark feeling as a voice whispered, Give up, Vickie, he's dead. But immediately there came another peaceful, loving whisper in her mind: "Be calm, and do the Heimlich maneuver."

She tried the maneuver but Kristopher did not respond. The Spirit whispered for her to check his throat. She did and was able to push the pennies down, opening his throat, and enabling him to breath again. "I know if I had not heard the Holy Ghost, my Kristopher would not be here," she said later. Eventually Kristopher would pass twelve pennies through the bowels. A loving Lord saw Kristopher's need, heard Satan's wicked attempts to confuse Vickie, and rushed to the rescue with divinely whispered guidance to a frightened mother, teaching her how to save her son. (see *Latter-day Sentinel*, June 3, 1983...16)

> Inspiration comes more as a feeling than as a sound. The Lord has a way of pouring pure intelligence into our minds to prompt us, to guide us, to teach us, to warn us. You can know the things you need to know *instantly!* Learn to receive inspiration. (Boyd K. Packer, *Ensign*, November 1979, 20)

As a young man, Art Berg suffered an automobile accident just a few weeks before his scheduled temple marriage. The accident broke his neck and paralyzed him from the chest down. Satan was delighted and boasted triumphantly to Art that he would use this tragedy to destroy Art's soul as well. During the first few days in the hospital, Art felt as though he was caught in the middle of a battle between two opposing forces. He said:

> On one side was all the good, right, and encouraging things in my life, led by the Lord himself. On the opposing side was Satan and his hosts, complete with all of the negative and degrading things the evil one would have me feel. In those first few days I came to understand and appreciate the vast difference in roles between these two opposing forces and the length and depth to which they would go to hurt me or to rescue me. (Art E. Berg, *Some Miracles Take Time,* American Fork, Utah: Covenant Communications, 1990, 22)

Satan will not stand by idly while the Holy Spirit places whispered inspirations in our minds. He marshals his own forces to whisper countering discouragements and defeating thoughts and temptations. For example, taking advantage of this young man's pain and fear, he reviled, "I've got you now. I have destroyed your life. Without your body you are nothing. You'll live a despicable life, and when it is over, I will have won." (Ibid., 22–23)

It is comforting to know that the Lord will not stand by idly watching Satan and his army place those kinds of whispered lies in a person's mind without counterbalancing them with whispered inspirations and assurances to lift and encourage us. Art received a wonderful "whispered" message from the Lord.

Into my mind and heart came some reassuring and powerful words I will never forget. A voice said, "Remember, Art, back a long, long time ago, when you and I sat in a great council in heaven. Remember, I said you could become like me. You thrilled at the idea. But, then I told you it would be hard, sometimes very hard. I promised you, however, with an oath and a covenant, that I would never leave you to suffer alone. Art, when you suffer, I suffer. When you hurt, I hurt. And, when you cry, I cry. I promised you then, and I will not leave you now." (Ibid., 28)

We might see another example of the balance the Lord provides when, in a moment of carelessness, one's spouse says or does something that, whether intentional or accidental, hurts us. This is a crucial time of vulnerability. We may rest assured that marital conflict will never go unnoticed by the enemy. He won't let us forget it for a moment. There are demons surrounding us constantly, just waiting for such a moment. How dare he *(or she)* say that, or do that, they whisper. He *(or she)* can't get away with that. Show him *(or her)* you will not be treated that way. Not recognizing the source of these vengeful thoughts, we may be filled with images of revenge, images of ways to turn the cold shoulder, images of ways to make the spouse pay for hurting us.

It has been said that "Forgiveness is giving up my right to hurt *you* for hurting *me.*" But that is a long way from the emotions now flooding into a wounded mind. Just on the other side of the veil there are demons casting fiery darts deep into the heart. Over and over they penetrate. Here comes a dart of anger, a dart of suggested resentment, a dart of withdrawal, a dart of calculated revenge, a dart of retaliation. Over and over the demons chant these wicked suggestions, hurling one dart after another until giving in seems the only alternative. And all this because we failed to recognize the source of the subliminal suggestions, and to defend ourselves with the shield of faith and the helmet of salvation.

If we are in tune with the Holy Spirit, we won't fall prey to these demonic suggestions. We will sense the divine warning: "You are being attacked by the devil. Don't give in to those feelings. They are beneath you. You love this person. Remember your covenants. Your marriage is more important than this moment of pain." We could shout back at the demons, "No. I recognize you. You don't own me. I won't give in to such feelings. I am the one who decides which thoughts will occupy my attention and I command you to leave me." President Kimball promised that if we live close to the Holy Ghost, "This member of the Godhead will guide, inspire, and warn, and will neutralize the promptings of the evil one." (*The Miracle of Forgiveness,* Salt Lake City, Utah: Bookcraft, 1969, 14–15) President Marion G. Romney taught:

> We know that there is available to each of us the gift of the Holy Ghost—the power of revelation which embraces the gift of discernment by which we may unerringly detect the devil and the counterfeits he is so successfully foisting upon this gullible generation. (*Ensign*, June 1971, 36–37)

Learning to ignore Satan's whisperings is very much like tuning a radio. The air is filled with radio waves broadcasting every conceivable type of program. Since a radio can play only one station at a time, however, we must decide which program to tune into. And so it is with our minds: either we tune into the Lord's frequency or Satan's. Both sides are "broadcasting" urgent messages to influence our thoughts, feelings, and choices. Neither side can compel us to listen to the messages they send. We have both the agency and the responsibility to choose which signals we allow our minds to focus upon.

Once we learn to recognize Satan's whisperings, it is as though we have taken off the blindfold and the battle is on even ground. He may catch us off guard from time to time, but never again will he be able to manipulate us in secret, undetected.

> Our Heavenly Father did not launch us on our eternal voyage without providing the means whereby we could receive from him guidance to ensure our safe return. Yes, I speak of prayer. *I speak, too, of the whisperings from that still, small voice within each of us.* (Thomas S. Monson, *Ensign*, May 1988, 55)

In Chapter 7, "The Battleground of Thought," and Chapter 20, "Putting on the Armor," we will learn how to use the Lord's helmet of salvation to protect our minds against Satan's whisperings.

5

Enemy Propaganda

"THERE IS NO DEVIL"

ONE OF SATAN'S MOST SUCCESSFUL STRATEGIES IS TO PERSUADE THE world that he does not exist. Day by day, week after week, year after year through the centuries, "He saith unto them: I am no devil, for there is none" (2 Nephi 28:22). President Marion G. Romney warned against the danger of being complacent about the devil:

> I know that there are some in the world who deny the existence of a personal Satan. This denial is false, *being sponsored by the father of lies himself.* The fact is, however, that Lucifer is a personage of spirit, just the same as Jesus and you and I were personages of spirit before we were born. Now, we may rest assured of this: if there is no devil there is no God. (*Ensign*, October 1983, 4)

One strategy is to make himself the object of ridicule so that he is not to be taken seriously. We have all seen portrayals of the devil in red, with horns on his head and a forked tail, but who would take such a creature seriously? Satan himself is the origin of this foolish depiction. It is but another attempt to deceive the world into believing he is only a myth. Elder Melvin J. Ballard explained:

> So far as the Latter-day Saints are concerned, we never conceived that the devil was a monstrosity, that he had long horns and a tail and forked hoofs. No sir, he is a gentleman in outward

appearance, and if you were to see him you would turn around to look at him. (*New Era,* March 1984, 35)

Elder David B. Haight warned:

> Many people who believe at least tentatively in the reality of God have a much harder time believing in the reality of the devil. Some even soft-pedal the subject and go along with the popular idea that the devil is a purely mythological creature. Some people roar with laughter as a television comic remarks, "The devil made me do it." Well, maybe he did! He will always try. To deny the existence of Satan and the reality of his evil power and influence is as foolish as ignoring the existence of electricity. (*Ensign,* July 1973, 56)

President Kimball was equally concerned that we take our spiritual enemies seriously.

> In these days of sophistication and error men depersonalize not only God but the devil. Under this concept Satan is a myth, useful for keeping people straight in less enlightened days but outmoded in our educated age. Nothing is further from reality. Satan is very much a personal, individual spirit being, but without a mortal body.
>
> *His desires to seal each of us his are no less ardent in wickedness than our Father's are in righteousness to attract us to his own eternal kingdom.*Yes, the devil is decidedly a person. He is also clever and trained. With thousands of years of experience behind him he has become superbly efficient and increasingly determined. (*The Miracle of Forgiveness,* 21)

The Book of Mormon teaches that many plain and precious truths have been removed from the Bible (see 1 Nephi 13:28–35). Satan, of course, was behind this and one of the things he caused to be removed or confused were the Biblical references to himself (see 2 Nephi 28:22; 2 Corinthians 4:3–4). The word "devil" appears in scripture 205 times and yet there is not a single reference to this word in the entire Old Testament. There is a total of 2,476 pages in all four current books of LDS scripture. The Bible comprises 1,590 pages, or 64 percent of the text and yet it only contains 29 percent of the references to Satan or the devil. The other three books of scripture contain 886 pages, or 36 percent of scripture and yet they contain 71 percent of all references to Satan and the devil. Clearly, Satan has not been successful in hiding himself in modern revelation as he was in the Biblical records.

The disparity between *length* of texts regarding Satan is even more compelling, because most Biblical references are brief and sketchy while Mormon scriptures contain lengthy dissertations warning us of his origin, goals, strategies, and powers. If it weren't for LDS scriptures and the teachings of modern prophets and apostles, the Latter-day Saints would be as uninformed about our adversary as the rest of the world is. But we are not ignorant of his devices, or at least, we should not be; we need not be if we will open our eyes and read what we have been given. Elder ElRay L. Christiansen said:

The truth is that Satan lives! Indeed, some have seen his satanic majesty in spirit form. President Harold B. Lee warned us to "make no mistake about his reality as a personality, even though he does not possess a physical body. Since the beginning of time, he, with his hosts . . . have waged relentless war to destroy the free agency of man."

> Those who teach that there is no devil or who declare him to be a figment of the imagination used only to frighten people are either ignorant of the facts or they themselves are deceived. (*Ensign*, November 1974, 23)

"How to Sin and Get Away with It"

Another of Satan's major strategies is to make us believe the lie that we can do anything we want and get away with it. Through one of his skilled representatives, an antichrist named Nehor, Satan taught the popular doctrine that:

> All mankind should be saved at the last day, and that they need not fear nor tremble, but that they might lift up their heads and rejoice; for the Lord had created all men, and had also redeemed all men; and, in the end, all men should have eternal life. (Alma 1:4)

Through Korihor, another antichrist, Satan taught just the opposite. Instead of all men reaping salvation upon their death, he taught that "when a man was dead, that was the end thereof (Alma 30:18). If that were true, then of course it might not matter so much what sins committed in this life.

In the hurry of these last days, Satan continues to present a dual line of propaganda. For those who will respond to direct enticement he boldly whispers, "Do this, or do that, and it mattereth not, for the Lord will uphold such at the last day" (Mormon 8:31). For those who may be troubled by conscience, Satan has many willing spokesmen who present his cunning appeasements:

> And there shall also be many which shall say: Eat, drink, and be merry; nevertheless, fear God—he will justify in committing a little sin; . . . there is no harm in this; . . . for tomorrow we die; and if it so be that we are guilty, God will beat us with a few stripes, and at last we shall be saved in the kingdom of God. (2 Nephi 28:8)

Satan's lie that "it mattereth not" is in direct opposition to the truth. It denies one of the most important laws of agency Heavenly Father has given us, the Law of the Harvest. When he presented this law, Paul was acutely aware of the appeal of Satan's doctrine that "it mattereth not," so he warned, *"Be not deceived;* God is not mocked: for *whatsoever a man soweth, that shall he also reap"* (Galatians 6:7). To think that what we do does not matter, does mock God; it mocks law and order and even cause and effect.

> For that same spirit which doth possess your bodies at the time that ye go out of this life, that same spirit will have power to possess your body in that eternal world. (Alma 34:34)

This inflexible law of justice, of cause and effect, requires God to "render to every man according to his works" (Proverbs 24:12). Satan would have us believe that we are victims of circumstance and environment and that we are stuck in our defeats. The Lord would have us realize that each person is in charge of his own choices and actions and is responsible for the harvest he reaps, regardless of circumstances. Satan is a liar. Everything we do matters. It not only matters, it has eternal consequences. If we would win our battles with Satan we must always remember our accountability and guard our actions carefully.

> And in one year were thousands and tens of thousands of souls sent to the eternal world, that they might reap their rewards

according to their works, whether they were good or whether they were bad, to reap eternal happiness or eternal misery, according to the spirit which they listed to obey, whether it be a good spirit or a bad one. *For every man receiveth wages of him whom he listeth to obey.* (Alma 3:26–27)

COUNTERFEITS AND DETOURS

As a master strategist, Satan uses a variety of campaigns in his war against mankind. The most obvious is the *direct appeal* to the gullible masses who will succumb to even the most deliberate evil suggestions. Of this direct, *undisguised* approach, Elder Mark E. Peterson said:

> Seduction is his greatest weapon. Do we realize that? I repeat: *seduction is the greatest weapon of the devil.* It is alluring; it falsely appears to be advantageous and desirable. He would have us think that bitter is sweet, that black is white, that sin is acceptable, that virtue is obsolete, archaic, and prudish. Because he revels in filth, he would tell us that to be clean is some naive concept of our grandmother's age which does not apply in this enlightened day.
>
> He says that evil is good and that standards have been relaxed. Go your way, he says; Fear no consequences; do your own thing; have fun; express your basest desires if you wish, and let yourselves go. That is his philosophy. Do we recognize it when it is flung at us by our angry foes, or when it comes with a soft voice and a disarming smile? Do we truly recognize evil when we see it? (*Ensign*, May 1980, 69)

However, we risk being deceived if we assume that Satan's temptations will always be so obviously evil that we will easily recognize him as the source. President Brigham Young warned:

> When the Devil cannot overcome an individual through temptation to commit wickedness, when he sees that a person is determined to walk in the line and travel straight forward into the celestial kingdom, he will adopt a course of flattery, will strive to exercise a pleasing influence and move along smoothly with him, and when he sees an opportunity he will try to turn him out of

the way, if it is only to the extent of a hair's breadth. (*Discourses of Brigham Young*, Salt Lake City, Utah: Deseret Book, 1951, 81)

There are millions of well-meaning, sincere, devoted Christians in the world who love the Savior as they know and understand him, who are unwittingly teaching false doctrines because they have been blinded by the traditions of men and the doctrines of the devil. One of the ways Satan detours people off the true path an inch or "a hair's breadth" at a time is by encouraging things which appear to be perfectly upright and acceptable, but which detour us from the best choices. For example, when the devil sees that a person loves the Lord and is determined to be in harmony with his will, he will try to guide that type of person into untrue religions, giving them a false sense of security. Rewarding their devotion with false feelings of salvation and spiritual ecstasy, the devil whispers, See how simple it is? All you have to do is profess belief in Christ. Accept him into your heart. See how good it feels. Now it's done. Don't be duped by all those man-made religions that demand strict ritual and obedience to an endless list of commandments. God is not like that. This is the real gospel. It's all in the heart. You are now saved. Don't express doubt of your salvation by trying to add good works.

Elder Gene R. Cook explained:

> The master of illusion teaches men to honor the Lord with their lips, while their hearts are far from the Lord. With others he disguises truth and equates spirituality with knowledge, with little or no emphasis on application of truths in personal lives. (*Ensign*, May 1982, 25)

We remember that Satan inspired some gullible people to build a tower whose top would supposedly give them access to heaven (see Genesis 11:4). Rather than submit themselves to the gospel plan which would provide for their honorable return to heaven, Satan offered them a substitute plan. Follow me and I'll show you how to get to heaven without having to obey all those commandments. Satan is a master at substituting imitations of Heavenly Father's plan.

> By every possible means he seeks to darken the minds of men and then offers them falsehood and deception in the guise of truth. *Satan is a skillful imitator,* and as genuine gospel truth is given the world in ever increasing abundance, so he spreads the counterfeit coin of false doctrine. (Joseph F. Smith, In Daniel H.

Ludlow, *Latter-day Prophets,* Salt Lake City, Utah: Bookcraft, 1948, 20–21)

Today he presents a wide range of substitute plans: psychology and philosophy in place of God's wisdom, the new age movement offering imitations of gospel principles without priesthood ordinances, reincarnation instead of resurrection, self-actualization in place of becoming like Christ, self-fulfillment instead of service in the kingdom, and astrology which presents the foolish idea that our lives are controlled by the alignment of heavenly bodies instead of by our agency and application of gospel principles. Ezra Taft Benson explained that another way Satan seeks to move us off the true path is to create confusion by twisting and distorting definitions.

> Freedom is a favorite confuser. Obscenities test the freedom of speech. Pornography, drugs, and immorality are claimed to be manifestations of personal freedom, along with miniskirts and nudity. (*Ensign,* December 1971, 55)

What's wrong with pornography? Lucifer sneers through a host of modern Korihors. Why are you ashamed of your body? Using clever, twisted logic, he tries to make it appear that those who support modesty and the sacredness of our bodies are the evil ones. Similarly, killing unborn children by abortion is done under the guise of freedom and the right to choose, making it appear that those who defend the sanctity of life are the ones against freedom and agency. Everything is cleverly twisted to redefine concepts to support sin.

> Satan . . . is the master of illusion. He creates illusions in an attempt to detour, dilute, and divert the power and the attention of the Latter-day Saints from the pure truth of God. He is particularly effective at creating spiritual illusions that cause a counterfeiting of spirituality . . . to lead them into sin and away from God. (Gene R. Cook, *Ensign,* May 1982, 25)

6

Enemy Ridicule

THE DEVIL AND HIS ANGELS ARE IN CONSTANT MISERY EXCEPT FOR the perverse pleasure they receive when they are successful in leading us into sin. "And because he had fallen from heaven, and had become miserable forever, he sought also the misery of all mankind" (2 Nephi 2:18; see also verse 27). It would appear the only time Satan gets relief from his misery is when he drags us into it as well. The guilt and suffering that we endure gives the devil so much pleasure that he actually laughs in lewd delight. For example, an excommunicated woman told me of her surprise to hear laughter in the motel room after her first act of adultery. She was startled, having thought they were alone in the room. Then the veil was removed from her eyes and she was allowed to see the room full of evil demons who were pointing at her in derision and laughing as they rejoiced at the fall of another of God's beloved children. Our choices would be far more valiant if we could just remember that we are always accompanied and observed by evil spirits who are anxious to ridicule our mistakes.

We are told that Satan made a friend of Cain. He spoke with him person to person and Cain "loved Satan more than God" (Moses 5:18). But Satan is no loyal friend to anyone. We see Satan's diabolical manipulations when he commanded Cain, saying, "Make an offering unto the Lord" (Moses 5:18). Why would Satan want someone to make an offering unto the Lord? Because he knew that he had taught Cain to do it improperly and that it was sure to be rejected by the Lord. He was deliberately setting Cain up to fail. In accordance with revealed instructions, Abel "brought of the firstlings of his flock . . . and the Lord had respect unto Abel, and to his offering." (Moses 5:20) Ignoring revealed priesthood procedures, Cain followed Satan's instructions and made a sacrifice of the produce he had raised (see Moses 5:19). Obviously, burning fruits and vegetables on an altar contains no proper symbolism of the shedding of Christ's blood and his Atonement. The imitation offering was unacceptable. When the Lord rejected his mocking sacrifice, "Cain was very wroth, and his countenance fell" (Moses 5:21). And did his personal friend, Satan, come to him with support and encouragement? No. Instead, he laughed and took delight in Cain's misery. Satan had tricked Cain into a defeating situation which led to God's rejection and Cain's unhappiness. "Now Satan knew this, and it pleased him" (Moses 5:21). In a similar manner the devil continually offers us pleasure and happiness in disobeying God's commandments, but he delivers nothing except suffering and misery: "And thus we see that the devil will not support his children at the last day, but doth speedily drag them down to hell" (Alma 30:60).

When Jesus came to America following his resurrection in Jerusalem, he told the people of Satan's delight in the cataclysmic destructions which had killed so many sinful unbelievers. "For the devil laugheth," Jesus told the survivors, "and his angels rejoice, because of the slain of the fair sons and daughters of my people" (3 Nephi 9:2).

Satan hates all who are faithful to God's plan because they are moving toward eternal happiness while he is moving toward eternal darkness and damnation. Yet he remains recklessly defiant and arrogant. After Enoch and his city were translated and taken from this earth, Enoch had a vision in which he saw that "the power of Satan was upon all the face of the earth. And he beheld Satan; and he had a great chain in his hand, and it veiled the whole face of the earth with darkness" (Moses 7:24, 26). And then, as if Satan was aware of the Lord and Enoch looking down upon him, "he looked up and laughed, and his angels rejoiced" (Moses 7:26).

An active LDS couple stayed a night in a motel which provided cable television. The husband fell asleep while the wife stayed up to watch the rest of a movie. At first she didn't realize it was R-rated. They never watched such movies, but by the time she realized the rating, she was intrigued and wanted to see the rest of it. "Turn it off now," the Spirit whispered. No. Don't turn it off. It's not so bad, Satan countered. Besides, it's so interesting. You can handle it. What can one time hurt? She gave in to the temptation and watched the rest of the movie. When it was over she felt defiled. She had compromised her integrity by deliberately watching a movie which was not conducive to the companionship of the Holy Spirit which had urged her to turn off the movie. And then she heard the laughter. Ugly, mocking laughter which came from Satan and his demons. It took over half an hour on her knees to drive the evil spirits away and feel safe again.

In Chapter 4 we introduced Art Berg, the young man who was paralyzed from the neck down after an automobile accident broke his neck. Satan used that opportunity to laugh at Art and ridicule his helplessness with such persistency that he was unable to sleep for the first four nights following his emergency surgery. He said:

> My body was exhausted from the trauma of the accident. However, as night would fall and I would try to sleep I began to hear voices in my mind. *I heard laughter; it was a hideous sound.* For a long time these voices and laughter were unrecognizable. All I knew was that the source must somehow be evil because of the fear it created in me. I fought sleep, terrified of the things I was hearing and feeling . . . the laughter . . . seemed to come from hundreds of voices.
>
> As I slowly understood the source of my fear, my family and I turned to the only power that could help us. In prayer, and through the power of the priesthood, we asked God to send his ministering angels to guard the way. Peace returned to our little room from that moment on, and I was free. Fear was destroyed, and faith, assurance, and hope were ushered in to be my constant companions. (*Some Miracles Take Time*, American Fork, Utah: Covenant Communications, 1990, 22–23)

Knowing that Satan laughs at our folly and rejoices in our mistakes should make us angry enough to resist him. It should create a greater determination not to be duped into sinful choices that cause him and his angels to rejoice (see Helaman 7:16). If we do not wish to be the object of his fun and ridicule, we will work diligently to recognize his attacks and protect ourselves by putting on the full armor of God every day of our lives.

PART TWO

———◆———

Determine Your Strategy

7

The Battleground of Thought

ASK SOMEONE TO NAME THE LOCATION OF THE GREATEST BATTLES ever fought and they will mention places like Gettysburg, Trafalgar, Iwo Jima, and Iraq. But the most frequent battles, the most intense and important battles occur within the mind. It is there that we wage hand-to-hand combat with Satan and his determined army of evil spirits.

> The greatest battle of life is fought within the silent chambers of your own soul. (David O. McKay, *Ensign*, May 1980, 56)

Every successful army has a command center from which the war is directed. It may be a special tent located a few miles behind the front line or it may be buried deep in the earth in a concrete bunker. Wherever it is, it is occupied by the general in charge, his assistants, and massive amounts of communication equipment. Our "command centers" are in our heads. We may choose to call it the mind or the brain, but whatever we call it, it is the part of us which controls our thoughts, focus of attention, and emotions, and selects our priorities, choices, and actions.

Just as every military man wears a helmet to protect his head from injury, it is vital to protect our own command centers in our battles with Satan. Every time the Lord has commanded us to "put on the whole armor of God," he has included the instruction to protect our minds by putting on "the helmet of salvation" (see Ephesians 6:17; D&C 27:18). Setting the example in all things, Christ himself put "an helmet of salvation upon his head" (Isaiah 59:17).

Imagine the quick victory an enemy would win if he could cause confusing and self-defeating orders to come from the opposing army's command center. One of Satan's foremost objectives is to gain control of our thoughts by drawing our attention away from the Lord and his commandments. He focuses his war on the battleground of the mind because he knows that "to be carnally minded is death; but to be spiritually minded is life and peace" (Romans 8:6). He knows that whoever controls the thought patterns controls the behavior patterns. The reason for this is simple. By influencing thoughts, Satan can influence attitudes and behaviors. Since all sin originates in thought, there is no deliberate thought too small to have an effect. No one cheats or steals without first indulging thoughts of greed. No one commits adultery without first entertaining thoughts of lust. If we think about an idea long enough, we are probably going to act it out because the thoughts we focus attention on are the blueprints of our future reality. The sin may not come for months or even years, but sooner or later we always reap in our physical lives what we first sow in our mental lives. Thus, whether we are obedient, valiant, and righteous, or mediocre, lukewarm, or even evil is first determined in the battleground of our thoughts.

To better understand Satan's attacks against our thoughts, we need to understand how the mind works. There is a law of mental function which is crucial to spiritual combat. The Bible states it this way: "As he thinketh in his heart, so is he" (Proverbs 23:7). There is another way to express this important law: "**What holds my attention holds me.**" Expressing the law of mental function this way is helpful because we all have difficulty controlling our thoughts, but every person can learn to control what holds his *attention*. Later we will explain how to do this. We may battle long and hard to control behavior using will power alone, but that is merely a surface battle against symptoms and ignores the fact that the mind is the control center. The real source of our faults lies within us, in the way the carnal mind thinks and directs our actions. Emmet Fox explained:

> The difference between a man of weakness and one of power lies not in the strength of the personal will, but in that focus of consciousness which represents their stage of knowledge. Whatever you give your attention to is the thing that governs your life.
>
> Attention is the key. Your free will lies in the directing of

> your attention. Whatever you steadfastly direct your attention to, will come into your life and dominate it. (*The Sermon On The Mount,* New York: Harper and Row, 109)

No matter how earnestly we attempt to break our bad habits and addictions, we are unlikely to succeed if we spend all our time and emotion focusing on the *sins* instead of the *solution,* which is changing the focus of our thoughts so that we have a closer relationship with Jesus Christ. When we pray about stopping our improper behaviors, without addressing our improper thought patterns, we unwittingly defeat ourselves. It will be, as James described: "Ye ask, and receive not, because ye ask amiss" (James 4:3). Our prayers can actually work in reverse because the more thought and energy we focus on the bad habits we are trying to conquer, the more they dominate our lives. **What holds my attention holds me.** When we get our attention off the symptoms we are compulsively acting out and learn to focus it on Jesus Christ and his promises of deliverance, our lives will be changed. Focusing our thoughts on Christ instead of on our sins opens the door to our hearts and makes it possible for him to reach inside and remove the compulsions and desires for evil. Only when our attention is focused in the right place can he give us a new heart and nature. When Christ holds your attention, he will at last hold your heart and be able to make you free.

> When we take time to look beyond our immediate problems and listen to the Spirit's promptings, we discover that our Heavenly Father is there protecting, guiding, and helping us every hour and every minute of every day. (Kellie Burrahm, *New Era,* January 1989, 11).

We will next consider several ways to think about the mind, or "command control center," which will help us understand how it works, how Satan attacks it, and why it is so important to protect it with a spiritual "helmet of salvation."

A THEATRICAL STAGE

Many writers have compared the mind to a stage. Unlike a theatrical stage, however, the stages of our minds are never empty. Something is always playing there. If we do not keep our stages filled with positive, spiritual thoughts, Satan will fill the void with negative, evil, and self-defeating thoughts. As we explained in Chapter 4, "Satanic Subliminals," placing whispered lies, temptations, and discouragements in our minds is Satan's most potent weapon. Undoubtedly every reader has experienced the sudden appearance of evil thoughts which had no possible origin in the previous train of thought. Such thoughts and feelings are triggered by Satan's whisperings. President Benson explained it this way:

> From one side of the wings the Lord, who loves you, is trying to put on the stage of your mind that which will bless you. From the other side of the wings the devil, who hates you, is trying to put on the stage of your mind that which will curse you. Usually with our hardly realizing it, he slips into our thoughts. (*Ensign*, April 1984, 11)

Using the same analogy, Elder Boyd K. Packer asked:

> Have you ever noticed that without any real intent on your part . . . a shady little thought may creep into your attention? These delinquent thoughts will try to upstage everybody. If you permit them to go on . . . they will enact for you . . . anything to the limits of your toleration. (*Ensign*, January 1974, 28)

We are distressed when Satan places unworthy thoughts and desires in our minds. We wonder, "Why do I think such things?" This is extremely dangerous, because if we fail to recognize the source of such thoughts we are vulnerable to Satan's next strategy. One of his most deadly devices is to first whisper unclean thoughts to us and then turn around and accuse us of being unworthy for having such thoughts. What a wicked person you are, he sneers. Look what you were thinking. You have an unclean mind. You are dirty. God couldn't possibly love you with such filthy thoughts in your mind. You should not pray. You should not attend church. You are not worthy. You are inferior.

Because we are surrounded by Satan's treacherous demons who constantly whisper evil thoughts and temptations to us, we must learn not to respond automatically to such thoughts with feelings of self-condemnation. All people experience unworthy and discouraging thoughts from time to time. It is a normal part of mortality, and we place ourselves in jeopardy if we automatically feel guilty just because an unworthy thought suddenly appears in our minds.

The important factor in judging a person's righteousness is not the *appearance* of unworthy thoughts, but his *response* to the thoughts once they have appeared. Does he or she enjoy the thoughts placed there by Satan? Does the person allow Satan to expand the ideas, contemplate, and wish for their fulfillment, or does he reject them and turn his attention to more holy considerations? Wearing the helmet of salvation will help keep evil thoughts off our mental stages and out of our conscious minds, but this requires constant vigilance. And sometimes, in spite of one's most diligent effort to prevent him, the devil manages to slip those thoughts into the mind. What do we do then? We must *replace* them with good thoughts. As Elder Boyd K. Packer emphasized:

> Bad thoughts often have to be evicted a hundred times, or a thousand. *But if they have to be evicted ten thousand times, never surrender to them.* You are in charge of you. Do not try merely to discard a bad habit or a bad thought. Replace it. When you try to eliminate a bad habit, if the spot where it used to be is left open, it will sneak back and crawl again into that empty space. It grew there; it will struggle to stay there. When you discard it, fill up the spot where it was. Replace it with something good. (*Speeches of the Year,* Provo, Utah: BYU Press, 1978–79, 39)

Let's remember that an individual is always in charge of what stays in the focus of his attention. While we cannot always control what *appears* on our mental stages, we can always control what *remains* there. President Benson emphasized that neither Satanic suggestions nor divine whisperings are forced upon us. "You are the stage manager," he said, "You are the one who decides which thought will occupy the stage. You are the one who must decide whose thoughts you will entertain." (Ezra Taft Benson, *Ensign*, April 1984, 11) Paul also emphasized that if we fight our battles the Lord's way, guarding our sacred minds with the helmet of salvation, we can have the total victory of "casting down imaginations . . . and bringing into captivity every thought to the obedience of Christ" (2 Corinthians 10:5). We will explain how to do this in coming chapters.

A TEMPLE

The Lord has told us to regard our bodies as temples. Surely the mind would be the holy of holies. "Know ye not that ye are the temple of God, and that the Spirit of God dwelleth in you? For the temple of God is holy, which temple ye are" (1 Corinthians 3:16–17). Just as the Lord is aware of what goes on inside each of our official church temples, he is also aware of what goes on inside our temple-minds. It is almost beyond mortal conception that God, who has a universe of innumerable worlds to oversee, actually monitors our thoughts to see what use we make of our minds each day, but he does. Because of his great love for us, "The Lord searcheth all hearts, and understandeth all the imaginations of the thoughts" (1 Chronicles 28:9). "He looketh down upon all the children of men; and he knows all the thoughts and intents of the heart" (Alma 18:32). The Lord said, "I know the things that come into your mind, every one of them" (Ezekiel 11:5).

Just as priesthood authority is used to guard temple buildings and assure the purity and worthiness of every person who enters, so we should guard what we allow to enter our temple-minds. H. Burke Peterson of the Presiding Bishopric has counseled:

> Our minds are tremendous reservoirs; they have the capacity to retain anything we put into them. We can put filth, garbage . . . or vulgarity into our minds—or we can fill them with beauty and spiritual experiences.
>
> Our minds, however, are not like our physical bodies. When we put something into our physical body that isn't right, that is dirty or trashy, that is not good for us, we can get rid of it in a brief period through natural bodily processes. But our minds will retain the trashy kinds of things for days and weeks, months and years, and sometimes for a lifetime. So the important thing to do, remembering that the mind has a hard time cleansing itself, is to be careful of what you put into it.
>
> Every time you look at something that would not have the approval of the Master, you are filling your mind with something that you will have a hard time getting rid of. Those who unceasingly fill their minds with things that are filthy and ugly are the ones who are led step-by-step into terribly destructive experiences. (*Ensign*, June 1981, 73–74)

Elder Joseph B. Wirthlin warned: "Experience teaches that when the will and the imagination are in conflict, the imagination usually wins." (*Ensign*, May 1982, 24) One way we can strengthen our helmets of salvation is to resolve: I will allow no picture to hang on the walls of my imagination that I would not hang on the walls of my home. And I will not allow myself to imagine something mentally that I would not do physically.

Another way to strengthen the spiritual helmets that guard our minds is to "Let this mind be in you, which was also in Christ Jesus" (Philippians 2:5). We know from the scriptures how Christ feels about the issues and challenges we face and we can train ourselves to face those daily choices with the ever-present question, "What would Jesus do?" As President Benson has counseled, "If thoughts make us what we are, and we are to be like Christ, then we must think Christlike thoughts" (*Ensign*, April 1984, 11).

> What you sincerely, in your heart, think of Christ will determine what you are, will largely determine what your acts will be. No person can study this divine personality, can accept his teachings without becoming conscious of an uplifting and refining influence within himself. (David O. McKay, *Gospel Ideals*, Salt Lake City, Utah: *Improvement Era* publication, 1953, 34)

Scripture reveals that there is a sacred record, a "book of remembrance" kept in heaven which contains the names of those who reverence and appreciate the Lord and think about him often (see Malachi 3:16). If we do not learn to control the thoughts which occupy our minds in *this* life, we will one day find ourselves standing before the Lord in great shame because:

> We will not be found spotless; and our thoughts will also condemn us; and in this awful state we shall not dare to look up to our God; and we would fain be glad if we could command the rocks and the mountains to fall upon us to hide us from his presence. (Alma 12:14)

What an awful, eternally damning consequence of allowing Satan to control our thoughts. On the other hand, the Lord has promised that if you will keep the stage of your temple-mind clean and occupy it with wholesome, spiritual things, if you will "let virtue garnish thy thoughts unceasingly; then shall thy confidence wax strong in the presence of God," and you will rejoice to be there (D&C 121:45).

AN ELECTROMAGNET

The mind often functions like a magnet. This attribute produces either one's greatest weakness or greatest strength. The thoughts and values we store in our minds are polarized, similar in effect to an electromagnet. They attract some things and repel some things, just like the opposite poles of a magnet. The helmet of salvation will help us to attract the things of the Spirit and to repel the evil tendencies of the carnal mind.

What holds your attention holds you is a powerful statement which can change your life, but only if you understand *why* this law is true and how it magnetizes or polarizes the mind. This principle can be explained by reviewing some simple high-school physics. A bar of metal in its dormant state is inert and inactive. It has no power to attract or repel another piece of metal. It is neutral. But when an electrical current runs through that same bar of metal the molecular structure is reorganized so that it becomes magnetized with positive and negative poles. That lifeless, inert piece of metal gains power because it is polarized. Now it will attract and repel other magnets and pieces of metal. The power of the electromagnet is not dependent upon the metal so much as on the amount of current running through it. The greater the flow of electrical current, the more powerful the magnet becomes.

The mind works the same way, with thoughts and feelings acting as the electrical current that runs through it. **What holds your attention holds you.** Focus on negative, self-defeating thoughts and your mind will be polarized to act out those commands. That is what an addiction is: a mind which has had so many evil, lustful, intense desires and thoughts run through it that it is polarized to attract the very things we are trying to resist. An addicted mind is like a giant, powerful magnet which attracts evil. And the strength of mental addiction is proportionate to the frequency and intensity of the thoughts and desires we run through our brain cells.

There is one important difference between the magnetism and

polarity of the metal and the magnetism and polarity of the mind. As soon as the current is removed from the bar of metal it returns to its former state of being, that is, lifeless and inert. The magnetism and power have vanished. But the mind is not like that. The polarizing, magnetizing, addicting power of the intellectual and emotional currents we run through our brain cells is cumulative. Every thought and feeling adds to those that went before. Every time we give in and indulge the unworthy thoughts and desires Satan is suggesting, the strength of the mind's polarity is increased. It accumulates and grows stronger, thought by thought, choice by choice, sin by sin, day by day. Consequently, what may have begun as a normal, human weakness can, repeated again and again with action, thought, and intense feelings, cause the negative, evil polarity of the mind to grow stronger and stronger until it becomes a monster we cannot control. The mind becomes so saturated, magnetized, or polarized that we are repelled by righteous things and attracted by every impulse or wicked suggestion that Satan whispers. Even the slightest thought or temptation unleashes the huge, accumulated power of this magnetic, mental monster so that over and over we are pulled into the sin we hate. This is the bondage of addiction. Satan would have us believe it is permanent, but through the power of Jesus Christ, every person who is willing to pay the price can reverse the current and repolarize the mind to attract and act on spiritual thoughts. Chapter 20 will explain how to take control of the mind's polarity, reverse the current, and undo the accumulated power of addictive thoughts.

The protective helmet of salvation is not something external that is put on the *outside* of the head. It is spiritual, created by what goes on *inside* the mind. Just as "God is mindful of every people," so he expects us to be mindful of him during our daily activities (see Alma 26:37). Wearing the helmet of salvation means using our minds to focus our thoughts and affections on the Lord, on the principles of spiritual combat he has revealed, and on his promises to be part of our battles. Alma said, "Let all thy thoughts be directed unto the Lord" (Alma 37:36). And Christ said, "Look unto me in every thought" (D&C 6:36). Not remembering the Lord in our day-to-day affairs leads to negative polarity and sin, while consciously remembering him leads to positive polarity and righteousness. Using the helmet of salvation to shut out worldly influence and focus our thoughts on Christ is so important that we are commanded to renew our covenants in the ordinance of the sacrament weekly, as we witness to the Father that we intend to always remember the Savior and pray for his Spirit to be with us (see D&C 20:79).

In Appendix B and Chapter 20, "Putting on the Armor," we will explain a proven program for driving away the most stubbornly entrenched thought patterns and for filling the empty chambers of our minds with power principles that guarantee victory on the battleground of thought.

8

The Battleground of Prayer

To wage a successful war it is necessary for the troops on the front lines to remain in communication with the general who is directing the battle. You and I are soldiers on the front lines of the war between Satan and God. Communication with our commander is called prayer. Our prayer lives determine whether we fight the war alone or with the help of the Lord. Our loving Father has shared many reasons why constant prayer is essential to winning our battles. To begin with, "Ye must watch and pray always *lest ye enter into temptation*" (3 Nephi 18:18). Being enticed by temptation is like getting shot at by the enemy. The Lord warns us to pray always against temptation because it is a real danger for all of us. The moment we stop praying about temptation is the moment we become vulnerable to spiritual injury.

> Humble yourselves before the Lord, and call on his holy name, and watch and pray continually, that ye may not be tempted above that which ye can bear, and thus be led by the Holy Spirit" (Alma 13:28)

Worse than being wounded by the enemy is being captured, so the Lord has also warned that "ye must watch and pray always, lest ye be tempted by the devil, *and ye be led away captive by him*" (3 Nephi 18:15). The mistaken idea that we can handle temptation without prayer leaves us without divine protection and greatly increases the likelihood of injury or capture. "Pray always, that you may come off conqueror; yea, that you may conquer Satan, and that you may escape the hands of the servants of Satan that do uphold his work" (D&C 10:5).

The counsel to pray always applies as much to the valiant and obedient disciple as it does to the sinner. Our Heavenly Father must be very disappointed when we turn our backs on him by not praying, saying, in effect, "Don't bother with this, Lord; I'll handle it myself."

The Lord understands the stress of continual battle and has provided opportunities for each weary warrior to temporarily retreat from the front line of conflict to renew his or her strength and determination. Jesus Christ has promised to shelter us and provide personal refuge when we need to regroup and recuperate. "The Lord also will be a refuge for the oppressed, a refuge in times of trouble" (Psalms 9:9). "God is our refuge and strength, a very present help in trouble. Therefore will not we fear, though the earth be removed, and though the mountains be carried into the midst of the sea" (Psalms 46:1–2) To show the tenderness and compassion with which the Lord seeks to protect us when we need relief he has promised, "For, behold, I will gather them as a hen gathereth her chickens under her wings, if they will not harden their hearts" (D&C 10:65).

> For thou hast been a strength to the poor, a strength to the needy in his distress, a refuge from the storm, a shadow from the heat, when the blast of the terrible ones is as a storm against the wall. (Isaiah 25:4)

Satan Says "Don't Pray"

A soldier who is isolated from his commander is one who is likely to be frightened, confused, and ineffective. Therefore, a major strategy of the enemy forces is to isolate us from the Lord by preventing prayer and breaking the line of communication with deity. To accomplish this objective, Satan's first suggestion is simply, Don't pray. It's stupid. You are too intelligent for such nonsense. Don't pray.

> For if ye would hearken unto the Spirit which teacheth a man to pray ye would know that ye must pray; *for the evil spirit teacheth not a man to pray, but teacheth him that he must not pray.* But

behold, I say unto you that you must pray always and not faint.
(2 Nephi 32:8–9)

We give a victory to Satan every time we neglect a prayer that should have been offered. If he cannot persuade us to *abandon prayer,* Satan's next strategy is one of *delay.* Okay, go ahead and pray, but don't do it right now. Wait awhile; wait until tomorrow. As an example, let's consider a prayer before going to bed. Drawing upon his vast manpower, Satan can quickly surround us with demons who chant unceasingly how tired we are. You've got to lie down, they whisper repeatedly. See how tired you are. You can hardly stay awake. It is important to take care of your body. You need your sleep. You can pray tomorrow. Get off your knees and into that bed now. If we don't recognize the source of these thoughts, they make perfectly good sense and into the bed we go, manipulated once again by our enemy, who then spends the night continuing to whisper frustrating, discouraging thoughts that fill our dreams with stress and cause us to awaken more tired than when we went to bed. We have all had those kinds of suggestions distract us when we are trying to pray.

A prayer delayed is almost as good a victory for Satan as a prayer never said because it is so easy for one delay to slip into another and days and weeks slip by as we struggle on our own and wonder why heaven seems so far away. Satan knows that if a person does not pray *in* his need, he will *remain* in his need.

Satan seems to have a contingency plan for every attack that fails. If he finds that he cannot prevent or delay a person's prayer, he will attack the person with confusion. He surrounds the person with evil spirits who whisper all kinds of distracting thoughts. Suddenly the person can't seem to focus on his prayer; his mind wanders off in every direction. This is simply because those whispered thoughts from our enemy are being conveyed through the spirit into the conscious mind. The thing to do in this situation is to pray for the ability to focus. Ask for a shield of light to surround you and shut out the demons so that you can communicate with your Heavenly Father.

Another strategy Satan uses to delay our prayers is trying to make us feel guilty about asking God for blessings, suggesting that the Lord is too busy to be bothered with us, or expects us to handle everything on our own. But God has given assurance that "I, the Lord, am merciful and gracious unto those who fear me, and *delight* to honor those who serve me in righteousness and in truth unto the end" (D&C 76:5). We do not bother God when we invite him to bless our lives. We bring him joy. What does bother God is when we avoid our prayers because we don't trust him enough to express our deepest desires. He has encouraged us to share our desires in prayer when he said that, "whoso believeth in Christ, doubting nothing, whatsoever he shall ask the Father in the name of Christ it shall be granted him; *and this promise is unto all, even unto the ends of the earth*" (Mormon 9:21).

> In every thing by prayer and supplication with thanksgiving let your requests be made known unto God. (Philippians 4:6)

OPENNESS AND HONESTY

If Lucifer cannot prevent or delay our prayers, he has yet another backup plan: encouraging superficial, repetitious prayers. He can defeat the purpose and effectiveness of one's prayer if he can move the person to pray superficially because he knows it is "counted evil unto a man, if he shall pray and not with real intent of heart; yea, and it profiteth him nothing, for God receiveth none such" (Moroni 7:9). Don't pray about the real problem. Just go through the motions and say the standard things, he whispers. An insincere prayer, a prayer that is dishonest in that it does not express one's real feelings, will only lead a person into spiritual bondage. Elder H. Burke Peterson taught the importance of making our prayers an honest expression of our feelings and desires. He said:

> As you feel the need to confide in the Lord or to improve the quality of your visits with him, may I suggest a process to follow: go where you can be alone, go where you can speak out loud to him. The bedroom, the bathroom, or the closet will do. Now, picture him in your mind's eye. Think to whom you are speaking, control your thoughts—don't let them wander, address him as your Father and your friend. Now tell him things you really feel to tell him—not trite phrases that have little meaning, but *have a sincere, heartfelt conversation with him.* Confide in him, thank him, ask him for forgiveness, plead with him, enjoy him, express your love to him, and then listen for his answers. (*Melchizedek Priesthood Manual,* 1974–75, 117)

Another way Satan attempts to harm a person's prayer life is by making the person think that Heavenly Father resents his or her problems. Most of us do not like to hear another person's problems. It makes us uncomfortable, but God isn't like that. An honest expression of a person's pain and confusion and sorrow does not drive him away. He rejoices when we bring our burdens to him because that gives him an opportunity to demonstrate his power on our behalf. As Sister Jayne B. Malan explained:

> Your Heavenly Father knows you and cares about what you are doing. Be on your knees daily and talk to your Heavenly Father. Share the happy times. Talk about what's hard for you. He'll be there to walk with you, and to comfort and protect you, for he has promised to those who seek him, "I will be on your right hand and on your left, and my Spirit shall be in your hearts, and mine angels round about you, to bear you up." (D&C 84:88) (*Ensign*, November 1989, 79)

It is no use pretending when we approach God. Like it or not, he knows us better than we know ourselves. Therefore, we must break ourselves, yes, break our very hearts, by coming to him just as we are, fully acknowledging our weaknesses, our faults, sins, bad habits, indeed, our entire unworthiness and need for him to change us. "Yea, acknowledge your unworthiness before God at all times" (Alma 38:14). Nothing will do but a full admission of how much we need him. Jesus praised the prayer of the humble man who "would not lift up so much as his eyes to heaven, but smote upon his breast, saying, God be merciful to me a sinner" (Luke 18:13). And the amazing and joyful truth is that when we do come to him honestly and openly, he responds much faster than he can when we attempt to hold our faults behind our backs, as if he didn't know about them.

Christ exemplified the importance of honesty in prayer in the Garden of Gethsemane where he wavered and wished to avoid completion of the Atonement. In the premortal counsel, Jesus Christ promised Heavenly Father and each of us that he would come to earth and sacrifice himself to pay for our sins and mistakes. Had he failed in this, we would have been doomed to eternal darkness and the torments of Satan. The New Testament demonstrates Christ's commitment to fulfill that promise. But as he entered the Garden of Gethsemane and the effects of our sins began to press down upon him, as he began to feel the guilt and shame and horror of *our* sins, the same as if he had committed them himself, he began "to be sore amazed, and to be very heavy" (Mark 14:33). He said to his apostles, "My soul is exceeding sorrowful, even unto death" (Matthew 26:38). No mortal words can convey the agony which he suffered, but we do know that his experience was not a picturesque, idealistic, peaceful kneeling at the side of a rock as we often see portrayed in art. The scriptures reveal that as his agony increased, "he went a little farther, and fell on his face, and prayed, saying, O my Father, if it be possible, let this cup pass from me: nevertheless not as I will, but as thou wilt" (Matthew 26:39).

The incomprehensible weight and agony of bearing the punishment for our sins was so great that not even Christ could accomplish it in one short session. Three times he rose from the terrible anguish and returned to the sleeping apostles. Three times he went back, alone, to feel and to suffer and to atone for us. And three times, in great, unbearable torment, he cried out to the Father for deliverance from the agony of that awful pain which was crushing down upon him because of my sins and yours. Three times he expressed his fear and dread and wavering, saying the same words: "O my Father, if this cup may not pass away from me, except I drink it, thy will be done" (Matthew 26:42).

Now we must ask why the Savior, who came to show us the perfect example of holiness and submission to the Father, would want us to know that this suffering caused "even God, the greatest of all, to tremble because of pain . . . *and would that I might not drink the bitter cup, and shrink*" (D&C 19:18). There are at least three reasons he wanted us to know of his desire for escape, and they have a lot to do with honesty in our own prayers. To begin with, when our mortal weaknesses cause us to waver in our duties, to shrink from our responsibilities and wish we could find an easier way, we can remember that Christ also had those same feelings. Jesus wants us to understand that there is neither shame nor disgrace in feeling tired or wanting to quit or hoping to escape the challenges we encounter. Not as long, that is, as we endure to the end and continue to pray, in spite of our feelings, "nevertheless, not my will, but thine be done."

Secondly, Jesus was not denied the help for which he asked. An angel appeared, "strengthening him," helping him to remain steadfast and true to his covenants (see Luke 22:43). We should realize that when fear, discouragement, or weariness is pulling us away from *our* duties, we too can pray for and receive divine assistance to remain faithful to our callings and duties. Joseph Smith counseled us to abandon our pride in those times of wavering or weakness, admit our needs and ask for help to stay faithful: "Help thy servants to say, with thy grace assisting them: thy will be done, O Lord, and not ours" (D&C 109:44). We must remember that if Jesus Christ had to call to his Father for help, there is no reason for us to feel ashamed when we follow that perfect, divine example.

And finally, a third message of this sacred account is that we must be totally honest with God in our prayers. The Savior did not try to fake the garden experience. He was in agony with unfamiliar feelings of shame and guilt and punishment for sins he did not commit. To his great alarm, he found himself afraid and shrinking from his duty, looking for a way of escape (see D&C 19:18). But he was honest and humble enough to tell his Father exactly how he felt. He certainly did not *want* to waver, so he asked for help. When a person is hurting and his commitment is weakening, he should say so in prayer. Urgent prayer. Immediate prayer. We must not allow foolish pride to try and hide our real feelings from God. He already knows how we feel—and he understands. He did not condemn Jesus, nor count his wavering as sin. Rather, he sent help to strengthen his son's resolve and keep him in the line of duty, and that is exactly what he will do for us when we are honest and submissive in prayer. Satan cannot defeat us on this battleground as long as we trust our Heavenly Father enough to be open and honest in our prayers.

ARE WE WORTHY TO PRAY?

Unfortunately, we are often reluctant to have an honest, open, heartfelt conversation because we are ashamed of our evil, selfish, or unworthy desires. Regrettably, many of us have come to feel shame over the problems of mortality, the very experiences we were sent here to encounter. It is precisely at the time when people seek to draw closer to Heavenly Father through repentance that Satan manipulates their lack of confidence to ruin their prayers. You can't talk to him now, he shouts. Wait till you've been good for awhile. Wait until after you've repented. But how can people repent and receive Father's help and strength and encouragement in that repentance if they are pretending they can hide their unworthiness from him? It is unfortunate when we allow our hurts, our sins, our feelings, or any other forms of spiritual sickness to come between us and the Lord.

When people have infections or diseases they do not feel ashamed to go to medical doctors for help, so why should they feel ashamed to admit to God that they need his spiritual help? We go for medical help when we have problems because we have faith in the doctor's ability to cure us. Why, then, when we have spiritual problems, are we reluctant to go to the greatest Physician of all? The medical doctor does not "look down" on a person for having a problem. Rather, he welcomes the opportunity to help restore the person's health. He respects that person for caring enough to take the appropriate action. Will God respect us less for coming to him for help? "Come unto me, all ye that labour and are heavy laden, and I will give you rest" (Matthew 11:28). Our repentance will be a thousand times more difficult without him than it would be if we humbly trust him to love us even in our imperfections. What a barrier to progress when we have so little faith and trust in God's love for us that we dare not reveal our innermost frustrations and pains to him. Bishop H. Burke Peterson testified:

> I know that whenever one of Heavenly Father's children kneels and talks to him, he listens. I know this as well as I know anything in the world—that Heavenly Father listens to every prayer from his children. I know our prayers ascend to heaven. No matter what we may have done wrong, he listens to us. (*Ensign*, June 1981, 73)

Elder Richard G. Scott said:

> If your life is in disarray and you feel uncomfortable and unworthy to pray because you are not clean, don't worry. *He already knows about all of that. He is waiting for you to kneel in humility and take the first few steps.* Pray for strength. Pray for others to be led to support you and guide you and lift you. Pray that the love of the Savior will pour into your heart. Pray that the miracle of the Atonement will bring forgiveness because you are willing to change. I know that those prayers will be answered, for God

loves you. His son gave his life for you. I know they will help you. (*Ensign*, November 1988, 77)

A man does not have to be perfect right now to receive an answer to his prayers, but he has to be humble in his heart and trying his best to fulfill the commandments. Then the Lord will assist him. (Gene R. Cook, *New Era*, December 1988, 7)

THE NEED FOR PERSISTENCE

If Satan cannot persuade us to abandon or delay our prayers, if he cannot persuade us to dilute and sugar-coat them, he will work to discourage us so that we will give up before the answers come. Look how long you've prayed. When will you realize there is no answer? he sneers. You are wasting your time depending on God. Take care of it yourself. Satan hopes we will believe that we are bothering God when we persist in our petitions. But persistent prayers do not bother God. What does bother him is when we don't trust him enough to keep asking until the response is given.

Someone has said that persistence is just another word for faith. When people persist in asking God to grant their righteous desires they are, in effect, bearing witness to him of their testimony of his goodness and grace. By persistently expressing our desires to him we are manifesting confidence in him. We are showing that we know he has the power and the willingness to grant our desires if they are right. We exhibit faith and trust in him when we claim his promise to grant unto us "according to our desires." On the other hand, consider the lack of faith we manifest if we do not continue to ask for the things we desire and need, thereby shutting him out of our lives.

Those who give up on their prayers not only forfeit the granting of their desires but, even more importantly, they lose the opportunity to grow closer to a Father and Savior who yearn to be part of their life. "Evening, and morning, and at noon, will I pray, and cry aloud: and he shall hear my voice" (Psalms 55:17). Unprecedented blessings were given to Jared and his brother through the personal ministrations of the premortal Jehovah who said, "And thus I will do unto thee because this long time ye have cried unto me" (Ether 1:43).

Persisting in our prayers, however, does not give us the right to demand an answer according to our personal timetable. Praying to Heavenly Father is not like putting coins in a divine vending machine. The spiritually mature person will exercise patience and trust, knowing that Father will respond according to the divine timing that will be for our best good. As Paul stated: "For ye have need of patience, that, after ye have done the will of God, ye might receive the promise" (Hebrews 10:36). Patience is the willingness to trust God to answer our prayers in his own way and in his own time, without demanding an immediate response. "For the people of the Lord are they who wait for him" (2 Nephi 6:13). When the faith we feel is rooted in the assurance of God's unceasing, unwavering love, we can willingly and patiently accept anything that happens as we trust his promises: Patience demonstrates that trust. Impatience and doubt deny it.

> Yea, I know that God will give liberally to him that asketh. Yea, my God will give me, if I ask not amiss; therefore I will lift up my voice unto thee; yea, I will cry unto thee, my God, the rock of my righteousness. Behold, my voice shall forever ascend up unto thee, my rock and mine everlasting God. Amen. (2 Nephi 4:35)

Satan cannot defeat us on the battleground of prayer as long as we persist in our prayers, trust the Lord's timing and refuse to give in. Don't ever let Satan tell you that your prayers make no difference, because the promise is that "the effectual fervent prayer of a righteous man availeth much" (James 5:16).

WHY ARE ANSWERS DELAYED?

Answers to prayer seldom come as quickly as we would wish and Satan knows how to use these delays against us. Persistent prayer is difficult when the heavens seem silent and the days, weeks, and months grind by without a discernible response. Prayer becomes an intense battleground as Satan takes advantage of the divine delay and jeers: I told you he is not listening. I told you he's too busy, that he doesn't care. If he really heard all these prayers, why hasn't he answered? At these times it is natural to get trapped in two Satanic falsehoods: that either God does not care or there is something wrong with you. It is helpful to realize that *everyone*, even the apostles and prophets, struggle with delayed answers to prayer. Bishop H. Burke Peterson confided:

> Have you ever knelt down alone and asked the Lord for something that is really important to you, and then gotten up and found that your prayer wasn't answered as you had hoped? I have. Have you ever prayed and prayed for days and days for something special and then found that it didn't work out? I have. In times past, on more than a few occasions, I have gotten up off my knees and wondered in despair, "What's the use? He isn't even listening," or "Maybe I'm not worthy." (*Ensign*, June 1981, 72)

We are better prepared to resist Satan's taunts when we realize that the Lord did not promise that we would receive according to our desires the *first time* we ask. Nor did he promise to open every door the first time we knock. When we pray properly—that is, with an honest pleading for our desires, tempered with a submissive "thy will be done" attitude, God will answer in the time and in the way that is for our best good. Elder Boyd K. Packer said:

> Sometimes you may struggle with a problem and not get an answer. What could be wrong? It may be that you are not doing anything wrong. It may be that you have not done the right things long enough. Remember, you cannot force spiritual things. Put difficult questions in the back of your minds and go about your lives. Ponder and pray quietly and persistently about them. The answer may come as an inspiration, here a little and there a little, "line upon line and precept upon precept" (D&C 98:12). (*Ensign*, November 1979, 21)

When we worthily petition the heavens, we can count on receiving one of three answers. It may be a "yes," or it may be a "no." But in many cases the answer is, "Let's wait awhile and see if you will still trust me." Elder James E. Talmage explained that "In mercy the Father sometimes delays the granting that the asking may be more fervent" (*Jesus The Christ*, Salt Lake City, Utah: Deseret Book, 1956, 435). Sometimes, when the answers to our prayers are deliberately delayed, it is the Lord's way of saying, "Why don't you show me how much you care, so that I can show you how much I care?" He knows that the more we plead, the sweeter the joy will be when the heavens do finally open to us. Sister Patricia Holland said:

> I want you to know that in my life, when I have had disappointments and delays, I have lived to see that if I continue to knock with unshakable faith and persist in my patience—waiting upon the Lord and his calendar—I have discovered that *the Lord's "no's" are merely preludes to an even greater "yes."* (*Speeches of the Year,* Provo, Utah: BYU Press, 1988–89, 73)

Sometimes the reasons for the delay in God's answers are as simple as our insincerity or disobedience. "They were slow to hearken unto the voice of the Lord their God; therefore, the Lord their God is slow to hearken unto their prayers, to answer them in the day of their trouble" (D&C 101:7).

> I don't believe he ignores his children when they talk to him. The problem in our communication with him is that not all of us have learned how to listen for his answers, or perhaps we are not prepared to hear him. I believe we receive his answers as we prepare ourselves to receive them. (M. Russell Ballard, *Ensign,* June 1983, 73)

At other times answers are delayed because even though what we ask for seems appropriate, we may be spiritually unprepared and would be harmed by premature answers. In such cases, God's divine love and foreknowledge will mandate that some prerequisites be resolved in our lives before he responds to those desires. At these times Father's delayed answers reflect an eternal perspective that may be difficult for us to perceive because we are so caught up in the urgency and desires of our immediate circumstances.

Many times we do not receive answers because we are incorrectly praying about *symptoms* instead of real needs. When Christ went to the pool of Bethesda, he said to a man who had lain there crippled and helpless for thirty-eight years, "Wilt thou be made whole?" (John 5:1–6) An interesting question. Of course the man wanted *healing,* but was he willing to give up all his bitter resentments and questions about God's love and be made *whole* spiritually as well as physically? Heavenly Father will not be detoured into dealing with symptoms. The Lord is always ready to respond to our needs, but it is difficult to answer superficial prayers that only deal with symptoms instead of causes.

Understanding these reasons God sometimes delays his answers will help us to persist in faith and trust, and to silence Satan's whispered discouragements. If we do not understand, then we need to pray about why our prayers are not being answered. If the heavens seem silent, there is always a reason and we can break through that silence by asking for further light and knowledge to correct our prayers. To solve this problem of praying about the wrong things, Bishop H. Burke Peterson has advised:

> May I suggest that when you pray for something very special, you pray for two things. First, pray for the blessing that you want, whether it's a new baby, or a job, or whatever; and second, ask the Lord for the blessing of understanding. Then, if he feels for some reason that the blessing isn't appropriate for that time, the blessing of understanding will come—and the frustrations that ofttimes come because we feel our prayers are not answered will blow away in the wind. (*Ensign*, June 1981, 74–75)

Satan cannot defeat us on the battleground of prayer when we trust God's timing and know that he is anxious to bless us.

> I know not by what method rare,
> But this I know, God answers prayer.
> I know that he has given his Word,
> Which tells me prayer is always heard,
> And will be answered, soon or late.
> And so I pray and calmly wait.
> I know not if the blessing sought
> Will come in just the way I thought;
> But leave my prayers with him alone,
> Whose will is wiser than my own,
> Assured that he will grant my quest,
> Or send some answer far more blessed.

(Eliza M. Hickok in *The Best Loved Religious Poems*, comp., James G. Lawson, New York: Fleming H. Revell, 169)

9

The Battleground of Temptation

It is on the battleground of temptation that we determine our eternal destinies as we grapple with Satan's daily, hourly, and sometimes moment-to-moment enticements. There is a line on this battlefield that divides good and evil. The Lord works hard to keep us on his side of the line and the devil tries to pull us to his side. If we remain on the Lord's side we are entitled to his help in our battles, but if we cross the line into the devil's territory, we become subject to his power. We cross this line by giving in to temptation. If we are to win our battles with Satan, we must learn to recognize this line and do all we can to stay on the Lord's side. President George Albert Smith said:

> There is a line of demarcation, well defined, between the Lord's territory and the devil's. If you will stay on the Lord's side of the line, you will be under his influence and will have no desire to do wrong; but *if you cross to the devil's side of the line one inch, you are in the tempter's power,* and if he is successful, you will not be able to think or even reason properly, because you will have lost the Spirit of the Lord. (Kimball, *The Miracle of Forgiveness,* 232)

Elder Joseph B. Wirthlin described a modern example of the line dividing safety from danger:

> While traveling along a mountainous road one evening through a driving rainstorm punctuated with frequent claps of thunder and flashes of lightning, Sister Wirthlin and I could barely see the road, either in front of us or to the right and the left.
>
> I watched the white lines on that road more intently than

ever before. Staying within the lines kept us from going onto the shoulder and into the deep canyon on one side and helped us avoid a head-on collision on the other. To wander over either line could have been very dangerous. Then I thought, "Would a right-thinking person deviate to the left or the right of a traffic lane if he knew the result would be fatal? If he valued his mortal life, certainly he would stay between those lines."

That experience traveling on this mountain road is so like life. *If we stay within the lines that God has marked, he will protect us, and we can arrive safely at our destination.* The Savior taught this principle when he said, "Enter ye in at the strait gate: for wide is the gate, and broad is the way, that leadeth to destruction, and many there be, which go in thereat: Because strait is the gate, and narrow is the way, which leadeth unto life, and few there be that find it." (Matthew 7:13–14) (*Ensign*, November 1990, 64)

Everyone Is Tempted

Satan tries to discourage us by making us feel guilty for being tempted. Aha! he shouts when we waver. You thought you were a disciple of Christ. You thought you were a righteous person, but you're not. The fact that part of you wanted to sin proves you are on my side instead of God's. Sooner or later you are going to give in. You are doomed. And we will be doomed if we believe such distorted lies. The Bible says: "Blessed is the man that endureth temptation: for when he is tried, he shall receive the crown of life, which the Lord hath promised to them that love him" (James 1:12). Nowhere do the scriptures say, or even hint, "Blessed is the person who never has temptations," because there is no such person. On the day of judgment it will not be our temptations which concern the Lord, but the responses we made to them. We should never allow Satan to trick us into feelings of shame for being tempted. The fact that people are tempted only shows they are human. As Elder Melvin J. Ballard said, "There is not a man or woman who lives that shall not be tried, whose position shall not be assailed, and if Satan can make an entrance, he will endeavor to capture that soul" (*New Era,* March 1984, 28).

Nobody is free from temptations of one kind or another. That is the test of life. That is part of our mortal probation.

Temptation of some kind goes with the territory. (Boyd K. Packer, *Ensign*, November 1990, 85)

TEMPTATIONS ARE NECESSARY

For a long time I held the opinion that this would be a much nicer world if Satan and his army were not here fighting against us. I was wrong. It might be a more pleasant world, but mortality would be a waste because, whether we are ready to admit it or not, we *need* Satan and the opposition that his army provides.

> For *it must needs be*, that there is an opposition in all things. If not so . . . righteousness could not be brought to pass, neither wickedness, neither holiness nor misery, neither good nor bad. (2 Nephi 2:11)

The words "it must needs be" show that the opposition provided by Satan's temptations is *mandatory* to our growth and progress toward exaltation. We simply cannot progress toward godhood without overcoming the imperfections that pull us in the opposite direction. One cannot have a tug of war unless there are opposing teams on each side of the rope. Whatever influence the Lord uses to win our souls, Satan must be allowed to balance that effort with his counterattacking temptations. If the Lord did not permit Satan equal time and access to mortals, the battle would be unfair and human agency would be diminished.

> Wherefore, man could not act for himself save it should be that he was enticed by the one or the other. (2 Nephi 2:16)

As much as we long for the day when we will be free of temptations and no longer have to wage that battle, we are advised, for now, to "count it all joy when ye fall into divers temptations" (James 1:2). President Brigham Young used to say, "I am happy, brethren, for the privilege of having temptation" (*Discourses of Brigham Young*, Salt Lake City, Utah: Deseret Book, 1951, 80). And Paul said, "Therefore I take pleasure in infirmities, in reproaches, in necessities, in persecutions, in distresses for Christ's sake: for when I am weak, then am I strong" (2 Corinthians 12:10). They understood that without the opposition of Satan's temptations, none of us could gain the experience which makes it possible to overcome our fallen natures and attain exaltation. Rather than hating Satan for tempting us, we could analyze the choices he places before us and feel grateful for his part in the development which makes it possible for us to return to our Father in Heaven.

> God allows Lucifer and his agents to tempt us so that we may more deliberately choose between good and evil. The Lord could banish Satan and his angels from the earth and remove temptations from men, but "it must needs be that the devil should tempt the children of men, or they could not be agents unto themselves" (D&C 29:39). (ElRay L. Christiansen, *New Era*, July 1975, 49)

It Is Not a Sin to be Tempted

Many people go into a panic of self-condemnation when they are tempted to sin—not because they actually crossed the line or did anything wrong, but simply because, for a split second or two, they actually wavered and considered the possibility of giving in. This is exactly what the devil hopes they will do because it weakens their confidence and increases their vulnerability. But the fact that evil sometimes appeals to us does not prove that we are unworthy. It is just a normal part of mortality. We all recognize the truth of President Kimball's words: "Because men and women are human and normally carnally minded . . . to do evil is usually easier than to do right" (*The Miracle of Forgiveness*, x). If we would win our battles with temptation we must recognize that the Lord does not reject people because of their fallen nature, but invites them to come to him for a new heart and transformation of character.

We all wish we were perfect and above temptation, and someday, if we remain faithful, that day will come. Meanwhile we must remember that it is by the resistance and conquest of temptations that we become holy. The more we resist, the more Christlike we become. President Kimball said,

> The difference between the good man and the bad man is not that one had the temptations and the other was spared them. It is that one kept himself fortified, and resisted temptation and the

other placed himself in compromising places and conditions and rationalized the situation. (*The Miracle of Forgiveness*, 231–32)

Instead of allowing Satan to erect barriers between us and the Lord simply because we feel tempted—instead of allowing him to make us feel evil or dirty because of temptations (even when we do not give in), we should understand that Lucifer does not tempt us because we are evil. He tempts us because he knows who we are and how good we will become if he can't stop us. Once we accept these truths and stop feeling condemned for every temptation that appeals to us, we become free to overcome our temptations in a new and wonderful way.

> Feeling the power of Satan does not make you evil. The fact that you're struggling does not mean that you are in his power or that the Spirit of God is not also striving with you. Evil consists, not of recognizing temptation, but of yielding to it. (Don Norton, *Ensign*, August 1978, 33)

"It Is Safe to Sin in Secret"

We will now uncover some of Satan's major strategies on the battleground of temptation. One of the ways Satan persuades people to yield to temptation is by whispering the lie that they can get away with it if they do it in secret. But the scriptures teach that there is no such thing as a secret sin. "For nothing is secret, that shall not be manifest; neither any thing hid, that shall not be known and come abroad" (Luke 8:17).

"There is nothing covered, that shall not be revealed; and hid, that shall not be known" (Matthew 10:26). Everything we do, whether in private or in public, is divinely recorded and will be presented as evidence for or against us in the final day of judgment. The Lord has warned, "you have many things to do and to repent of; for behold, *your sins have come up unto me*" (D&C 56:14).

> But behold, ye cannot hide your crimes from God; and except ye repent they will stand as a testimony against you at the last day. (Alma 39:8)
>
> Some may think the Almighty does not see their doings, but if he does not, the angels and ministering spirits do. They see you and your works, and I have no doubt but that they occasionally

> communicate your conduct to the Father, or to the Son. (Joseph
> F. Smith, *Gospel Doctrine,* Salt Lake City, Utah: Deseret Book,
> 1919, 435–36)

Smoking is prohibited in the buildings where I work. I am always amused by the naive people who think they can smoke undetected because they are hidden in the safety of rest room stalls where no one can see them. A nonsmoker can detect the evidence of their violation the instant the door is opened. Satan's efforts to convince us that our "secret" sins will go undetected by an omnipotent God are equally lamentable, but we will not be deceived if we remember that "All things are naked and opened unto the eyes of him with whom we have to do" (Hebrews 4:13). "For the ways of man are before the eyes of the Lord, and he pondereth all his goings" (Proverbs 5:21).

To encourage sinful indulgences, Satan also whispers that people will be safe in their sin if they do it in remote places where there are no prying eyes to judge or hold them accountable. But scripture says of the Lord's awareness: "Thou knowest my downsitting and mine uprising, thou understandest my thought afar off . . . and art acquainted with all my ways" (Psalms 139:2–3).

> There are no corners so dark, no deserts so uninhabited, no canyons so remote, no automobiles so hidden, no homes so tight and shut but that the all-seeing One can penetrate and observe. (Kimball, *The Miracle of Forgiveness,* 110)
>
> Behold, ye have sinned against the Lord: and be sure your sin will find you out. (Numbers 32:23)

In addition to his deception regarding sinning in remote places, Satan also whispers that we are safe in our sins if we do them at night, under the cover of darkness, as if the Lord wouldn't notice because he is asleep. But the Lord doesn't keep office hours, for "Behold, he that keepeth Israel shall neither slumber nor sleep" (Psalms 121:4). Nor does the dark of night prevent God from seeing what we do, for "There is no darkness, nor shadow of death, where the workers of iniquity may hide themselves" (Job 34:21–22).

> If I say, Surely the darkness shall cover me; even the night shall be light about me.
>
> Yea, the darkness hideth not from thee; but the night shineth

as the day: the darkness and the light are both alike to thee. (Psalms 139:11–12)

If we are not deceived by Satan's lies about hiding in darkness or remote places, he whispers, There is no God, but even if there were, he is so far away that he couldn't possibly see you or observe your sins. Do whatever you want. No one is watching. But Christ has told us that he is not a faraway, isolated shepherd. Even when Christ must leave the earth for duties elsewhere, we still remain under his observation and watchful care. "The Lord looketh from heaven; he beholdeth all the sons of men. From the place of his habitation he looketh upon all the inhabitants of the earth." (Psalms 33:13–14)

> For mine eyes are upon all their ways: they are not hid from my face, neither is their iniquity hid from mine eyes. (Jeremiah 16:17)

Let us consider Bishop Vaughn J. Featherstone's sobering challenge:

> Would you picture a huge scroll sliding down from the ceiling? On it are listed the names of those who purchased pornographic literature. The list is large enough so that all may see. Is your name on the list? Now suppose those names are removed, and the names of all those who attended or viewed X-rated movies are presented so that all who are in the congregation may see. Again, is your name on the list?
>
> Now . . . how about all those of you who have a masturbation problem? If the names of those who had the problem were projected across this huge scroll, would your name be there, or would you be able to sit back confident and pure in heart?
>
> And . . . what if we had the names of those who had a homosexual problem? What if their names were on this huge scroll? Their names removed, then we had those who are adulterers, who are serving in priesthood positions, unbeknownst to many, unbeknownst unto anyone except themselves and the partner in sin? How about all of you who have committed fornication? Or have you been involved in petting? Suppose their names were on this huge scroll, so that all may see.
>
> Now I can tell you this. I bear my solemn witness that if you do not self-inflict a purging in your lives, the time may well come when there might not be a scroll, but it will be as though there

were. It may be as though it had been shouted from the tops of the houses. People cannot hide sin. You cannot mock God and hold the Lord's holy priesthood and pretend that you are his servant. (*Ensign*, May 1975, 66)

Finally, when the devil sees we will not be deceived by lies about secret sins, he counters, Okay, so you can't hide. But how can you possibly love a God who vindictively watches for every little mistake you make? Once again, Satan is trying to place barriers between us and God by inferring that his watchfulness is only to punish wickedness, when in reality, he is anxiously watching for opportunities to bless. Elder Horacio A. Tenorio of the Second Quorum of Seventy said, "Our Heavenly Father loves us dearly and watches over us in all our needs and cares, following us through life step by step" (*Ensign*, May 1990, 79). Remembering that God is ever mindful of us and watching us day by day, deed by deed, choice by choice will help us ignore Satan's enticing lies that we can hide our sins because no one would know or care. It helps us strive more diligently to honor the trust God has given us through personal agency and to give him happy, obedient lives to observe and reward.

The eyes of the lord are in every place, beholding the evil and the good. (Proverbs 15:3)

DISGUISED TEMPTATIONS

Hiding behind the protection of the veil, Satan always seeks to increase his odds by cloaking his temptations in clever disguises. If Satan were stupid he might say, Here's a wonderful sin. Why don't you forget God and indulge yourself? But he is much too cunning to make his invitations so obvious. The devil is a master of disguise and imitation. He can make his offers seem so appealing and desirable that even the very elect, if they are not in tune with the Holy Spirit, can be deceived. General Primary President Michaelene P. Grassli pointed out how Satan's suggestions "often appear inviting. If he came to you looking ugly and scary, you'd turn and run as fast as you could. So he has to trick you by making bad things seem good." (Frie*nd*, July 1991, 1)

Be aware and warned of the subtle workings of Satan, for he never stops trying to lead us astray. He is an expert on making things seem appealing and right, when actually they can bring about our moral destruction. (Delbert L. Stapley, *Ensign*, May 1975, 22)

As he offers the pleasures of the world, Satan taunts: God doesn't want you to have any fun. All he does is issue commandments to keep you from enjoying life.

Even though you have a testimony and want to do what is right, it is difficult not to be drawn to the great and spacious building. From all appearances, the people in the building seem to be having a great time. The music and laughter are deafening . . . don't mistake telestial pleasure for celestial happiness and joy.

The people in that building have absolutely nothing to offer except instant, short-term gratification inescapably connected to long-term sorrow and suffering.

The commandments you observe were not given by a dispassionate God to prevent you from having fun, but by a loving Father in Heaven who wants you to be happy while you are living on this earth, as well as in the hereafter. (Glenn L. Pace, *Ensign*, November 1987, 40)

Bishop Robert D. Hales presented an interesting example of Satan's appeal:

Some years ago, as a young man, I had an opportunity to work summers on a ranch with my wise Uncle Frank, who taught me an important lesson about shepherding. He described to me how lambs are enticed and led away from the safety of their mother's sides and the flock that loves and cares for them.

Cunning coyotes send their pups to play near the flock-running, frolicking, tumbling—it looks so inviting to the little lambs. The frolicking pups look like they are having so much fun that the lambs are enticed to wander from the protective environment of the flock and their mother's nurturing sides. In their innocence, they fail to observe that the adult coyotes are moving in a circle, ready to pounce and cut them off from the flock, ultimately killing and devouring them.

This is also Satan's way. He uses our free agency to entice us with apparent "good times." Soon we may become entrapped and, if not eventually brought back to the flock, we will not be able to go to the temple, enter into the covenants, and receive the ordinances necessary to attain eternal life, that we might live in the presence of God the Father and Jesus Christ. (*Ensign*, May 1987, 75)

Elder Richard G. Scott warned, "Satan will use rationalization to destroy you. That is, he will twist something you know to be wrong so that it appears to be acceptable and thus progressively lead you to destruction." (*Ensign*, May 1991, 35)

> Lucifer in his diabolical scheming deceives the unwary and uses every tool at his command. He will use his logic to confuse and his rationalization to destroy. He will shade meanings, open doors an inch at a time, and lead from purest white through all the shades of gray to the darkest black. (Spencer W. Kimball, *Ensign*, November 1980, 94)

GRADUAL TEMPTATIONS

If he could do it, the devil would lure us from the straight and narrow path a mile at a time. If not by a mile then by a yard or a foot. But Satan knows that he cannot expect us to leap from a righteous life into the depths of depravity in one sudden decision, so in most cases his enticements will be so subtle, so unnoticeable, that he may only gain an inch at a time. It's only a little sin, he mocks. What can such a tiny indiscretion hurt? It's harmless. Enjoy yourself. This is not important enough to deny yourself. Go ahead and try it this once. But through repetition of our sins those tiny inches soon add up to miles as we drift gradually into more serious sins.

> The most favorite method the enemy of our souls has employed in ages past and that he will employ today is to capture souls by leading them gently, step by step. Men and women do not go far wrong in an instant. It is by slow degrees, step by step. (Melvin J. Ballard, *New Era*, March 1984, 38–39)
>
> Serious sin enters into our lives as we yield first to little temptations. Seldom does one enter into deeper transgressions without first yielding to lesser ones, which open the door to the greater. (Kimball, *The Miracle of Forgiveness*, 215)

EXPLOITING OUR WEAK POINTS

In preparation for attack, an army always looks for the weak spots in the enemy's defenses, and so it is with Satan. Why should he attack where we are strong when he knows all our weaknesses? President David O. McKay said, "Your greatest weakness will be the point at which Satan will try to tempt you . . . and if you have made yourself weak, he will add to that weakness" (*Improvement Era,* July 1968, 3). In addition to making temptations appear harmless and appealing, and offering them in gradual, carefully calculated, progressive steps, Satan's forces also know exactly how to *customize* their temptations to our individual desires.

> Lucifer and his followers know the habits, weaknesses, and vulnerable spots of everyone and take advantage of them to lead us to spiritual destruction. (Kimball, *The Miracle of Forgiveness,* 218–19)

Our defenses will be vastly improved when we understand *how* Satan knows us so well. Satan and his army of evil spirits are free to roam the world, free to follow us into our schools, places of work and worship, free to be in our homes and entertainment facilities, free to follow us anywhere on this earth except when we enter the temples. Working in darkness, on the other side of the veil, hidden from our view, they are watching us carefully, noting our likes and dislikes, our weaknesses and vulnerabilities.

Imagine how much you could learn about someone if you were invisible and could be with that person everywhere he went, twenty-four hours a day throughout his entire life, just as Satan's spirits can do. By carefully observing what people do with their time and what catches their attention, by listening to the words they speak, observing their likes and dislikes, choices and preferences, and the things they read, Satan's spirits can easily deduce their weaknesses, motives, ambitions, and desires. By finding the most vulnerable spots in one's character, they can then drive a wedge deep into those flaws to pull that person away from Father and down toward the dark. Lawrence R. Peterson Jr. explained:

> It is possible that Satan can at least determine our susceptibility

to a particular temptation from our words and actions, which reveal our thoughts. As the Savior taught, a tree is known by its fruit. (Luke 6:43–45) Satan can see our fruits as well as any person—and we can be certain that he'll be quick to take advantage of the weaknesses we exhibit. (*Ensign*, July 1984, 31)

The devil knows where to tempt, where to put in his telling blows. He finds the vulnerable spot. Where one was weak before, he will be most easily tempted again. (Kimball, *The Miracle of Forgiveness*, 171)

Satan plays dirty in this war of temptation. Not only does he know how to take advantage of our weaknesses, he does not hesitate to kick us when we are down. Elder Howard W. Hunter said:

There are times in our struggle with the adversities of mortality when we become weary, weakened, and susceptible to the temptations that seem to be placed in our pathways. Such a time is always the tempter's moment—when we are emotionally or physically spent, when we are weary, vulnerable, and least prepared to resist the insidious suggestions he makes. (*Ensign*, November 1976, 17)

To win our conflicts on the battleground of temptation, we must carefully guard our weaknesses by avoiding all places, situations, and people that could inflame the desire to satisfy those weaknesses.

A PROTECTIVE BREASTPLATE

The war between Satan and the Lord is a battle for the emotions and loyalties of the heart (see 2 Nephi 28:20; Mosiah 3:6). Satan knows that it matters very little what we *believe* if he can pierce our hearts with unworthy desires, for the heart is the control center which governs what we do, often in spite of what we know or believe in our minds. As Elder Joseph B. Wirthlin said, "Most of us don't mind doing what we *ought* to do when it doesn't interfere with what we *want* to do, but it takes discipline and maturity to do what we ought to do whether we want to or not" (*Ensign*, November 1980, 69).

Our hearts need spiritual protection because they represent the center of emotion, commitment, values and priorities. "For where your treasure is, there will your heart be also" (Matthew 6:21). As the prophets describe the strategies of defense we should use against Satan's temptations, one of the things they have stressed is that we protect our hearts by putting on "the armor of righteousness" (see 2 Nephi 1:23; 2 Corinthians 6:7). The scriptures are precise in their description of spiritual armor. The "armor of righteousness" we are commanded to wear is intended to be used as a breastplate—"the breastplate of righteousness" (see Ephesians 6:14; D&C 27:16), reinforced with additional layers of protection from "the breastplate of faith and love" (1 Thessalonians 5:8).

A breastplate is a defensive shield worn to protect the vital organs, such as the heart, because if the heart is injured the entire body suffers or dies. The breastplate of righteousness, faith, and love protects our hearts from being pierced with Satan's fiery darts of temptation. Always eager to set the example, Christ himself "put on righteousness as a breastplate" (Isaiah 59:17).

There are many definitions of righteousness, faith, and love. In terms of the spiritual armor we are developing, we could say that the more we are like Christ, and the more we love him and exercise faith in him, the more righteous we will be, and the more protection we will receive from our spiritual breastplates. On the other hand, the less we are like Christ, the more worldly, unrighteous, and vulnerable we will be. No heart could possibly be wounded by Satan's attacks when it is protected by a triple breastplate of spiritual strength comprising personal righteousness, faith in Christ and a love that insists that we honor the Savior with diligent obedience to his commandments. "And because of the righteousness of his people, Satan has no power" (1 Nephi 22:26). As Elder Delbert L. Stapley emphasized, "The only way Satan can be bound is for people to forsake his temptations and enticements to do evil, and to walk uprightly and circumspectly before the Lord" (*Ensign*, December 1971, 94–95).

> And it came to pass that I, Nephi, beheld the power of the Lamb of God, that it descended upon the saints of the church of the Lamb, and upon the covenant people of the Lord, who were scattered upon all the face of the earth; and they were armed with righteousness and with the power of God in great glory. (1 Nephi 14:14)

THE SAVIOR UNDERSTANDS OUR TEMPTATIONS

One of the keys to overcoming our temptations is discovering that Christ understands what we are going through because he has been there before us. What an amazing discovery to learn that Jesus Christ not only understands temptation because he is God and knows everything, but that he also understands because he personally, in the flesh, encountered and conquered the exact same temptations that we struggle against. As Alma prophesied:

> He shall go forth, suffering pains and afflictions *and temptations of every kind;* and this that the word might be fulfilled which saith he will take upon him the pains and the sicknesses of his people . . . And he will take upon him their infirmities, that his bowels may be filled with mercy, according to the flesh, that he may know according to the flesh how to succor his people according to their infirmities. (Alma 7:11–12)

Christ did not come to earth to skim over the surface of mortality as a mere spectator. He agreed to come as a full participant so that we could never have a temptation, experience, or sorrow that he cannot understand from his own personal experience. There is nothing Satan can confront us with on the battleground of temptation which Christ hasn't already faced and conquered. Christ could have chosen to view our sorrows, temptations, weaknesses, and pains *vicariously.* He could have chosen to know them second hand, through the influence of the Holy Ghost which "knoweth all things." But because of his infinite love, because he wanted no barriers to exist between his understanding and our needs, because he wanted to be perfect in his Atonement, and because he wanted to be perfect in his ability to empathize with us in carrying our burdens, he chose to encounter the experiences of mortality firsthand, in the flesh, exactly as we do. And so it was that "the Son of God *suffereth according to the flesh* that he might take upon him the sins of his people, that he might blot out their transgressions *according to the power of his deliverance*" (Alma 7:13). The "power of his deliverance" is built upon that foundation of his personal, firsthand exposure, in his own flesh, to every kind of human pain, affliction, infirmity, and temptation possible. His exposure included physical afflictions as well as spiritual, mental, and emotional ones. President Benson explained:

> Even though he was God's Son sent to earth, the divine plan of the Father required that Jesus be subjected to all the difficulties and tribulations of mortality . . . Indeed there is no human condition—be it suffering, incapacity, inadequacy, mental deficiency, or sin—which he cannot comprehend or for which his love will not reach out to the individual . . . There is no human problem beyond his capacity to solve. Because he descended below all things (see D&C 122:8), he knows how to help us rise above our daily difficulties. (*Ensign*, November 1983, 6, 8)

To have faith in Christ's understanding and compassion for our battles with temptation, we must ask: Was Jesus so holy that it was easy for him to resist his temptations? Was his exposure to temptation "in all points" merely an academic overview or was it a real encounter that pulled and tugged at his desire as it does ours? The answer given in the scriptures is that his battles with constant temptation were so real that they formed a major part of his "sufferings." Many of the scriptural references to the Savior's temptations include the word "suffer" in their descriptions.

For example:

> He shall go forth, suffering pains and afflictions and temptations of every kind. (Alma 7:11)
> He suffered temptations. (D&C 20:22)
> And thus the flesh becoming subject to the Spirit, or the Son to the Father . . . suffereth temptation, and yieldeth not to the temptation. (Mosiah 15:5)

How would it be possible for the Son of God to actually "suffer" in his resistance to temptations unless they were real encounters? His temptations would not have caused him to suffer unless there was a genuine possibility of giving in. Perhaps we cannot comprehend the intensity and determination with which Satan marshaled his evil forces against the Lord, but we can be certain that he tried harder to destroy him than he did to destroy any other person who ever lived. The point of all this is that when Satan tries to use our temptations to put barriers between us and the Lord, we can have faith in the truth that our temptations are not a barrier, but a common bond between us and the Lord.

For we have not an high priest which cannot be touched with

> the feeling of our infirmities; *but was in all points tempted like as we are,* yet without sin. Let us therefore come boldly unto the throne of grace, that we may obtain mercy, and find grace to help in time of need. (Hebrews 4:15–16)

Think about the implications of that remarkable statement. Paul presents the reality of Christ's temptations as the very reason we can have confidence, and even boldness, in approaching God for help in overcoming our own temptations. Because Christ experienced in his flesh what we experience in our flesh, he not only understands and has compassion for us, but knows exactly how to help us. He said, "Fear not, little children, for you are mine, and I have overcome the world" (D&C 50:41). The fact that he has overcome every possible temptation we can face should reduce our fears as we encounter our own temptations because what he has done in his own flesh, he can teach us to do in ours.

> For verily he took not on him the nature of angels; but he took on him the seed of Abraham.
>
> *Wherefore in all things it behooved him to be made like unto his brethren,* that he might be a merciful and faithful high priest in things pertaining to God, to make reconciliation for the sins of the people.
>
> For in that he himself hath suffered being tempted, he is able to succour them that are tempted. (Hebrews 2:16–18)
>
> How grateful we should be for a kind, wise, loving Savior who will help us overcome our faults, our mistakes, and our sins. He loves and understands us and is sympathetic to the fact that we face temptations. (Theodore M. Burton, *Ensign,* August 1988, 9)

DON'T BATTLE TEMPTATION ALONE

The devil would have us believe that we are helpless before his awesome powers of temptation, but we are not. A person will not feel hopeless or afraid of Satan when he remembers God's promise to protect him from every temptation beyond his power to resist and conquer. In our day the Lord told Joseph Smith:

> Yet you should have been faithful; and he would have extended his arm and supported you against all the fiery darts of the

adversary; and he would have been with you in every time of trouble. (D&C 3:8)

The promise applies equally to each person. Elder ElRay L. Christiansen stated: "No person will ever be given more opposition than he has the potential to overcome or endure" (*Ensign*, December 1971, 60). God has never promised to intervene by reducing the size or strength of our temptations. He fulfills his promise of divine protection by joining us in the battle, expanding and adding to our ability to resist until we can stand face to face against temptations which tower above us like a giant, and win the battle because his strength is added to ours. Elder Eldred G. Smith stated:

> God would be very unjust if he were to turn Lucifer loose to tempt man without giving him help to overcome. God will not permit Satan to have power over you, to tempt you beyond the strength he will give you if you will seek and accept his help. (*Ensign*, January 1974, 63)

Satan tries to isolate us on the battleground of temptation so that we attempt to conquer his enticements with our own powers alone. He tries to make us believe that giving in is inevitable, but it is not. Christ himself is "the way" of deliverance. That is why the Saints are taught "to withstand every temptation of the devil with their faith on the Lord Jesus Christ" (Alma 37:33). President Kimball emphasized:

> He who has greater strength than Lucifer, he who is our fortress and our strength, can sustain us in times of great temptation. And the man who yields to the sweet influence and pleadings of the Spirit and does all in his power to stay in a repentant attitude is guaranteed protection, power, freedom, and joy. (*The Miracle of Forgiveness,* 176)

In Chapter 12, "Strategies of Defense," we will explore proven procedures for winning every conflict on the battleground of temptation.

10

Prisoner of War

WHEN WAR IS FOUGHT BETWEEN OPPOSING NATIONS, EACH COUN-
try's army has two objectives: kill the enemy or capture him. If enemy
forces are captured, they are bound and placed in prison. Satan has
the same objectives in the spiritual war he is fighting against God and
mankind.

> Satan would convert divinely independent spirits into creatures
> bound by habit, restricted by appetite, and enslaved by transgres-
> sion. He has never deviated from his intent to enslave and destroy.
> (Richard G. Scott, *Ensign*, November 1981, 11)

There are dozens of scriptural warnings against the dangers of being
taken captive by Satan, being placed in spiritual bondage and being literally bound with his chains of death, darkness, and hell. While it may
be unpleasant to study some of these references, the Lord must feel it
is important for us to do so, because this subject has been a recurring
theme throughout the history of recorded revelation. If we would avoid
our own capture by spiritual enemies, we must be aware of their enslaving objectives and techniques and take steps to protect ourselves.

> Verily, verily, I say unto you, ye must watch and pray always, lest
> ye be tempted by the devil, and ye be led away captive by him. (3
> Nephi 18:15)

A captive is a prisoner, a person who has lost his freedom and is
under the control of others. No conscientious soldier would remove his

armor and needlessly expose himself to enemy fire, but that is exactly what happens when we choose to break the commandments.

> Satan's power over a person increases as that person becomes more wicked, until eventually the person is "taken captive of the devil" and bound with the "chains of hell." (Alma 12:11) (Lawrence R. Peterson Jr., *Ensign*, July 1984, 30)

DEMON POSSESSION

It is one thing to admit we have been tempted, or even addicted and held captive to the point that we lost our agency to the devil, but it is a long reach from there to admitting the potential for actually being possessed by evil spirits. That possibility is revolting and repugnant. We protest, "No way. Not me. That only happened back in Bible times." That is exactly what Satan wants us to think, but the truth is that demon possession probably occurs as much today as it did then. Indeed, because of the rampant wickedness in our modern world, it may be even more common today than it was then. In our own dispensation the Lord has declared, "And these signs shall follow them that believe . . . in my name they shall cast out devils" (D&C 84:65, 67). Why would he declare this to the members of his church if there were no demon possessions to be expelled? Among others, one of the modern restrictions of the use of the priesthood in our generation is that we "Require not miracles, except I shall command you, *except*, casting out devils" (D&C 24:13). In other words, the Savior is acknowledging that the problem of Satan having a possessive hold on the hearts of the members is so prevalent that we do not need permission to use the priesthood in casting demons out of our lives. "And whoso shall ask it in my name in faith, they shall cast out devils" (D&C 35:9).

Being denied physical bodies of their own, Lucifer's spirit soldiers will do anything they can for the privilege of possessing our bodies. "Satan is insanely jealous of your body. He would like to possess and destroy it." (Carol J. Wood, *New Era*, June 1978, 9) Once inside a person's body, the evil spirits become very possessive about the flesh they have stolen and present great resistance before surrendering it back to the rightful owner. For example, on one occasion, upon being commanded to leave the body of a young boy, "Straightway the spirit tare him; and he fell on the ground, and wallowed foaming . . . And the spirit cried, and rent him sore, and came out of him" (Mark 9:20, 26) On another occasion the Savior commanded an evil spirit to leave the body of a man. "And when the unclean spirit had torn him, and cried with a loud voice, he came out of him" (Mark 1:26).

It would appear that evil spirits are so desirous of the physical sensations which we take for granted that they would prefer to inhabit the bodies of pigs to having no flesh at all (see Mark 5:1–13; Luke 8:26–33). Commenting on these verses, Elder Talmage said, "To gain for themselves the transitory gratification of tenanting a body of flesh, these demons are eager to enter even into the bodies of beasts" (*Jesus The Christ*, 183). Their eagerness to capture and possess bodies of flesh is easier to understand when we realize that one's capacity to experience joy and pleasure is reduced when the spirit has no tabernacle of flesh (see D&C 93:34). Indeed, those who have experienced the magnified capacities made possible by the union of flesh and spirit are said to look upon the loss of their physical bodies as a form of bondage (see D&C 138:50). Surely the frustrations would be just as great for Satan's unembodied spirits.

It appears that if evil spirits can inhabit your body even temporarily, they can share in the sinful thrills that come as you act out their evil instructions. These spirits may compel the person to abuse the body by overeating, by indulging in the artificial thrills of drug or alcohol abuse, or sexual escapades. The almost involuntary compulsions acted out by those who are captive to such possessions make it appear that these demons will do anything they can to amplify and heighten the sensations denied them without a body of flesh. And each time the spirits are successful in this invasion, they become all the more determined to return and repeat the experience (see Matthew 12:43–45). You may regain control and force them to leave for a time, but they will return as soon as your body is capable of repeating the sin and your frame of mind permits their entrance. Thus you can fall into addictive cycles of endless repetition even as you wonder why they are so difficult to escape.

> The demons that take possession of men, overruling their agency and compelling them to obey Satanic bidding, are the unembodied

angels of the devil, whose triumph it is to afflict mortals, and if possible to impel them to sin. (Talmage, *Jesus The Christ*, 183)

There are two ways to be possessed by evil spirits. One is by a strong, compelling presence and mental control, while the other is by having them actually enter and dwell inside our physical bodies. "Therefore the spirit of the devil did enter into them, and take possession of their house" (Alma 40:13). A person's body may be invaded and possessed by only one spirit at a time, or by several. Mary Magdalene, for example, had seven devils cast out of her body (see Mark 16:9). One man was possessed of so many evil spirits that when Jesus demanded to know who had afflicted the man, they gave no name but arrogantly replied, "My name is Legion: for we are many" (Mark 5:9). I am certain, however, that the most common form of demon possession is not physical habitation, but in having our hearts, emotions, and desires captive to the strong, manipulative influence of the evil spirits assigned to defeat us.

Perhaps you have observed someone temporarily possessed by a spirit of anger or hatred. Or perhaps you, yourself, have felt suddenly transformed from your normal, rational attitude to an insane fit of rage, ranting, and raving, perhaps screaming at someone who has done something displeasing. And then the rage passes as quickly as it came. You find yourself back to your normal self, left with terrible feelings of guilt and wondering, "How can this be?" You may have been temporarily possessed; if not physically, then at least controlled by evil spirits who have a need to express their anger and misery by striking out at their physically embodied brothers and sisters. This is why it is so vital to "pray always lest that wicked one have *power in you*, and remove you out of your place" (D&C 93:49).

Each time we give in to evil enticements we open the door to the possibility of possession. For example, those who allow their thoughts to wander into sexual fantasies will find their thoughts more and more difficult to control. Having deliberately opened the door to unworthy thoughts, the person has unknowingly invited the unclean devils to enter and take control of his or her mind. When we allow our imaginations to focus on evil, one possibility is that evil spirits will guide our thoughts into progressively downward spirals of filthiness until the incessant thoughts compel us to seek wicked fulfillment by acting out the lewd desires. As Elder Melvin J. Ballard said, "Secret weaknesses and vices leave an open door for the enemy of your souls to enter, and he may come in and take possession of you, and you will be his slave" (*New Era*, March 1984, 38). These temporary possessions are also made possible by participation in mind-altering drugs, alcohol, pornography, masturbation, petting, and lewd acts of sexual lust. These unfortunate choices open the door to mental and emotional possession as surely as if we had posted a welcome sign. It appears that accepting these sins enables the evil spirits to use our bodies temporarily to act out their wishes. They probably receive vicarious pleasures as they become our partners and manipulate our emotions and sinful actions, urging us on and on to repeat the debased actions. "It is as though Satan ties strings to the mind and body so that he can manipulate one like a puppet" (Richard G. Scott, *Ensign*, May 1986, 10–11).

The spiritual bondage which Book of Mormon prophets speak of so frequently is simply being in a state wherein we have auctioned away our agency thrill by thrill, sin by sin, until we are under the control of evil spirits who delight in manipulating us to repeat our sins, degrading us as they laugh and mock.

> Satan would have all of the children of Father in Heaven behave like robots . . . Through subtle, tempting influence, he encourages us to gratify desire for personal power and influence or to succumb to appetite. He progressively binds those that follow carnal desire. Unless they repent, they are effectively converted into robots who no longer exercise control over their eternal destiny. (Richard G. Scott, *Ensign*, November 1981, 11)

Most readers will be aware of people who are possessed in the sense that they respond like robots to the enticements of the evil ones. These unfortunate victims are so addicted to cycles of self-indulgence and defeat that whenever Satan or his evil spirits desire to participate vicariously in the person's addiction, they have only to whisper stimulating suggestions which move the captive to act out his fantasies. Is this not a form of possession? Whenever we find ourselves out of control, unable to prevent ourselves from doing the sin we hate and want to abandon, we are seeing evidence of possession. Whether it is actual habitation, or merely control over our hearts, the result is the same: loss of agency, spiritual captivity, and enslavement, hurting ourselves and the ones we love. We are prisoners of war, but Jesus Christ can set us free. Just as we opened the door by yielding to temptation, we can slam the door shut and lock Satan out by saying no to our temptations.

> It is extremely difficult, if not impossible, for the devil to enter a door that is closed. He seems to have no keys for locked doors. (Kimball, *The Miracle of Forgiveness*, 215)

PRISONERS TO ADDICTION

In our first yieldings to temptations we are only creating a vulnerability or disposition to say yes to future temptations. The more often we yield, the stronger Satan's influence becomes. However, when we allow our habits to deteriorate into compulsive addictions, we have been taken prisoner. We have been *captured* and *imprisoned* by Satanic enticements as surely as any soldier in a P.O.W. camp. The devil's goal is to "deceive and to blind men, and to lead them captive at his will, even as many as would not hearken unto my voice" (Moses 4:4). Whether we say yes to temptations deliberately or only unintentionally, we are then in danger of being "taken captive by the devil, and *led by his will* down to destruction. Now this is what is meant by the chains of hell." (Alma 12:11) When our hearts are hardened in disobedience to the point that we are not only "led according to the will of the devil," but actually taken captive by him, we are often chained by habit and addiction to the point that Satan has "all power" over us.

> But remember that he that persists in his own carnal nature, and goes on in the ways of sin and rebellion against God, remaineth in his fallen state *and the devil hath all power over him*. (Mosiah 16:5)

As we struggle against the enslaving possessions of evil habits and addictions, as we try to resist, but fail, falling back into endless cycles of defeat, repeating the sin we hate, we are only seeing the determination of our enemies to hold us in captivity. So it was in the Book of Mormon:

> The people having been delivered up for the space of a long time to be carried about by the temptations of the devil whithersoever he desired to carry them, *and to do whatsoever iniquity he desired they should*. (3 Nephi 6:17)

When I was a young boy, it was my assignment to put a rope around our goat and lead it out to the field where it could graze. It went willingly, even eagerly. But when it was time to bring the animal back to the confines of the pen for the night, it dug in its feet and refused to be led. It would shake its head and fight every step of the way. Falling into spiritual captivity is something like that. At first we go willingly. The pleasures of sin bring thrills of excitement. They are adventurous. They give us a "high." But soon we find ourselves going beyond what we would have ever thought possible. We never meant to go so far. We must stop. We must retreat. We must repent. We must return to the Lord. But we can't. Every time we try to resist, those chains of habit pull at us and drag us back into the cycles of sin we have grown to hate. Unknown to us there are dozens of evil spirits around us, whispering, shouting that we can't win, that we must do as they bid.

When people are being pushed into repeated cycles of sin they can't control, they naturally feel terrible about themselves. They wonder what is wrong with them and why they can't change when they want to so desperately. Satan delights in that misery and encourages it with his diabolical whisperings. What a weak person you are. You say you want to stop doing this, yet you do it over and over. What an insincere hypocrite you are. You are helpless. You will never be free of this. You may as well give in and enjoy it. In his cunning, Satan stays in the background, never revealing his influence in the addiction, allowing the captive to assume it is all his own doing. Because the addict doesn't recognize the forceful manipulations coming from the evil spirits who surround him day and night, he is helpless to defeat them by himself and wastes his energy hating himself.

> Many thousands of people are living a tortured existence. Attached to thousands of individuals is some galling, oppressive handicap which is sapping their energy, exhausting their mental and spiritual resources, and depleting their ability to live happy, productive lives. They are compelled to carry each newly acquired torment with them wherever they go until eventually, exhausted and defeated, they give up the struggle and fall into . . . discouragement, failure, and death. (Sterling W. Sill, *New Era,* October 1976, 5)

The most miserable, hopeless, depressed, anguished people I know are those who are living lives of cyclical defeat as they return again and again to act out the very sins they hate and want to overcome, but haven't learned how. The following scripture describes what the devil can do to us, or make us do, when we have surrendered our wills and given him power over us.

> But now, behold, they are led about by Satan, even as chaff is driven before the wind, or as a vessel is tossed about upon the waves, without sail or anchor, or without anything wherewith to steer her; and even as she is, so are they. (Mormon 5:18)

This is a compelling description of a person made helpless by mental and emotional possession. Step by step, sinful indulgence by indulgence, we surrender our agency and cross the combat zone into the enemy trenches and say, in effect, "Here I am. Bind me and take me away." And thus, "he leadeth them by the neck with a flaxen cord, until he bindeth them with his strong cords forever" (2 Nephi 26:22).

A person in spiritual bondage is continually amazed by the wicked things he does in spite of every intention to repent and obey. Family members are confused and angered by the repeated promises of their loved one to repent, only to see him or her return to the sin again and again. What neither the wayward person nor the family seems to understand is the power of Satan to hold people in captivity once their repeated, sinful choices have gradually led them into Satan's territory and they have forfeited their agency.

Before people who are caught in addictive cycles of defeat can draw upon the Savior's unlimited power of deliverance, they must first recognize the overwhelming power and possessive influence of the evil spirits who are getting vicarious pleasure through human sin. People must realize that the unrelenting pressure to act out their addictive compulsions comes from more than their own habitual desires. Take courage if you are one who has been taken prisoner in this manner. No one needs to remain prisoner to such enslavements, because Jesus Christ has unlimited power to free us if we will only learn to open our hearts and allow him to. In later chapters we will discuss how to tap into his infinite power of deliverance.

> One may ask, "What must I do to break the chains that bind me and lead me away from the path our Savior would have us follow?" These chains cannot be broken by those who live in lust and self-deceit. They can only be broken by people who are willing

to change. We must face up to the hard reality of life that damaging chains are broken only by people of courage and commitment who are willing to struggle.and weather the pain. (Marvin J.
Ashton, *Ensign*, November 1986, 15)

SATAN CANNOT TAKE YOU PRISONER BY FORCE

We close this unpleasant chapter with the good news that there are
divine limitations placed upon the enemy. As powerful as they are,
Satan and his demons are not allowed to do everything they want to
do. Joseph Smith said, "The devil has no power over us only as we
permit him" (*Teachings of the Prophet Joseph Smith,* sel. Joseph Fielding
Smith, Salt Lake City, Utah: Deseret Book, 1938, 181). Satan and his
spirits have great power of persuasion and, if we allow it, even possession, but there are boundaries beyond which they are not allowed
to go—unless we invite them. Their ability to tempt, for example, is
strictly controlled. If they were allowed to overpower us with temptations so compelling that we were incapable of resisting, our agency
would be violated and we could not be held accountable for the sin.
Thus, "God is faithful, who will not suffer you to be tempted above
that ye are able, but will with the temptation also make a way to escape,
that ye may be able to bear it" (1 Corinthians 10:13). What a wonderful, comforting promise.

Here's another limitation: As much as Satan would like to grab
control of children before they can defend themselves, the Lord has
declared that "power is not given unto Satan to tempt little children,
until they begin to become accountable before me" (D&C 29:47).
Similarly, when the three Nephites were translated, their mortal probation was pronounced over, and they were placed "off limits" just like
innocent children. "There was a change wrought upon them, insomuch
that Satan could have no power over them, that he could not tempt
them" (3 Nephi 28:39). If we persist in righteousness, the day will
come when that pronouncement will apply to us as well. Meanwhile,
we should remember that it is not Satan who makes the rules, but God,
for it is he "who controllest and subjectest the devil, and the dark and
benighted dominion of Sheol" (D&C 121:4).

Job was an extremely righteous disciple. He was protected by that righteousness, just as we are when we learn to wear the armor of God. Satan challenged God. He boasted that he could break Job's faith. If that were really so, why didn't he just do it? Why did he challenge God to a spiritual duel? It was because he needed divine permission to penetrate the protective shield formed by Job's righteousness. "Wicked spirits have their bounds, limits, and laws by which they are governed" (Joseph Smith, *History of the Church*, vol. 4:576). Elder Eldred G. Smith explained:

> Lucifer can do on this earth only what he is permitted to do. Remember the story of Job? In each trial Job was subjected to, Lucifer asked for permission to test Job. He was given permission to go just so far, one step at a time. Job lost his wealth on one test, his family on another, his health on another. The Lord gave Satan full control over Job, except he could not destroy his soul. As with Job, so with us, *the Lord will not permit Satan to try us beyond our ability to resist or withstand his efforts, if we will accept his help.* (*Ensign*, December 1971, 45–46)

Satan is clever and cunning. He knows he cannot force his will upon us, but he also knows that most of us are asleep and unprepared for Satanic warfare and that gives him the opportunity to catch us off guard and manipulate us into choices which give him power over us. Nevertheless, the demonic possessions we have discussed can never happen unless we allow them to happen. Satan cannot force his will upon us unless we surrender our agency to him.

> Satan and his aides no doubt may know of our inclinations, our carnal tastes and desires, *but they cannot compel a righteous person to do evil if he seeks help from the Lord.* Too many try to blame Satan when in reality the fault lies within themselves because they yield to his enticements. (ElRay L. Christiansen, *New Era*, July 1975, 49)

If we are taken captive, it is either because we deliberately made the choices which led to that imprisonment, or we unwittingly allowed ourselves to be taken captive because we failed to arm and protect ourselves with the armor of God. And so the prophets plead with us, be on guard, watch yourselves, make your choices carefully so that you do not "choose eternal death, according to the will of the flesh and the evil which is therein, which giveth the spirit of the devil power to captivate, to bring you down to hell, that he may reign over you in his own kingdom" (2 Nephi 2:29).

> In all his evil doings, *the adversary can go no further than the transgressor permits him to go,* and we can gain complete power to resist the evils caused by Satan through adherence to the principles of the gospel of Jesus Christ.
>
> Members of the Church may have the blessing of the Holy Ghost, the prompter, as a companion as well, and *when the Holy Ghost is really within us, Satan must remain without.* (ElRay L. Christiansen, *Ensign*, November 1974, 24)

11

The Battleground of Immorality

SEX IS A SACRED, DIVINE, AND BEAUTIFUL GIFT FROM GOD TO BE enjoyed between man and wife. Whenever we teach about the laws of chastity, immorality, and sexual restraint, it is easy to convey the misconception that sex is evil and ugly, which it is not—unless perverted and defiled through Satanic misapplications. "It is important . . . that we impress upon our children's minds and hearts the beautiful and eternal nature of their sexuality" (Editorial, *Ensign*, December 1986, 57).

> Properly understood, the scriptures and the prophets counsel us to
> be virtuous not because romantic love is bad, but precisely because
> romantic love is so good. It is not only good, it is pure, precious,
> even sacred and holy. For that very reason, one of Satan's cheapest
> and dirtiest tricks is to make profane that which is sacred. (Bruce
> C. Hafen, *Ensign*, October 1982, 66)

Lucifer has successfully twisted and distorted this most precious part of humanity until the world has been persuaded to view sex as the biological equivalent of quenching thirst, satisfying the hunger for food, or passing waste materials from our bodies. He has made it commonplace, non-private, even cruel, torturous, and enslaving; the theme of endless ridicule, humor, and entertainment; something not only accepted in unmarried relationships but to be sought and expected from as many partners as one desires. Alma stated that adultery and fornication are the "most abominable above all sins save it be the shedding of innocent blood or denying the Holy Ghost" (Alma 39:5).

Sexual sin—the illicit sexual relations of men and women—stands,

103

in its enormity, next to murder. The Lord has drawn no essential distinctions between fornication, adultery, and harlotry or prostitution. Each has fallen under his solemn and awful condemnation. Those who would palliate this crime and say that such indulgence is but a sinless gratification of a normal desire, like appeasing hunger and thirst, speak filthiness with their lips. Their counsel leads to destruction; their wisdom comes from the father of lies. ("Messages of the First Presidency," *Improvement Era*, November 1942, 686)

While Satan is continually enticing people to defile the sexual part of their nature through experimentation and indulgence outside of marriage, the Lord has asked us to reverence these feelings, to keep them sacred and reserved for the marriage partner.

The law of chastity requires total abstinence before marriage and full fidelity afterward. It is the same for men and women. It is the cornerstone of trust so necessary to the precious happiness of the marriage relationship and family solidarity. (Spencer W. Kimball, *Ensign*, November 1978, 105)

One of the standards on which your happiness is based, now and in the future, is moral purity. The world would tell you that this standard is old-fashioned and out of date. The world would have you accept a so-called *new morality*, which is nothing more than immorality. In the church and kingdom of God, chastity will never be out of date, regardless of what the world may do or say. So we say to you, young men and women—maintain your self-respect. Do not engage in intimacies that bring heartache and sorrow. You cannot build happy lives on immorality. (Ezra Taft Benson, *Ensign*, November 1977, 30–31; emphasis in original)

President David O. McKay said, "Your virtue is worth more than your life. Please young folk, preserve your virtue even if you lose your lives." (As quoted in Kimball, *The Miracle of Forgiveness*, 63) When a woman has been sexually defiled, she has been deprived of "that which was most dear and precious above all things, which is chastity and virtue" (Moroni 9:9). "Chastity is of more value than anything else in all the world," said President Heber J. Grant. "There is no true Latter-day Saint who would not rather bury a son or a daughter than to have him or her lose his or her chastity" (*Gospel Standards,* compiled by Homer Durham, Salt Lake City, Utah: *Improvement Era,* 1941, 55).

If sexual passions are not controlled, they will overpower and destroy the feelings of true love. As Alma said, "see that ye bridle all your passions, that ye may be filled with love" (Alma 38:12). Without a bridle to direct the horse's powerful energy, the animal would leave the rider's desired path and wander wherever it chose. So it is with our sexual passions and appetites. Without the bridle of self-control, our appetites can run wild, taking us into degrading experiences that we later regret. "We must not let the attractions of the moment bring disaster for the eternities" (Kimball, *The Miracle of Forgiveness,* 1969, 246).

> God implanted the physical magnetism between the sexes for two reasons: for the propagation of the human race, and for the expression of that kind of love between man and wife that makes for true oneness. His command to the first man and woman to be "one flesh" was as important as his command to "be fruitful and multiply."
>
> The Bible makes plain that evil, when related to sex, *means not the use of something inherently corrupt, but the misuse of something pure and good.* It teaches clearly that sex can be a wonderful servant but a terrible master: that it can be a creative force more powerful than any other in the fostering of a love, companionship and happiness, or it can be the most destructive of all life's forces. (Billy Graham, as quoted by Spencer W. Kimball in *Ensign,* May 1974, 7–8)

President Kimball wisely explained what every person troubled with sexual desires knows: As soon as one gives in to a small temptation, he is faced with a larger and stronger desire. Each sin feeds on itself, so that the hunger is never satisfied but grows with each experience. He said:

> Sin in sex practices tends to have a "snowballing" effect. As the restraints fall away, Satan incites the carnal man to ever-deepening degeneracy in his search for excitement until in many instances he is lost to any former considerations of decency. (*The Miracle of Forgiveness,* 78)

Temporary thrills of illicit pleasure quickly evolve into an uncontrollable monster which demands more and more of the person's time and emotions. The excitement and thrills wear away, but the gnawing hunger for repetition remains. The sexual addict is caught in a swirling nightmare of descent into ever-increasing frequency and degrees of sin. The more he feeds the passions, the stronger and more demanding they become as evil spirits gain more and more power over the victim. As Brigham Young said, "If the spirit yields to the body, the devil then has power to overcome the body and spirit of that man, and he loses both" (*Discourses of Brigham Young,* Salt Lake City, Utah: Deseret Book, 1951, 70). The person thus driven by lust loses his sense of reality. When desires are aroused, he forgets the eternal implications of his sin and the cost involved in the inevitable feelings of shame, guilt, and remorse which always follow sinful indulgence. Responding almost automatically to demonic encouragement and manipulation, as if he were in a trance, he acts out the lust the demons have aroused, doing things he would never dream of doing when he was "in his right mind." There are probably more spiritual casualties in this combat zone than on any other battleground.

> The most favorite method the enemy of our souls has employed in ages past and that he will employ today is to capture souls by leading them gently, step by step, towards the greatest and most destructive sin against spiritual life—immorality, the ultimate end of self-indulgence. (Melvin J. Ballard, *New Era,* March 1984, 38)

The challenge people face on the battleground of immorality is to choose carefully and prayerfully when, where, how and with whom they will express their sexuality. In a very real sense, our eternal destinies depend on whom we kiss, embrace, and give our love to—and when it is given. The way people handle the sexual part of their lives will determine whether or not they attain the godhood intended by Heavenly Father.

> *Sexual experiences were never intended by the Lord to be a mere plaything or merely to satisfy passions and lusts.* We know of no directive from the Lord that proper sexual experience between husbands and wives need be limited totally to the procreation of children, but we find much evidence from Adam until now that no provision was ever made by the Lord for indiscriminate sex. (*Ensign,* October 1975, 4)

Elder Richard G. Scott explained the difference between real love and Satan's counterfeit of lust:

Love, as defined by the Lord, elevates, protects, respects, and enriches another. It motivates one to make sacrifices for another. *Satan promotes counterfeit love, which is lust. It is driven by a hunger to appease personal appetite.* One who practices this deception cares little for the pain and destruction caused another. While often camouflaged by flattering words, its motivation is self-gratification. (*Ensign*, May 1991, 35)

We are surrounded by the enemy on the battleground of immorality. Clothing fashions, popular music, advertising, literature, and entertainment are so saturated with sexual immorality that its degrading influence is inescapable. *Every person living in this generation will have to face sexual temptations and choose between virtue and lust.* Living in today's sexually wicked world is like walking through a battlefield which Satan has heavily mined with booby traps. These traps have been carefully, cleverly placed in today's social structure to destroy the noble sons and daughters of God. Just as a military mine can injure and cripple one's body, Satan's sexual traps can destroy a person's virtue and cripple him or her spiritually.

To defend himself against a particular weapon, a soldier must understand how it works, how it inflicts damage, and how to recognize and protect himself against its threat. And so it is in our spiritual conflicts on the battleground of immorality. If we are not aware of the subtle and cunning devices Satan uses to entice our thoughts and passions, if we do not recognize and understand the deadly weapons he uses against virtue and chastity, we are fighting without armor and are vulnerable to his attacks. In this chapter we will learn how to protect ourselves against his lethal weapons of lust, necking and petting, pornography, masturbation, fornication, adultery, and homosexuality.

That the Church's stand on morality may be understood, we declare firmly and unalterably, it is not an outworn garment, faded, old-fashioned, and threadbare. God is the same yesterday, today, and forever, and his covenants and doctrines are immutable; and *when the sun grows cold and the stars no longer shine, the law of chastity will still be basic in God's world and in the Lord's Church.* Old values are upheld by the Church not because they are old, but rather because through the ages they have proved right. It will always be the rule. (Spencer W. Kimball, *Ensign*, November 1980, 96)

SATAN'S WEAPONS OF NECKING AND PETTING

President Kimball taught that "Among the most common sexual sins our young people commit are necking and petting" (*The Miracle of Forgiveness,* 65). "Necking" might be defined as bodily contact between unmarried partners from the neck up, such as a kiss, or stroking the other person's hair. While this may hold no evil in itself, it is often the prelude to dangers beyond imagination when thoughts and hands wander below the neck to touch intimate, sacred parts of the body. "Petting" might be defined as unmarried couples touching each other anywhere that would normally be covered by modest clothing. A couple may have no intention of "going all the way," but petting feeds the fires of passion which demands progression and further exploration. Fondling each other's body may seem perfectly justified if you really love each other, but petting is one of the devil's most effective weapons for destroying virtue.

> Any sexual intimacy outside of the bonds of marriage—and I emphasize that means any involvement of the sacred, private parts of the body—is a sin and is forbidden by God. (Richard G. Scott, *Ensign*, May 1991, 34–35)

Who would say that he or she who pets has not become lustful, has not become passionate? Is this not the most abominable practice that God rebuked in his modern reiteration of the Ten Commandments: "Thou shalt not . . . commit adultery . . . *nor do anything like unto it* (D&C 59:6). What, may I ask you, is like unto adultery if it is not petting? (Spencer W. Kimball, *Ensign*, November 1980, 96)

No girl owes a boy kisses or other intimacies just because he spends a lot of money and shows her a good time on the date, and no boy has the right to expect or demand such favors of his date. To demand intimacies before marriage is wicked, cruel and unworthy of a priesthood holder who is supposed to be using his mortality to prepare for exaltation. We could profit by remembering Solomon's counsel: "If sinners entice thee, consent thou not" (Proverbs 1:10).

Many people believe there is nothing terrible about necking and petting as long as sexual intercourse doesn't follow, but there are many reasons why these preliminary intimacies are sinful. One reason is found in the Ten Commandments: "Thou shalt not steal" (Exodus 20:15). When you arouse sexual passions in a person you are not married to, by fondling his or her body, you are creating emotional memories that can last a lifetime and you are *stealing* precious, irreplaceable purity and innocence from that person's future spouse. No amount of love, no intensity of caring for another person can justify the fondling of that person's body before marriage. To do so arouses extremely sacred feelings and we have no right to steal them from another by sharing such intimacies before marriage. Someday, when the veil is removed, we will have the capacity to remember everything we have ever done (see Alma 5:18). In each date and social contact with the opposite sex, we are choosing the kind of memories we will live with for eternity. Make them pure and clean.

Perhaps the greatest danger in petting is the progression of desire it creates as it leads one first into mental, and then into physical fornication or adultery.

> Our Latter-day Saint boys and girls are the finest in the world. There is no group anywhere from ocean to ocean that can even compare with them ... And yet ... the devil knows how to destroy them. He knows, young men and women, that he cannot tempt you to commit adultery immediately, but he knows that he can soften you up by lewd association, vulgar talk, immodest dress, sexy movies, and so on. He knows too that if he can get them to drink, or if he can get them into his "necking, petting" program, the best boys and girls will finally succumb and will fall. (Kimball, *The Miracle of Forgiveness*, 230–31)

The automobile is undoubtedly one of the greatest tools Satan has for destroying virtue. It is a wonderful experience for couples to be alone together, to talk, explore ideas, feelings and goals, but this must never be done in the darkness of a "lover's lane." Satan will not let such a perfect opportunity go by without his attention. President Kimball reported that "one survey revealed that seven out of nine girls who lost their virtue suffered that loss in cars after dances" (*The Miracle of Forgiveness*, 64).

The couple's intentions may be totally honorable, but Satan is a skilled adversary and knows how to arouse desires in even the most innocent of situations. When a boy and girl get in a car for a date, they should not assume they are alone. It is quite probable that evil spirits accompany them, hoping for the opportunity to suggest unworthy thoughts and deeds. If that boy and girl take physical liberties with each other, their passions could be inflamed into a raging fire by the demons who have been perfecting their seductive skills for thousands of years. President Kimball described this danger when he acknowledged that even though a couple "intended no evil . . . the privacy made easy the passionate intimacies which crept upon them stealthily as a snake slithers through the grass" while "legions of vicious, hovering tempters" make the automobile, thus used, "Satan's near perfect setting for sin." (*The Miracle of Forgiveness,* 225)

Prevention and avoidance are the keys. President Kimball said, "As I study the story of the Redeemer and his temptations, I am certain he spent his energies fortifying himself against temptation rather than battling with it to conquer it." (*The Miracle of Forgiveness,* 217) Don't give Satan the opportunity to smother you in an avalanche of unexpected desires. If you would keep your virtue, decide now, ahead of temptation, that you will do nothing that would embarrass you if others knew about it. Don't wait for the moment of passion when desires are pulling at you and clouding your mind. Decide now, in the calmness and safety of the Holy Spirit's companionship exactly what you *will* do and what you *will not* do. Make the promise to yourself, to your Heavenly Father and to your future spouse. Make that line so clear that Satan will never be able to pull you across. President Kimball related a tragic experience in which a young couple described their unexpected, but-oh-so typical fall into immorality:

> The simple kisses we had often exchanged gradually developed into petting. We loved each other so much that we convinced ourselves that it was not so wrong merely to pet since we sort of belonged to one another anyway. *Where we ended one night became the starting point for the next night,* and we continued on and on, until finally it happened-almost as though we could not control ourselves—we had intercourse. We had even talked about it and agreed that whatever else we did, we would not go that far. And then when it was late—so late—so everlastingly late—we woke

up to the meaning of what we had done. (*Ensign*, November 1980, 94–95)

SATAN'S WEAPON OF PORNOGRAPHY

One of the great debates in modern society is the definition of pornography. Whatever else pornography may or may not be, for the purpose of learning to overcome Satan's influence in our lives, this book will define pornography as the inappropriate intent to stimulate sexual excitement through the provocative display of the body, usually with nudity or carefully calculated partial nudity. Being against pornography does not mean there is something evil or ugly about bodies, per se—including nude bodies. It simply means that every aspect of God's sacred gift of sexuality is reserved exclusively for marriage. There is a fine line between the natural feelings of appreciation for the beauty of the bodies God created and allowing those natural feelings to progress into desire and lust. Pornography defiles the private, intimate nature of sexuality by putting it on public display and making it common and non-private. No one has the right to invade the sacred privacy of another person's nudity unless invited to within the marital relationship. To do so involves consequences of eternal importance.

> It's perfectly natural to be attracted to a good-looking young woman. It's the way God planned that it should be. Satan knows this, however, and will ever so quietly sneak bad thoughts into your mind. (Editorial, *New Era*, May 1989, 17)

As one mission president counseled his elders, "There's nothing wrong with thinking, 'She's sure pretty.' But let the thought stop there" (*New Era*, May 1989, 18). While there is nothing wrong with admiring an attractive woman, we are commanded, "Lust not after her beauty in thine heart" (Proverbs 6:25).

One of the obvious evils of pornography is the mental adultery it incites. The Savior's familiar words, "whosoever looketh on a woman, to lust after her, hath committed adultery with her already in his heart," show his concern for mental adultery (Matthew 5:28). Can there be any doubt that looking longingly at pictures of nude men or women is included in this warning? While *mental* adultery does not have the physical dangers of disease and unwanted pregnancy, it has eternal consequences that are just as terrible as the physical act. The nervous system cannot tell the difference between a real experience and one that is vividly imagined. Anyone who has responded to an imagined fear knows that the body reacts just the same as it would have if the emergency had been genuine. The pornographic memories and other internal effects on our brains are equally damaging, whether committed physically or mentally.

Pornography could be likened to the atomic bomb of spiritual warfare. Just as fire and radiation from a nuclear explosion consume the flesh of its victims, pornography consumes its victims with lust, blinding its users to eternal consequences. Pornography creates an unquenchable yearning for ever-increasing cycles of artificial stimulation. It is perhaps the most devastating, addicting weapon Satan has used in these last days before the millennium.

Pornography is one of the devil's most effective weapons for softening the conscience. Satan uses pornography to attack virtue because he knows that if he cannot persuade God's children to indulge in sexual sins *physically,* with pornography he can induce them to participate in those activities *mentally,* thereby establishing damaging mental habits and preparing the way for future indulgence. It doesn't matter as long as you just look, he whispers, knowing that the longer we watch, the more likely we are to participate.

Each time we pollute our minds with pornographic material we are planting the seeds of lust that will eventually grow into a harvest of filthy, wicked deeds as we act out the things we have fantasized. As Elder H. Burke Peterson warned, "Those who unceasingly fill their minds with things that are filthy and ugly are the ones who are led step-by-step into terribly destructive experiences" (*Ensign*, June 1981, 74). Pornography is a proven method of leading people into the sins of masturbation, fornication, adultery, homosexuality, bestiality, sexual violence, child abuse, and other lewd acts. Many active church members who would never have considered committing such sins find themselves welcoming and seeking these filthy practices because, through the accumulating poison of pornography, their minds have been captured by the enemy and they have lost the Spirit of the Lord. The effects of pornography are both progressive and cumulative. Each image viewed adds to those of the past, inciting ever-increasing lust and desires for adventure and excitement.

> That person who entertains . . . pornographic pictures and literature records them in his marvelous human computer, the brain, which can't forget this filth. Once recorded, it will always remain there, subject to recall. (Spencer W. Kimball, *Devotional Speeches of the Year*, Provo Utah: BYU Press, 1974–75, 241)

I once worked in a factory where we built autopilot systems. Each "black box" was filled with subcomponents which had their own assembly and quality control history. To track these components we printed a serial number on the metal chassis with a black ink that contained acid, so that the number would actually etch its way into the metal. One day as I sat at the white Formica work bench, I accidentally spilled a bottle of this ink. To my horror, the bench was quickly covered with a huge black splotch. By the time I found some rags it was too late. The acid had done its work and the bench was permanently stained with ugly black marks which would forever testify to my careless mistake.

Viewing pornography is something like pouring acid-etching ink into the fibers of our brains, etching images that will stain our memories almost forever and which can suddenly erupt in convulsions of desire years later. The pornographic images may be entirely unnoticed and forgotten by the conscious mind. We may not be bothered by the memories for weeks, months, or even years, but they are still recorded there in the brain cells, occupying space that could have stored spiritually uplifting material. Those memories and seductive images are hidden in our minds like a time bomb, ticking away, waiting for the right moment of lust to unleash their explosive power over our actions. Satan knows how to stimulate recall of those pornographic time bombs. Sooner or later, perhaps many years after abandoning the use of pornography, in an unguarded moment of lustful thought, the person unintentionally opens the door to the past. Perhaps it is only for a brief moment that the mind is accessible to Satan, but he can instantly trigger a recall of those long-forgotten images. All that past filth can be suddenly unleashed in an astonishing explosion of overwhelming memory. We are confused. How could we be filled with such powerful and unexpected desires for sexual gratification which are so far in excess of the stimulation that would otherwise have resulted from that momentary indiscretion? We are swept away in a wave of accumulated past memories, wondering why we feel so compelled to sin when we only indulged such a momentary, tiny wicked thought.

> The body has defenses to rid itself of unwholesome food, but the brain won't vomit back filth. *Once recorded it will always remain subject to recall,* flashing its perverted images across your mind, and drawing you away from the wholesome things in life. (N. Eldon Tanner, *New Era,* January 1977, 32)

To win our battles with Satan it is imperative that we have the Lord's Spirit with us to expand and strengthen our efforts. **To lose the Lord's Spirit is to lose our battles.** Viewing pornography and indulging in sexual fantasies drive the Spirit away, for "the Spirit of the Lord doth not dwell in unholy temples" (Helaman 4:24). "And he that looketh upon a woman to lust after her . . . shall not have the Spirit" (D&C 42:23). This is one of the main reasons why mental adultery is so serious. Entertaining lustful thoughts drives the Spirit away, even if we do not act upon them. We cannot expect to enjoy the companionship of the Holy Spirit when we dump filth and sensuality into our sacred temple-minds. As Elder Joseph B. Wirthlin said:

> Pornography in all its forms . . . constitutes a spiritual poison that is addictive and destructive. Every ounce of pornography and immoral entertainment will cause you to lose a pound of spirituality. And it will only take a few ounces of immorality to cause you to lose all of your spiritual strength, for the Lord's Spirit will not dwell in an unclean temple. (*New Era,* May 1988, 7)

As pornography rots away the conscience and readies us for other sins, it also destroys our relationships with loved ones and with God. Just as the radiation from an atomic blast spreads outward from the center of the explosion, the effects of pornography also radiate outward from the user into the lives of family and friends, leaving marriage and family relationships empty and hollow, stripped of the love, warmth, and intimacy God meant them to have. A person addicted to pornography cannot sustain meaningful relationships because his capacity for love has been destroyed, burned away by the flames of lust, leaving him hollow and empty inside. He is incapable of giving love to others while his thoughts are constantly dominated by a gnawing hunger for the illusionary fulfillment that pornography promises but never delivers. In a subconscious effort to hide this emptiness, the person addicted to pornography grows cold, distant, and hostile because deep inside, the eternal spirit recognizes the enormity of the sinner's filth and fears discovery. However, people who turn from pornographic substitutes and fill their lives with meaningful relationships with loved ones and with the Lord can be healed of pornography's gnawing hungers and will no longer need its empty illusions. In later chapters we will discuss exactly how to accomplish this. Elder H. Burke Peterson warned:

> Our mind, like a tremendous reservoir . . . is capable of taking in whatever it may be fed—good and bad, trash and garbage, as well as righteous thoughts and experiences. It has a capacity to store whatever we will give it. Unfortunately, what our mind takes in, it keeps—sometimes forever. It's a long, long process to cleanse a mind that has been polluted by unclean thoughts. (*Ensign*, November 1980, 38)

Fortunately, through the cleansing Atonement of Jesus Christ, there is a way for those ugly memories to be removed from one who sincerely repents. It is not something we can do for ourselves, but it is something the God of the impossible can do, leading us back to purity and holiness before our maker. The Savior promised, "Return, ye backsliding children, and I will heal your backslidings" (Jeremiah 3:22).

As we fight our battles with Satan's pornographic lures, we not only have to conquer the desires and lust of the flesh, but also *the lust of the eyes*" (see 1 John 2:16). Peter referred to wicked men and women who have "eyes full of adultery . . . that cannot cease from sin" (2 Peter 2:14). And Paul explained that the "lust of the eyes" is really the mental adultery Christ spoke about as sinners act out "the lusts of our flesh, fulfilling the desires of the flesh *and* of the mind" (Ephesians 2:3). Job indicated an understanding of the relationship between the lust of the eyes and mental adultery when he said, "I made a covenant with mine eyes; why then should I think upon a maid?" (Job 31:1).

Alma challenged: "all you that are desirous to follow the voice of the good shepherd, come ye out from the wicked, and be ye separate, *and touch not their unclean things*" (Alma 5:57). We are not "separate" from the wicked things of the world and we are surely touching and clinging to their "unclean things" when we look at pornographic magazines or indulge in other sexually immoral entertainments. What army would be stupid enough to invite the enemy to infiltrate its computer command center and allow that enemy to tamper with the computer files? That is exactly what we do when we accept the devil's treacherous weapon of pornography into our lives. Is it any wonder that President Benson said:

> We counsel you . . . not to pollute your minds with such degrading matter, for *the mind through which this filth passes is never the same afterwards*. Don't see R-rated movies or vulgar videos or participate in any entertainment that is immoral, suggestive, or pornographic. (*Ensign*, May 1986, 45)

After condemning mental adultery, Jesus introduced a cure when he said, in stark, frightening imagery:

> And if thy right eye offend thee, pluck it out, and cast it from thee: for it is profitable for thee that one of thy members should perish, and not that thy whole body should be cast into hell. (Matthew 5:29)

It is not likely that Jesus intended for people to actually destroy their vision by literally ripping their eyes from the sockets, although, as he said, even that drastic measure would be preferable to losing their exaltation. He was most likely using this suggestion to indicate the necessity for strict self-discipline, the need for taking whatever action is required to control the lust of the eyes. We can apply the spirit of this lesson by "plucking away" the unacceptable *inputs* to our eyes and thereby eliminating the visual offenses to the Lord's Holy Spirit. For example, we are "plucking away" visual offenses from our eyes and reducing sexual struggles when we refuse to view sensual movies, videos, and television shows that are incompatible with the Lord's Spirit. We are "plucking away" our eyes when we change the television channel to avoid sexually provocative advertisements, or walk out of a theater at the first sign of inappropriate entertainment. We are also spiritually "plucking away" our eyes when we refuse to look at magazines presenting nudity or even near-nudity, or when we turn our eyes away to prevent lusting toward an attractive person of the opposite sex.

Alma said that if you would "forsake your sins," you must "go no more after the lusts of your eyes" (Alma 39:9). To be in harmony with the Savior's admonition to avoid mental adultery, we must learn to prevent our eyes from lingering on *anything* and *everything* which can fuel the appetite for more explicit stimulation and imagination. Once we identify and eliminate the visual stimuli that trigger our lust, we have eliminated or greatly reduced the severity of our struggles, even before the battle begins. You know in your own heart what it is that you must personally "pluck away."

> *We must stop the flow into our minds of these unhealthy and unwhole-some streams of experiences and thoughts.* Evil acts are preceded by unrighteous thoughts. And unrighteous thoughts are born of vulgar stories, jokes, pictures, conversation and a myriad of other Satanic products. There should not be any X- or R-rated movies that we participate in viewing or talking about. There must be no pornographic magazines, pictures, or stories, no re-telling of filthy jokes or crude experiences.
>
> Once in a while we should stop and ask ourselves, "In whose army are we fighting? Whose battle lines are we defending?" Do you have the courage to walk out of an off-color PG-rated movie? Have you the courage to keep out of your home some television shows that are filled with suggestive sexual conversation-and even experiences? Have you thought lately how effective these shows are in piercing even the strongest spirits? Brethren, we do not feed ourselves a diet of trash! (H. Burke Peterson, *Ensign*, November 1980, 38–39)

In Chapter 7, "The Battleground of Thought," we learned how the helmet of salvation can protect our sacred minds and eyes from the evils of pornography and lust. In Chapter 20, "Putting on the Armor," we will learn how to drive the ugly, filthy memories and images from our brain cells and replace them with clean, righteous thoughts and principles of spiritual power.

Satan's Weapon of Masturbation

Masturbation can be defined as "manipulating one's own sexual organs to produce sexual excitement" (Editorial, *Ensign*, December 1986, 58). This practice is one of Satan's most common and deadly weapons, causing tremendous heartache to both the sinner and the loved ones who struggle to understand the problem. President Kimball described masturbation as "a rather common indiscretion" (see *Ensign*, November 1980, 97). And Bishop Vaughn J. Featherstone indicated that any boy who successfully avoided doing this throughout his teenage years "would be quite a rare young man" (see *Ensign*, May 1975, 66–67). During the October 1980 semi-annual world conference, President Kimball gave a lengthy sermon on the temptations of immorality. Expressing deep regret for having to mention such sins as masturbation in public he said:

> We would avoid mentioning these unholy terms and these reprehensible practices were it not for the fact that we have a responsibility to the youth of Zion that they be not deceived by those who would call bad good, and black white. (*Ensign*, November 1980, 97)

So great is the need for understanding of this subject that an *Ensign* article entitled "Talking With Your Children About Moral Purity" stated:

> Some parents feel embarrassed to speak frankly to their children about sexual intimacy. However, the world is not embarrassed . . . It is important, therefore, that we impress upon our children's minds and hearts the beautiful and eternal nature of their sexuality.
>
> In modern society, it is far too common a tragedy for young people to cultivate a strong sexual appetite even before they begin to date. One cause of this serious problem can be the sin of masturbation. *Children should be taught, at around the first signs of puberty, what masturbation is and why it is wrong.* Parents who avoid guiding their children in this matter do them a disservice. (*Ensign*, December 1986, 57–58)

President Kimball said:

> Prophets anciently and today condemn masturbation. It induces feelings of guilt and shame. It is detrimental to spirituality. It indicates slavery to the flesh, not the mastery of it and the growth toward godhood which is the object of our mortal life. Our modern prophet has indicated that no young man should

be called on a mission who is not free from this practice. (*The Miracle of Forgiveness,* 77)

Paul taught the importance of not misusing the sexual parts of our bodies when he said, "Every one of you should know how to possess his vessel in sanctification and honour" (1 Thessalonians 4:4). Treating sexuality with "sanctification and honour" means total abstinence before marriage and tender, loving self-control and purity of thought within marriage. David asked, "Who shall ascend into the hill of the Lord? Or who shall stand in his holy place?" His answer was, *"He that hath clean hands,* and a pure heart" (Psalms 24:3–4). "Entangle not yourselves in sin, *but let your hands be clean"* (D&C 88:86). The moral responsibility not to use our hands to abuse our bodies applies to every person. This may be one of the things Isaiah had in mind when he said, "Blessed is the man that . . . *keepeth his hand from doing any evil"* (Isaiah 56:2). The Savior suggested a remedy which we could apply to masturbation:

> And if thy right hand offend thee, cut it off, and cast it from thee: for it is profitable for thee that one of thy members should perish, and not that thy whole body should be cast into hell (Matthew 5:30).

Again, it is not likely that Christ really intended for us to grab a knife and start hacking a limb off. Rather he was showing the importance of controlling both our thoughts and the actions of our hands as they carry out our unclean thoughts. "If iniquity be in thine hand, put it far away" (Job 11:14).

In order to conquer this vile habit, it is important to understand that the reasons for compulsive masturbation are not limited to the gratification of sexual desire. Many are held captive in this addiction because it has become a self-perpetuating method of coping with *non-sexual* problems covering a wide spectrum of social inadequacies. The hidden, often subconscious, reasons for turning to masturbation are varied and complex. For example, masturbation is often used as an attempt to escape from the stresses of academic, employment, marital or family problems, feelings of loneliness, discouragement, and depression. For some it provides a quick sedative for sleep. Subconsciously it is used by many in an attempt to compensate for the feelings of inadequacy, inferiority, lack of self-worth, and even as a form of self-punishment for feelings of unworthiness.

The roots of this addiction can range from the physical simplicity of an escape from idle time and boredom to the spiritual complexities of lust and demonic possession or manipulation, as was discussed in the last chapter, "Prisoner of War." It is quite likely that whenever we find ourselves out of control and unable to prevent ourselves from doing the sin we hate and want to abandon, we are seeing evidence of the possessive influence of evil demons who are using their victim's body of flesh to act out the desires they cannot fulfil in their own spirit bodies. It's your body, the demons whisper, and no one has the right to tell you what you can or can't do with your own body. It is no different from eating when you are hungry. Almost everyone does it. Don't be ashamed of your feelings. You will feel better if you do this.

In addition to the complex mental and emotional reasons why masturbation is so addicting, there are additional *biological* reasons why it is difficult for men, especially, to break this habit. The Lord designed the husband's body to produce semen to carry the life-giving sperm into the wife's body. Each time the semen is released, the body goes into production to replace it. The more often a man masturbates, the higher the rate of production and the resulting urge to release it again. It can become a continual cycle rather like winding and unwinding the mainspring in a clock. The tighter the spring is wound, the greater the stored energy and need to unwind. Masturbation releases that pressure temporarily, but in so doing starts the next cycle, like rewinding the spring tighter and tighter, until it seems every cell in the mind and body is screaming for release.

Satan knows how to use this physical biology against us. Look, he says, your body has these natural sexual desires and it is your duty to gratify them. It will harm you if you don't. You have to make provision for the sexual desires of your flesh. It's not reasonable to deny these appetites just because you're not married. Scripture answers, "Put ye on the Lord Jesus Christ, and *make not provision for the flesh,* to fulfil the lusts thereof (Romans 13:14). Every time we choose to view pornography we are "making provisions" to stimulate the lusts of the flesh, which has the same effect as throwing gasoline on a raging fire. It is not *necessary* to gratify sexual desires or "make provision for the flesh" because the Lord has built into the male body the capacity to shut down the production so that abstinence itself regulates the body and unwinds the spring, as it were.

The prophets have exposed Satan's scheming rationalizations for the cunning entrapments they are meant to be. President J. Reuben Clark said, "The sex urge does not have to be satisfied. Satan's old lie is that it does have to be satisfied" (*Ensign*, April 1975, 66).

The body can regulate itself as long as it is not tampered with, but one of the difficulties experienced by men who try to abandon this habit is that the body responds to change slowly. If there have been months or years of frequent masturbation, it is going to take some time before the body is convinced that it no longer needs such an artificially high rate of production. Depending upon the frequency of the man's abuse, it could take months before these sensitive parts of the body slow down as the Lord designed them to do during abstinence. This struggle is serious and difficult, much like the withdrawal pains endured by newly abstaining cigarette smokers. But if the repentant person understands this process as a natural consequence of past abuse, he can have the patience to endure the withdrawal period and look forward to the reward of greater self-control and less pressure or fewer urgings once the body is restored to its proper condition. However, if the person attempting to repent of this sin slips and repeats the act, the cycle of production is started all over again and the difficulties of withdrawal are renewed and prolonged. Perhaps this helps explain why Satan's lie to the repenting masturbator, You've been good for a long time, just once more won't hurt, is so cunning and cruel.

People who declare war on this habit often express surprise that the problem gets worse before it gets better. This is to be expected. It is a sign that you are moving in the right direction and the demons are trying to stop you. When soldiers are captured as prisoners of war, the guards are quite willing to allow them to wander about the camp *dreaming* of escape. But when they actually *attempt* escape, that is a different matter. When Satan sees a person putting on the armor of God and preparing to replace the habit of masturbation with spirituality, he raises every possible defense to keep that person in captivity.

Experience shows that people who focus all their energies on condemning themselves for this problem and fight it with will power alone are not likely to succeed because they are concentrating on *symptoms* rather than *solutions*. The habit of masturbation is almost always an attempted remedy, an attempted self-medication for the spiritual sickness that has driven the sinner inward, filled him with loneliness, and isolated him from a healthy relationship with the Lord, the spouse, family members, and friends. Thus, contrary to what one would naturally assume, sex, lust, and masturbation are usually not the *real* problems, but only *symptoms* of deeper problems, such as the inadequacies previously described. Remember the spiritual law: **What holds your attention holds you.** Will power cannot heal spiritual sickness even if it is sufficient to control the unworthy behavior. Another reason for failure to conquer this habit is focusing one's attention on the sins of the past and lacking faith in Jesus Christ to rescue and heal the spiritual problems which separate us from Heavenly Father.

If masturbation has been a problem, why not decide right now to take up your spiritual armor and fight against the Satanic influences which hold you in that captivity. "Watch ye, stand fast in the faith, quit you like men, be strong" (1 Corinthians 16:13). "I beseech you therefore, brethren . . . that ye present your bodies a living sacrifice, holy, acceptable unto God, which is your reasonable service" (Romans 12:1). In Chapters 12 and 20 we will discuss the principles which enable us to conquer the mental and spiritual habits which addict us to pornography and masturbation. Appendix A presents an effective seven-step plan for breaking the *physical* cycles which hold us in this captivity in spite of our desires to repent.

SATAN'S WEAPON OF FORNICATION

Fornication is defined as sexual intercourse between unmarried partners. It is ranked in seriousness of sin next to adultery, which is second only to murder (see Alma 39:5). This practice is strictly forbidden by the Lord, "For this is the will of God, even your sanctification, that ye should abstain from fornication" (1 Thessalonians 4:3).

> The world may countenance premarital sex experiences, but the Lord and his Church condemn in no uncertain terms any and every sex relationship outside of marriage, and even indecent and uncontrolled ones within marriage. And so, though many self-styled authorities justify these practices as a normal release, the Church condemns them. Such unholy practices were condemned by ancient prophets and are today condemned by the

Church. (Spencer W. Kimball, *Faith Precedes the Miracle*, Salt Lake City, Utah: Deseret Book, 1972, 175)

In these last days, fornication has become the standard of conduct expected by the world, even in casual dating. Those who respect the sanctity of sexuality and prefer to preserve their virtue by waiting for marriage are considered old-fashioned, prudish, and unworthy of company. If someone you are dating even *hints* at fornication, that should be your last date with him or her, for as Paul reminded the Saints of his time, "I wrote unto you in an epistle not to company with fornicators" (1 Corinthians 5:9). Elder Neal A. Maxwell said, "Do not company with fornicators—not because you are too good for them, but, as C. S. Lewis wrote, 'because you are not good enough.'" "Remember," Elder Maxwell warned, "that bad situations can wear down even good people." (*New Era*, June 1979, 42) If the person you are with urges petting or fornication, you are with the wrong person—because he or she is suggesting that you trade a few moments of pleasure for an eternity of joy. The price is too high. No one is worth that cost.

There are two major strategies used by Satan to trick couples into fornication. The first is calculated to separate the sex act from the deep and tender feelings of love and oneness which God meant it to have in marriage. Satan accomplishes this by promoting casual, recreational sex between couples with no commitment to each other. This is his perverted logic: Making love is just as natural as eating, drinking, or sleeping. The body was made for pleasure. Make love and you will be loved. To these lies the devil adds, Abstinence is outdated. In today's modern world; there is no harm in "making love" because you are perfectly safe from the dangers of disease and pregnancy if you use condoms and birth control. Such are the devil's lies, so eagerly accepted by a lustful world. But the Lord has declared that intercourse is a sacred gift reserved strictly for the sanctity of marriage. "Now the body is not for fornication, but for the Lord" (1 Corinthians 6:13). "Abstain . . . from fornication: from which if ye keep yourselves, ye shall do well" (Acts 15:29). Satan's cunning rationalizations are calculated to distract people from the truth that the most harmful consequences of fornication are not the physical perils, but the loss of the Holy Spirit and the spiritual damage to our relationship with Heavenly Father.

Satan's second strategy is designed to entice couples who are committed to each other not to wait until marriage. It's okay, he whispers, because you're in love and you already belong to each other. Why should you deny your love by waiting for the formality of a marriage license? What possible difference could a piece of paper make? Of this Satanic philosophy, Jeffrey R. Holland counseled:

> Sexual expression is a high and holy physical gratification we were designed and created to enjoy. It is given of God to make us like God. But it is not ours without price. Not instantly. Not conveniently. Not with cozy corruption of eternal powers. It is to be earned, over time, and with discipline. It, like every good thing, is God's right to bestow, not Satan's. When faced with that inherent appetite, a disciple of Christ must be willing to say, "Yes, but *not this way*." In time, with love, after marriage. (*Ensign*, February 1984, 69; emphasis in original)

Waiting until marriage may be one of the most difficult things people will be challenged with during mortality. But we came here to learn to conquer and control the desires of the flesh, not to be ruled by them. "Therefore endure hardness, as a good soldier of Jesus Christ" (2 Timothy 2:3). It is only natural that two people in love will desire each other. And it is only natural that the relationship will grow toward more intimacy after the couple formalizes their commitment to each other with an engagement ring and plans for marriage. Temptations toward sexual intimacy tend to increase the deeper the feelings of love, and the longer the wait for marriage. Such feelings are cause for joy and not for shame. However, even though God instilled those desires in us, we have no right to fulfill them until that union has been sanctioned by priesthood authority. To do so prematurely will only tarnish and diminish that which could have been treasured for eternity by carefully guarding each other's virtue and waiting for marriage.

> Self-control, self-mastery . . . may not be popular in this age of license and lack of restraint, but what is needed is self-discipline. Can we imagine the angels or the Gods not being in control of themselves in any particular? The question is of course ludicrous. Equally ridiculous is the idea that any of us can rise to the eternal heights without disciplining ourselves and being disciplined by the circumstances of life. The purity and perfection we seek is unattainable without this subjection of unworthy, ungodlike

urges and the corresponding encouragement of the opposites. (Kimball, *The Miracle of Forgiveness*, 28)

No matter how difficult the struggle, marriage is worth waiting for. Nothing can replace the feeling of cleanliness and integrity one experiences by going to the temple altar clean and undefiled. No momentary thrill is worth giving up the treasure of being able to look each other in the eye across the temple altar with no shameful past to hide, knowing that both partners are virgins, both physically and mentally.

> Many rationalize that this attraction of two unmarried people is love, and they seek thereby to justify their intimate relations. *This is one of the most false of all Satan's lies.* It is lust, not love, which brings men and women to fornication and adultery. No person would injure one he truly loves, and sexual sin can only result in injury.
>
> The God of yesterday, today, and tomorrow continues to demand continence and to require that people come to the marriage altar as virgins, clean and free from sex experience. (*The Miracle of Forgiveness*, 65, 66–67)

SATAN'S WEAPON OF ADULTERY

For thousands of years the Lord's commandment of marital fidelity has been emphatically clear and inflexible: "Thou shalt not commit adultery" (see Exodus 20:14). We have already discussed the seriousness of acting out one's lust in necking, petting, masturbation, pornography, and fornication, which the prophets have declared are all "like unto" adultery. While these weapons are primarily used to destroy *individuals,* Satan's weapon of adultery is calculated to destroy *families* and *marriages.*

Under the laws of ancient Israel, adultery was considered worthy of punishment by death (see Leviticus 20:10). In today's world, religious societies are not allowed to take life, but in a sense the adulterer takes his own life, for "when lust hath conceived, it bringeth forth sin: and sin, when it is finished, bringeth forth death" (James 1:15). Jesus said, "he that looketh on a woman to lust after her, or if any shall commit adultery in their hearts, they shall not have the Spirit, but shall deny the faith and shall fear" (D&C 63:16).

> But whoso comitteth adultery with a woman lacketh understanding: he that doeth it destroyeth his own soul. (Proverbs 6:32)

Many who face church courts because of adultery have expressed confusion as to how it happened when they never intended to go so far. It is extremely rare that an active church member falls into an adulterous relationship in one sudden abandonment of the marriage vows. Almost always this awful circumstance comes into one's life as the natural result of a series of progressive compromises and improper choices, something like moving down a long flight of stairs. We start at the top, working toward a happy, fulfilling marriage. Through very minor errors we take a step or two downward as we make selfish and immature choices that damage the marriage. Step by step we descend through the emotions and choices that eventually cause us to abandon our covenants. Each step leads to another, adding such minimal damage that for a long time we don't even notice as the harm begins to accumulate.

> Infidelity is a subtle process. It does not begin with adultery; it begins with thoughts and attitudes. Each step to adultery is short, and each is easily taken; but once the process starts, it is difficult to stop . . . Like most illnesses, infidelity is easier to prevent than to remedy, and the best prevention is to work hard at developing a good marriage. (Veon G. Smith, *Ensign*, January 1975, 58, 61)

If this descent continues over weeks and months, without even realizing it the person's thinking becomes distorted and he or she loses perspective. Such persons actually believe Satan when he whispers that the adultery is justified because the spouse is an uninteresting or inadequate partner. The truth is that no marital difficulty can justify infidelity. The problem with a wayward partner is not the spouse, but that partner's own greedy, self-centeredness and carnal desires.

> Whatever the rationalizations and arguments, there are no circumstances which justify adultery. (Kimball, *The Miracle of Forgiveness*, 69)

126

The steps leading to adultery are easy to recognize when we are not blinded by Satan's deceptions. Let us consider some of the pivotal decisions which lead us away from the Lord and toward the greedy clutches of Satan. The following steps do not necessarily occur in the same order for every person, but each compromise listed can serve as a measurement of one's present position and a gauge of how far Satan may have enticed one down the path toward adultery.

1. We begin by losing appreciation for our blessings.
2. We take our spouses for granted.
3. We seek opportunities to spend time with others instead of with our families.
4. We grow isolated and stop communicating with each other.
5. We grow in resentment toward family responsibilities.
6. We begin brooding over the things we dislike in our spouses.
7. We replace courtesy and compliments with criticisms and put-downs.
8. We allow the marriage to deteriorate and either deliberately or subconsciously reach a point where we stop trying to make it work.
9. We justify indifference by telling ourselves we just don't care anymore, or that we never loved the spouse in the first place.
10. We lose the companionship of the Holy Ghost.
11. We avoid going to the temple.
12. We stop holding Family Home Evening.
13. We stop reading the scriptures and church magazines.
14. We allow our negative feelings to override gospel knowledge, testimony, and conscience.
15. We stop communicating with our Heavenly Father in prayer.
16. We neglect, then resent, and finally resign from church assignments.
17. We stop attending church.
18. We begin justifying our sins instead of repenting.
19. We give up trying to live the gospel and accept Satan's lie that it is too late for us.
20. We try to relieve our guilty consciences by blaming our spouses for the self-imposed misery we feel instead of accepting it responsibly.
21. We begin looking for escapes instead of solutions.
22. We begin allowing attractions to other people to occupy our thoughts.

23. We indulge "what-if" dreams and fantasies about what it would be like to be with another person.
24. We begin to move toward the fulfillment of those fantasies by flirting with prospective partners.
25. We entertain thoughts of escaping the misery we feel by leaving the marriage and living with someone else.
26. We allow the pleasures of the present moment to become more important to us than the realities of eternity.

The final act of adultery is not the only sin. For any man or woman to begin to share affection or romantic interest with any other than the spouse is an almost certain approach to ultimate adultery. There must be no romantic interest, attention, dating, or flirtation of any kind with anyone so long as either of the participating people is still legally married, regardless of the status of that marriage. (Kimball, *The Miracle of Forgiveness*, 70)

Satan knows how to seize upon the opportunities provided by our compromises. Using his power to surround us with evil spirits who whisper defeating suggestions, he bombards us with constant temptations and lies. He directs attention away from the memories of the good times we had together and fills our minds with memories of past disappointments, difficulties, and wounds we have experienced with our companions. He amplifies the spouses' imperfections in our minds until our companions seem so ugly and undesirable that we can't even imagine why we married them in the first place. Consider some of the lies the devil uses for attacking marriages and leading to adultery:

1. You are unhappy because you married the wrong person. It is his (or her) fault you are not happy. Find a new partner and you will be happy.
2. He (or she) doesn't treat you right. You owe it to yourself to find a better situation.
3. She (or he) will be better off without you. You never really loved her (or him) anyway. She (or he) deserves the chance to find a better person.
4. You are so wicked there is no chance of attaining the Celestial Kingdom, so you owe it to yourself to get a new partner and enjoy this life as much as you can.

Warning bells should be sounding if you have heard some of these lies recently, because once you have eroded your resolves by accepting these lies and compromising yourself, Satan will find an opportunity to present you with both "the perfect partner" and the circumstances to make the adultery possible. How easy it is to mistake the attraction we feel for such a person as *love,* when in reality, all it amounts to is *lust* and the selfish desire for excitement and escape. In our self-imposed loneliness we reach out to that person, not to give, but to take and to try to fill the emptiness we have caused in our own lives.

No matter how far one has descended toward adultery, because of the sacrifice and Atonement of Jesus Christ, he or she can always choose to repent. It will be difficult to heal deep wounds, change habits, and rebuild the damaged marriage, *but it can be done.* The difficult path to repentance is infinitely easier to endure than is the guilt and pain of sexual sin. And even if one has gone all the way and broken the marriage and temple vows, the adultery can still be forgiven with proper confession and repentance. **Don't ever let Satan persuade you it is too late to change.**

> But he that has committed adultery and repents with all his heart, and forsaketh it, and doeth it no more, thou shalt forgive. (D&C 42:25)

SATAN'S WEAPON OF HOMOSEXUALITY

Homosexuality and lesbianism—sexual relationships between members of the same sex—are unquestionably two of Satan's most deadly weapons. Advocates of same-sex preference try in vain to present it as nothing more than an "alternate lifestyle" and to divorce it from the category of sexual sin, but "the seriousness of the sin of homosexuality is equal to or greater than that of fornication or adultery" (Kimball, *The Miracle of Forgiveness,* 81–82).

> It is wrong! It is unnatural; it is abnormal; it is an affliction. When practiced, it is immoral. It is a transgression. There appears to be a consensus in the world that it is natural, to one degree or another, for a percentage of the population. Therefore, we must accept it as all right. Do not be misled by those who whisper that it is part of your nature and therefore right for you. That is false doctrine! (Boyd K. Packer, *Devotional Speeches of the Year,* Provo, Utah: BYU Press, 1978, 33–34)

The scriptural condemnations of this sin are unmistakably clear: "Thou shalt not lie with mankind, as with womankind: it is abomination" (Leviticus 18:22). The Lord warned of the suffering resulting from homosexuality when he said, "If a man also lie with mankind, as he lieth with a woman, both of them have committed an abomination: they shall surely be put to death" (Leviticus 20:13). In today's society we do not punish immorality with physical death, but the homosexual is often crippled by depression, self-pity, and hopelessness, which are manifestations of the spiritual death resulting from this empty perversion.

> If an individual tries to receive comfort, satisfactions, affection, or fulfillment from deviate physical interaction with someone of his own gender, it can become an addiction. *At first it may fill a need and give comfort of some kind, but, when that has faded, feelings of guilt and depression soon follow.* A greater need emerges. A cycle begins which sets that individual on a long, sad, destructive skid into emotional and physical disintegration, and ultimately spiritual oblivion. (Boyd K. Packer, *Devotional Speeches of the Year,* Provo, Utah: BYU Press, 1978, 36)

Loneliness is one of the major tragedies of the "gay" lifestyle because very few homosexual encounters provide long-lasting satisfaction. One study showed that 50 percent of the male homosexuals surveyed in one American city had used at least 500 sexual partners and 28 percent had 1,000 partners (see Allen Bergin, *BYU Studies,* 1979, 464). Once the initial thrill of adventure has passed, most encounters leave the partners feeling empty and cheated, used and abused. It is the bitter sting of sin. One bishop described the agony felt by gays who were active in his San Francisco ward:

> I have probably interviewed over forty gay men and six gay women—good wholesome experiences—and I've never had one person say, "I'm glad I'm a homosexual." They feel sorrow about their sexuality, not once in a while, but twenty-four hours a day, seven days a week. (*Sunstone,* February 1990, 15)

It would be irresponsible to discuss homosexuality without exploring its causes and origins. While it is true that some men and women have deliberately chosen this perversion, I do not believe this is true of most. It is certainly true that the majority of people who seek help in overcoming this problem have no memory of choosing or consciously doing anything that could account for its origin. With tears of despair they relate that from their earliest childhood memories they cannot remember a time when they did not feel attracted to members of the same sex. Unable to identify a turning point or cause of their reversed sexual preference, they often become victims of two of Satan's cruelest deceptions: that God created them that way; and that their orientation is permanent and irreversible.

It is unthinkable that God would cause a certain percentage of his children to be born into mortality with unchosen homosexual desires that would compel them to act contrary to the sexuality he intended. To even suggest God as the cause and origin of homosexuality is to accuse him of being responsible for the very sin he condemns. How could our loving Heavenly Father condemn and punish his children for a trait which he had placed within them and which they would therefore be helpless to change? "Let no man say when he is tempted, I am tempted of God: for God cannot be tempted with evil, neither tempteth he any man" (James 1:13–14). President Kimball said:

> Many have been misinformed that they are powerless in the matter, not responsible for the tendency, and that "God made them that way." *This is as untrue as any other of the diabolical lies Satan has concocted.* It is blasphemy. Man is made in the image of God. Does the pervert think God to be "that way?" (*The Miracle of Forgiveness*, 85)

If a person is not *born* homosexual and cannot remember choosing this path, then how does it happen? It happens, at least in major part, because of Satan's clever manipulations. While there are many theories attempting to account for a person's vulnerability to homosexual desires, science has not been able to prove any biological or cultural factors that would explain it consistently. Same-sex preference is treated by science as if it is nothing but a *behavioral* issue, but the truth is that it is a *spiritual* conflict. It is no surprise that science does not understand the cause or cure of this dilemma because science does not accommodate the role of Satanic influence in manipulating the sexual nature and using it as a weapon against us.

It is my opinion that, while there certainly could be factors in the biological makeup, and while there are often inadequate relationships in one's early home life that might predispose a person toward a gender confusion, the most logical explanation for the strength of this compulsion is the influence of Satan. Just like all the other sins of immorality, *homosexuality is a Satanic weapon* which has been perfected over the centuries to ruin the sexuality which God gave us, prevent marriage and children, and isolate the victim from God and church. It is but one of the many ways in which Satan "seeketh that all men might be miserable like unto himself (2 Nephi 2:27).

Satan would love to have us occupy our time and emotions probing the past for some tiny clue to the origin of the homosexuality, because he knows that as long as we are looking backwards we cannot look forward. To win their conflicts with Satan on this battleground, victims must realize that *origins are not the issue.* Even if we understood *how* Satan tricked us into this situation, it would not relieve us of the responsibility to change. It can certainly prove beneficial in therapy to understand how early childhood resulted in undeveloped maturation of the gender identity. It is, however, largely a self-defeating mistake to spend all one's time probing into the complex puzzle of *why* and *how* one was tricked into homosexual perversions, because preoccupation with this misdirected focus blinds us to the solutions and drains away energy from the application of the principles of spiritual healing.

Let us not forget the law of mental function: **What holds my attention holds me.** For example, no matter how committed a person is to losing weight, he will never succeed in his diet as long as he tells himself, "I am fat, I am fat." The brain always works to sustain the self-image we have defined. When the obese person learns to separate himself from his body and say something like, "I am a thin person trapped in an overweight body," he will move toward success because the battle has been changed from "me" battling "me," to "me" battling "it." In the same way, the person troubled with homosexual compulsions must stop defeating himself by continually programming his brain to believe "I am gay." The identity must be changed. *He* is not a homosexual. He is a beautiful, precious child of God, *trapped* in a body of flesh that has homosexual desires. Even if one's identity and sexual preference have become confused, the *real person,* the spirit body inside the physical body still has the same divine gender it received as the offspring of God. The battle is not against the self alone, but also against

Satan and the influence he has temporarily gained over the mind and the flesh. Elder Packer said:

> Your battle is two-thirds won, or three-fourths or four-fifths won, when you take charge of your identity. Accept yourself as belonging in the tabernacle that God has provided you. (*Devotional Speeches of the Year*, Provo, Utah: BYU Press, 1978, 39)

To escape the terrible captivity of same-sex preference, the attention and emotion must be focused not on the *problem*, but on the *solution*—our relationship with Jesus Christ. Whether people deliberately *choose* the path of homosexuality, or feel themselves to be the victim of an *unchosen* preference, there is only one path to freedom. When Jesus said "I am the Lord, the God of all flesh" (Jeremiah 32:27), and "I am the way" (John 14:6), he did not say, "except for homosexuals." Those readers who are angry because they feel they have been victimized by an unchosen environmental deficiency, or by Satan and his evil spirits, should feel encouraged to remember that there is a principle of justice and compensation which guarantees that the less responsible a person is for his suffering, the more right he has to claim God's help in correcting it.

Once they understand that Satan is at least involved in the *development*, if not the actual *origin* and *cause* of homosexuality and lesbianism, victims of these deadly weapons are able to move from the confusing, enslaving emotions of self-condemnation to the rescuing, life-changing powers available through our Savior. It is encouraging to know that men and women are not tempted with homosexual desires because of how wicked they are, but because of how good Satan knows they can be. Satan tries to prevent homosexuals from repenting by providing them with a number of seemingly logical rationalizations to justify their behavior. We will consider three examples:

1. His first justification is: There has always been, throughout the centuries, a certain percentage of the population with this preference. It is true there have always been homosexuals, but to believe that this justifies the sin would be like saying that murder and rape are also justified, if that is what one prefers, because there has always been a certain percentage of the population which felt compelled to commit those sins.

Let us emphasize that right and wrong, righteousness and sin, are not dependent upon man's interpretations, conventions, and attitudes. Social acceptance does not change the status of an act, making wrong into right. If all the people in the world were to accept homosexuality . . . the practice would still be a deep, dark sin. (Kimball, *The Miracle of Forgiveness*, 79)

2. As a second justification he whispers, It is your right to be this way. It was caused by conditions beyond your control. You are not responsible. There is no more reason to change this than there is to change the color of your eyes. It is simply an alternative lifestyle and the problem is not in you, but in those narrow-minded people who don't understand. Unrepentant homosexuals who publicly lobby for "gay rights" have become experts at proclaiming the seeming injustice of their situation, claiming to be helpless victims of unchosen preferences and desires. This is to be expected because:

If someone is heavily involved in perversion, it becomes very important to him to believe that it is incurable. Can you not see that those who preach that doctrine do so to justify themselves? (Boyd K. Packer, *Devotional Speeches of the Year*, Provo Utah: BYU Press, 1978, 35)

I have often wondered if we would not discover, could we accurately measure and compare desires, that a person's vulnerability to *homosexual* desires is really no more difficult to overcome than the vulnerability to lust that troubles many *heterosexuals*. Heterosexuals have to struggle against the lustful desires they feel just as the homosexual does. Homosexuals have no monopoly on the difficulty of resisting temptations. The Lord is not asking any more of them than he is of unmarried heterosexuals, widows, or people who are divorced. Everyone has a "predisposition" to some kind of emotional sin, but predisposition is no justification for surrender to the enemy. The fact that sinful desires might come upon us due to an environmental circumstance, or even an inherited genetic tendency, makes no difference in our duty to conquer and rise above them. Even though Satan may attack us with different sexual weapons, the Lord expects us to conquer our personal inappropriate desires of the flesh and learn to live in the spirit regardless of our individual sexual orientations.

3. In addition to whispering that there is no *reason* to change,

"The tempter will claim that such impulses *cannot* be changed and should not be resisted. Can you think of anything the adversary would rather have us believe?" (Boyd K. Packer, *Ensign*, November 1990, 86) You've been this way so long it is too late to change, Satan whispers. Look how hard you've tried to change and you never could. You'll always be this way. Unfortunately, these lies are supported by many therapists who feel that if the patient reports no heterosexual attraction, impulse, or arousal, they think a change is impossible And they are correct—as far as their own skills warrant—for in most cases homosexual desires cannot be changed by psychology's behavioral modification techniques because they are not *behavioral* problems—they are *spiritual* problems. Homosexuality is no different or more difficult for God to heal than any other lust or compulsive addiction.

Elder Boyd K. Packer explained the starting point for change when he said, "You may not be able, simply by choice, to free yourself at once from unworthy feelings. You *can* choose to give up the immoral expression of them." (*Ensign*, November 1990, 86; emphasis in original) The presence of an unworthy desire is never a justification for indulgence nor does it evidence that change cannot be made.

No matter how long people have been held hostage by homosexual desires, their continued imprisonment is totally unnecessary. The ransom has already been paid by the Savior, the gates are open wide, and we have but to take his hand and walk into freedom. Every homosexual who wants to be healed, who truly wants to break free from this overwhelming compulsion, can do so through the grace and miraculous heart-changing power of God's love. Don't offend your Savior by accepting Satan's lie that you are trapped and cannot be changed, because it simply isn't true. By learning to wear the armor of God and defending yourself with the spiritual weapons he has provided, you can be free if you want to be free.

> To those who say that this practice or any other evil is incurable, I respond: "How can you say the door cannot be opened until your knuckles are bloody, till your head is bruised, till your muscles are sore? It can be done.
>
> Men have come to their Church leaders dejected, discouraged, embarrassed, terrified, and have gone out later full of confidence and faith in themselves, enjoying self-respect and the confidence

> of their families . . . Men have come first with downward glances
> and have left the final interview months later looking the inter-
> viewer straight in the eye. (Kimball, *The Miracle of Forgiveness*,
> 82–83)

In many cases Satan persuades the homosexual that he *cannot*
change simply because he does not know *how* to change. It seems that no
matter how hard he tries to resist, the desires not only remain but inten-
sify. This simply shows how desperately Satan is fighting against losing
his prisoner. All the complexities of homosexuality boil down to one
simple fact: The victim is captive to a situation he cannot change by
himself. Therefore, he needs and is entitled to the help of Jesus Christ
to change the defect. What is needed is not a Band-Aid treatment, but
major surgery—a complete transformation of one's heart and nature—
and *no one* can perform his own heart surgery.

The *origin* of same-sex preference is not nearly as important as
the fact that every person can get out of it and achieve total victory
through the power of Jesus Christ, who said, "My grace is sufficient"
(see Ether 12:27). What good news for sorrowing sinners, to know
that it is not they who must do all the changing. God does not expect
us to change our preferences and desires all by ourselves. Nowhere
do we find a prophet saying, "Take away your own sin. Save yourself.
Transform your own nature. Make yourself into a new creature." That
is for Christ to do as we sincerely place our lives and wills in the Savior's
hands and work to obey the commandments. He is the Shepherd. He
is the Savior. It is he who came to save us from our sins (see John 1:29).
Our part is to view ourselves as we truly are, in our "own carnal state,
even less than the dust of the earth," and to ask God to "have mercy,
and apply the atoning blood of Christ that we may receive forgiveness of our sins, and our hearts may be purified" (Mosiah 4:2). As we
sincerely do our best to repent of the *sinfulness* as well as the sin, as we
express the desire to be clean and pure, and as we give the Lord permission to reach inside and change the things we want to change but
are unable to change by ourselves, we will be able to testify with King
Benjamin's converts, that "the Lord Omnipotent . . . has wrought a
mighty change in us, or in our hearts, that *we have no more disposition
to do evil*, but to do good continually" (Mosiah 5:2).

I am not suggesting that Jesus Christ will do everything for us, only that he will do everything that needs to be done and which we are *willing* but *unable* to do for ourselves. The battle will not be easy or short. It will be a marathon, not a hundred-yard dash, but it can be won. Remaining in sexual captivity is infinitely more painful than the process of overcoming it.

To win these battles, all immoral relationships must be broken off immediately. It will be hard. There will be loneliness. There will, for a time, be an unfilled void. This is to be expected. The withdrawal pains might be likened to the labor pains of the coming rebirth. However, if Satan is to be defeated on this battleground, every tie with those who indulge and encourage this behavior must be cut. No one can quench the flames of desire while continuing to put wood on the fire. If one has to change his job or school, even move to get away from his part-ners in sin, he must do it. It is a small price to pay for freedom.

The number of failures experienced in the past is irrelevant to the achievement of success—once you allow Christ to be in charge of your escape and to have his power added to yours. The Savior does not fail. His power is perfect and infinite. He has promised to share his power with us: "As many as received him, to them *gave he power* to become the sons of God" (John 1:12). Once we place ourselves in his care, the only reason we might continue to fail is because we remain too dependent upon ourselves and not sufficiently in tune and dependent upon him. Elder Boyd K. Packer gave this assurance of the Savior's concern for those who have been captured by the weapon of homosexuality:

> You yourself can call upon a power that can renew your body. You can draw upon a power that will reinforce your will. If you have this temptation—fight it! Oh, if I could only convince you that you are a son or a daughter of Almighty God! You have a righteous, spiritual power—an inheritance that you have hardly touched. You have an Elder Brother who is your Advocate, your Strength, your Protector, your Mediator, your Physician.
>
> I bear witness that great, healing, cleansing power is extended now to you. And that great power is set against that intruding power of perversion which now raises its head in society. Come away from it, and one day you will be in his presence. *He will welcome you with outstretched arms and you and he will weep for*

> *joy over the one who has returned.* (*Devotional Speeches of the Year,*
> Provo, Utah: BYU Press, 1978–79, 40)

There is always a way out. Let us not continue to waste our lives in misery while Satan's filthy devils dance about with glee over the way they have manipulated us. Let us rise up like the sons or daughters of God that we really are, fulfill the identity Father chose for us, and become the person that Jesus suffered and died for us to become.

Heterosexuals must guard against allowing their revulsion toward this sin to be reflected in their attitude toward its victims. It is not the role of the church member to judge, condemn, or reject homosexuals, nor to cast them from us into the arms of the triumphant enemy. While it is our duty to teach the truth that homosexuality is a sinful perversion of God's intention for our sexuality, it is also our duty to offer encouragement, love, and acceptance to people troubled with this affliction. Rather than shunning or condemning, we must lead them to Christ so they can receive healing and the change of heart that will set them free from this affliction. We must remember that loving the sinner is not the same as condoning the sin. Jesus Christ repeatedly opened his arms and welcomed every person who would accept the invitation to come to him in repentance and so must we. President Kimball gave the assurance that:

> The Lord loves the homosexual person as he does all of his other children. When that person repents and corrects his life, the Lord will smile and receive him. (*The Miracle of Forgiveness,* 89)

YOU ARE WANTED

Some readers may have already crossed the line between virtue and immorality. While sexual sin is enormously serious and even ugly and offensive to the Lord, you must realize that *you* are not ugly or unwanted. Even though Satan's enticements have lured you into making wrong choices, these can be reversed by making new choices that will return you to the Lord's side of the line. No matter what you have done, no matter how long or deliberately you have sinned, God still loves you and wants you back with a stubborn love that is infinite and unceasing. Paul was amazed to discover that Christ not only "died for the ungodly," but that even "while we were yet sinners, Christ died for us" (Romans 5:6, 8). This should certainly give us hope, "For the Son of man is come to seek and to save that which was lost" (Luke 19:10). Because of Satan's whisperings, most people who are seeking to repent of sexual sins have an absolute conviction that they are worthless and incapable of divine notice or rescue. In one way that is a good sign because it evidences their conviction of guilt and remorse. But Satan knows how to use these feelings of self-loathing to prevent the repentance and victory these people strive for so earnestly. Always, inescapably, **what holds your attention holds you**. When we allow Satan to focus all our attention on the ugliness of the sins we have committed, he successfully blocks us from focusing on the way back—the Atonement and gospel of Jesus Christ. *The Lord does not consider anyone worthless.* As terrible as impurity is in the Lord's sight, and as much as he may be hurt by what we have done, the wonderful truth is that his attention is not on the sin but on helping us to escape and return to him so that we may be transformed into new creatures in Christ and stand before our Heavenly Father in perfect beauty and holiness.

What we must learn to do when we are bombarded with doubts about the Lord's compassion, mercy, and forgiveness is to turn to the scriptures and base our hope and confidence on what God has said rather than on our personal feelings while we are still trapped in guilt and shame. John testified that "God sent not his Son into the world to condemn the world; but that the world through him might be saved" (John 3:17). Christ himself promised, "Him that cometh to me I will in no wise cast out" (John 6:37). Offering praise to the Lord, Lehi testified, "Because thou art merciful, thou wilt not suffer those who come unto thee that they shall perish!" (1 Nephi 1:14). And Peter testified that God is "long-suffering to us-ward, not willing that any should perish, but that all should come to repentance" (2 Peter 3:9). Truly, such magnificent promises should encourage every repentant sinner and provide the strength to shun Satan's lies.

Some haughty, self-righteous Scribes and Pharisees caught a woman in the act of adultery, dragged her through the streets of Jerusalem and threw her at Jesus' feet, demanding punishment. Christ's response demonstrated that he is not looking for opportunities to punish, but for ways to change hearts and lead people back to Heavenly Father. After driving the crowd away with the embarrassing challenge, "Let him that is without sin cast the first stone," he revealed his love and mercy to the woman when he said, "Woman, where are those thine accusers? Hath no man condemned thee?" She said, "No man, Lord." Jesus replied, "Neither do I condemn thee. Go and sin no more." (see John 8:1–11.) He could have sternly demanded, "How did you ever sink so low? How could you do this terrible thing? Don't you know that adultery is second only to murder?" But Christ wasn't interested in condemning the woman, only in helping her to repent so that she could receive forgiveness and stand clean before her Heavenly Father.

Don't let Satan make you feel worthless just because you struggle with inappropriate sexual desires. Gird up your loins and fight back. Make the effort necessary to apply Christ's Atonement to your sins and learn to stand tall as the infinitely valuable son or daughter of God that you are.

CLEAN AGAIN

To emphasize the serious consequences of deliberate sin, the Savior warned, "I the Lord cannot look upon sin with the least degree of allowance," yet in the very next verse he emphasized that there is always a way back and that every remorseful and repentant person will be accepted: "Nevertheless, he that repents and does the commandments of the Lord shall be forgiven" (D&C 1:31–32). That couldn't possibly apply to you, Satan counters, because you've repented before and yet you always go back to your sin. Moroni demonstrated, however, that there is always hope, because even the ungrateful Nephites, who were continually wavering between righteousness and wickedness, were patiently forgiven. "But as oft as they repented and sought forgiveness, with real intent, they were forgiven" (Moroni 6:8). That statement was carefully placed in the Book of Mormon's witness of Christ so that we, in this modern day of sexual and other battles, would have hope in spite of Satan's lies.

Satan will challenge those who are repenting of sexual transgression: God may forgive, but you will never be the same. You will always be regarded as an inferior disciple, so you may as well come back to the pleasures of (whatever your sexual vulnerability is). If all we could do was to stop sinning, then Satan would be right; we would be stained and inferior for the rest of eternity, because no mortal can cleanse himself nor undo his sins and stand clean and guiltless before the Father. But Satan's logic does not allow for the infinite power of Christ's Atonement to erase one's sins after repentance and forgiveness. Once forgiven, cleansed by the Atonement and transformed by the new birth Christ is seeking to give us, our forgiven sins will be blotted from the record of our personal lives. Not only will they not be mentioned in the day of judgment, but they will not even be remembered by the Lord when he looks upon us in joy and welcomes us back to his presence. (see Jeremiah 31:34; Ezekiel 18:21–22; Hebrews 8:12; D&C 58:42.) The celestial kingdom will not be filled with people who never made a mistake, but with people who recognized their weaknesses and overcame them through the Atonement of Jesus Christ. "And because thou hast seen thy weakness thou shalt be made strong, even unto the sitting down in the place which I have prepared in the mansions of my Father" (Ether 12:37).

12
Strategies of Defense

SATAN DOES EVERYTHING POSSIBLE TO LURE US OFF THE STRAIGHT and narrow path, to wander and explore the broader paths of enticements so appealing to our lesser selves. In this chapter we will explore proven methods of defending ourselves on the various battlegrounds of spiritual combat. One effective way to counter these enticements is to visualize a line dividing God's territory and the devil's and simply ask, "Which side of the line am I on?" When we are being pulled by unworthy desires or temptations and our resolves are wavering, another effective defense is to visualize the demons grabbing at us and trying to pull us across that line. We can also visualize angels coming to our defense to help drive the evil spirits away. Remember, Satan can never pull us across that line unless we agree to go.

DON'T CREATE UNNECESSARY TEMPTATIONS

Some temptations come from the devil and some from the natural desires of the flesh, but many are created by our own foolishness. If we would win our battles with temptation, we must learn not to put ourselves in situations which will entice and inflame desire, creating unnecessary temptations. For example, I can go into the break room at work with no appetite and not the slightest desire for "goodies." But if I pause to gaze into the enticing vending machine, I am soon seized with almost irresistible hunger pangs for candy or pastries which but a moment ago were not even in my thoughts. I am responsible for that temptation because I know that **what gets my attention gets me.**

By deliberately focusing my attention on the goodies in the vending machine, I have created an unnecessary struggle with the desires of my flesh. In the same way, we create temptation when we choose to listen to inappropriate music or view pornographic magazines, movies, or videos. Perhaps we go to the magazine stand or video display telling ourselves, "I'm not going to buy or rent any pornography, but I think I'll just take a look at the covers." We tell ourselves "I'm not going to watch an R-rated movie on cable television, but I think I'll just check the movie guide and see what's playing." Or, "I'm not going to snack between meals, but I think I'll just take a peek in the refrigerator and see what's there." In each of these examples we are being dishonest with ourselves. We don't admit we want to sin, but set ourselves up with foolish rationalizations: "I'm just going to check it out." Subconsciously we know that we will be tempted and probably give in, but we are pretending that we did not deliberately choose to sin. We cannot conquer the fires of temptation when we deliberately throw gas on the flames.

Perhaps you have enough will power to look at the vending machine, the kitchen pantry, the television guide or magazine stand without giving in to the resulting temptations. But why take the chance of becoming unnecessarily entangled in desire? Why place yourself in the position of possibly giving in when it is so much better to avoid the enticement? Even if you do resist the temptation, the Holy Spirit will not be with you when you step over the line dividing good and evil, just to "check things out." President Kimball counseled, "The best way to resist temptation is to avoid it. Prevention is far, far better than repentance" (*The Miracle of Forgiveness,* 61).

> Avoid, as well as possible, unholy places, unwholesome music, friends who do not uphold similar standards, and entertainment that depicts immorality and vulgar language. As you do this you will drive away the unclean, evil thoughts. *Thus Satan and his hosts with their subtle whisperings will have no power over* **you.** (Ronald A. Dalley, *New Era,* August 1984, 45)
>
> Satan leaves his fingerprints. They are quite distinguishable to any who are warned. Accordingly, the danger sign is placed

prominently where it is always visible to the educated eye. (Kimball, *The Miracle of Forgiveness*, 232)

In the book of Proverbs we are told that a "prudent man" learns to recognize Satan's fingerprints so that he can avoid all places, people, situations and influences which contribute to his weakness and temptations. On the other hand, the foolish person ignores the warning signs and moves right into the damaging environment and falls. "A prudent man foreseeth the evil, and hideth himself: but the simple pass on, and are punished" (Proverbs 22:3). By refusing to create our own temptations, we can have greater confidence in winning our battles with Satan.

Let us now examine five proven plans of action that will prepare us against every temptation: learning to choose our responses ahead of time; learning to separate ourselves from the temptation; learning to say "it's not worth it"; learning to drive the devil away from us; and learning to defend ourselves with the shield of faith.

DECIDING AHEAD OF TIME

Few generals would attack an enemy before their own army was prepared. Military preparation for battle includes deciding in advance how to respond to the various alternatives the enemy might use in its offense and defense. What will my army do if the enemy does *this?* What will we do if he does *that?* One of the most important strategies in spiritual combat is to prepare ourselves to meet our temptations ahead of time, *before* the crisis of desire arrives.

> A term commonly used by safe-driving experts is "defensive driving," implying the recognition that other cars on the road are a potential threat and that hazardous situations should be anticipated. Waiting to react until a danger is actually present may be too late.
>
> So it is with temptation. Once we decide we want to do right and then pray for the constant influence and prompting of the Holy Ghost, *we can anticipate situations that could sorely tempt us. We can then look ahead and be prepared.* It is during our stronger moments that we should prepare a plan of action for the moment of temptation. (Jon M. Taylor, *New Era*, November 1972, 38)

It is difficult to refuse temptations at the time of presentation, when we are caught in the strong pull of desire to give in and indulge. If we wait until that moment of passion to decide whether or not to give in, we will often lose the battle because our choices will be swayed by the desires we *feel* more than by what we *believe* we should do.

> Temptations come to all, but long before we are faced with them, we . . . must determine what our course will be. It is too late if we wait until the moment of temptations before making our decision. (N. Eldon Tanner, *Ensign*, December 1971, 34)

When a person resolves and prepares to stay on the right path *before* temptations come, he or she will not stray to the devil's side of the line when being pulled by carnal desires. Elder Sterling W. Sill taught that "we can solve all our problems when we correctly and firmly make up our minds about them in advance." He related this example:

> A man came to talk to me about a moral problem. I asked him, "What are you going to do when the next temptation comes along?" He said, "How can I tell until I know what the temptation is?"
>
> I said, "You say you don't know what you will do. But I can tell you right now what you are going to do. You are going to succumb. *If you can't make up your mind while you are here talking to me, what chance will you have when the temptation is beating you over the head with some desire to which you have already committed yourself?*"
>
> If we can learn to solidly make up our minds against evil, we can make ourselves stronger than anything that can happen to us. If we can decide once and for all against those things we are not going to do, then we will be free to spend all of our time doing those things we ought to do. (*Making the Most of Yourself*, Salt Lake City, Utah: Bookcraft, 1971, 19–20)

By deciding ahead of time, when we are not under the stress of conflicting desires, we can always choose the right because we are not doing battle with our carnal desires for the wrong. Then, when the passion of temptation does arrive, our struggles will be less because we already have a predetermined course of action and will not have to decide based on the way we feel at the moment.

Separate Yourself from the Temptation

Temptations are much easier to resist when we regard them as part of "the carnal nature" instead of part of ourselves. Then it becomes "I" resisting "it" instead of "I" resisting "me." Consider three suggestions for separating the desires of temptation from yourself.

1. Think of temptations as nothing more than a wind from Satan. As it blows past us we feel the wind, but it is not part of us and cannot affect us unless we hoist our sails to catch it.

2. Instead of automatically assuming the temptation is your own desire, visualize the demons who surround you. See them chanting the temptation over and over as they laugh and mock at your struggle with the ideas and desires they have planted in your mind. Resolve that you will not allow them to manipulate you.

3. Think of your body as a space suit worn by your spirit in this foreign environment of mortality. The flesh is not *you*, it is a suit you wear. Upon death you will temporarily discard that suit as surely as an astronaut sheds his space suit. The space suit is a servant to the astronaut, not the master. In the same way, our bodies should be our servants, not our masters. "And why should I yield to sin, because of my flesh?" Nephi asked. "Yea, why should I give way to temptations, that the evil one have place in my heart to destroy my peace and afflict my soul?" (2 Nephi 4:27).

> The greatest conflict that any man or woman will ever have will be the battle that is had with self. I should like to speak of spirit and body as "me" and "it." "Me" is the individual who dwells in this body, who lived before I had such a body, and who will live when I step out of the body. "It" is the house I live in, the tabernacle of flesh and the great conflict is between "me" and "it." (Melvin J. Ballard, *New Era,* March 1984, 35)

It's Not Worth It

The brain controls behavior but it does not give the orders; it only follows instructions. Not the instructions of what we say at the time we are facing a temptation, as much as the instructions of what we *feel* as our desires are being enticed by the enemy. If we are living in cycles of repeated failure that cause us to give in to the temptations we are trying to resist, it is because we have trained our brains to believe that is how we *want* to respond. In effect, every time we give in to temptation, we are teaching our brains, "I don't care how much I suffer for this later, right now I want to do this because *it is worth it to me.*"

If we have been giving in to our sinful desires every time we feel lonely, discouraged, or tempted, our brains can hardly reach any other conclusion than believing this is the best way we have of coping with the stress. After all, if it wasn't worth it to us, why would we have yielded to so many temptations in the past? If we have spent years developing the habit of deriving pleasure from our sins, our brains develop conditioned response patterns. They become "magnetized," or "polarized" to this inclination, as we described in the "Electromagnet" portion of Chapter 7, "The Battleground of Thought." This is how we get trapped in the vicious cycles of habit and defeat that keep us on the frustrating up-and-down roller coaster ride of despair, in spite of our best intentions to repent.

As our thought and behavioral command centers our brains have to weigh the pain and guilt we suffer against the pleasures we derive from giving in. As long as the brain believes that giving in gives us pleasure, or fills some deep need that is more important to us than the guilt we suffer after doing the sin, it is going to continue leading us into indulgence, no matter how hard we try to resist the temptations.

When the moment of temptation arrives and pulls at our desires, our simply saying or thinking "I don't want to do this" doesn't work because it is not honest. We can't fool our brains. Repeated disobedience trains them to recognize the pleasure our sins give us. No matter how sincerely we intend to repent, until we receive the new birth and transformation from Christ that removes the *desire* for evil, part of us will continue to crave the fulfillment of our old habits, and our minds know that. But we can change those results by learning a new way to instruct the brain's conditioning By being honest we can teach our brains or minds to respond to the old habits in a new way. When temptations arouse our desires, the first thing to do is admit that we *are* tempted and that part of us, the lesser, carnal part, *would like* to give in. Instead of lying to ourselves by pretending it wouldn't feel good or that we don't want to do it, we can admit, "Yes, I would like to do that," or "Yes, that would feel good," or similar words that fit our temptations. But immediately after that honest admission, we then give the new instruction: **"But it is not worth it to me anymore."**

Now the mind has a valid reason to cancel all previous choices and listen to the new instructions. When we say, "Sure, that would feel good, **but it is not worth it to me anymore,**" our brains or minds will feel justified in ignoring the established pattern of past responses and work to support the new decision to resist. Repeating these words as we encounter temptation helps our mental conditioning accept that we are giving up something we want for something we now want more. Once our minds believe this, they will work with us to resist our temptations instead of pulling us back into old patterns of response because they mistakenly believe we still want to give in. Responding to our temptations with "**it is not worth it to me anymore**" also entitles us to receive the special grace and strength Christ has promised to add to our own limited will power when we allow him to be a partner in our battles.

Until we develop the habit of using this powerful phrase to defend ourselves against the enticements of the enemy, we could, for instance, post 3 x 5 cards with this affirmation in the locations where we face the greatest temptations. The affirmation "**it is not worth it to me anymore**" can help defeat every enemy on the battleground of temptation.

SEND THE DEVIL AWAY

The Apostle James made a promise that is sometimes hard to believe. He said, "Resist the devil, and he will flee from you" (James 4:7). Everyone has had the experience of resisting the devil and then feeling that he was not fleeing at all, but attacking with even greater intensity. This is not because the promise is false, but because we did not resist in the proper way. Trying to fight the devil with nothing but one's own limited will power makes certain that Satan will not leave, but will surround him or her with even more demons, whispering evil suggestions and laughing at the misery they have caused. But when we respond to those temptations with faith in Christ's power to win our battles, the devil will indeed flee.

Teach them to withstand *every temptation* with their faith on the Lord Jesus Christ. (Alma 37:33)

One of the reasons Christ's temptations are described in scripture is to teach us the way to resist our own temptations. As we study the Savior's example, it is important to know that:

> *The Power is given to every man and woman that lives to speak as Christ did:* "Get thee hence, Satan;" and he will leave you as quickly as he left the Master. He cannot capture a single soul unless we are willing to go. He is limited. He must win men and women. (Melvin J. Ballard, *New Era,* March 1984, 37)

Affirming Elder Ballard's words, President Spencer W. Kimball said, "He has to leave when you say, 'Depart from me Satan'" (*New Era,* June 1978, 9). Nothing defeats an enemy like discouragement. Show the devil that you are aware of his cunning devices and that they are not going to work anymore. Tell him to leave. You might say something like:

> I am a disciple of Christ and with his help I will defeat this temptation. Satan, 1 am going to keep my covenants no matter what you do. I am not helpless. I can say no to this temptation.

DEFENDING OURSELVES WITH THE SHIELD OF FAITH

We are commanded to "Take upon you my whole armor, that ye may be able to withstand the evil day" (D&C 27:15). The armor of God includes a spiritual helmet to protect our minds from Satanic whisperings and a breastplate to protect our hearts from the enticements of evil desires. As the Lord described the armor we should wear, however, he always placed one item above all others in importance. *"Above all"* he said, take "the shield of faith, wherewith ye shall be able to quench all the fiery darts of the wicked" (Ephesians 6:16). The "fiery darts of the wicked" are the whispered temptations and discouragements which Satan and his evil army use to entice us into sin (see 1 Nephi 15:24). No matter how strong and complete his armor is, no warrior would want to stand helpless while the enemy beat upon him with blow after merciless blow. Why should a person allow Satan's flaming, poison darts to penetrate his armor and create unworthy desires within him when he can deflect the blows with the shield of faith?

Normally, when we think of a shield we picture something that the ancient knights of the round table used, a strong metal plate that one holds in front of himself. That image does not adequately symbolize the protection made possible by the spiritual shield of faith which the Lord has commanded us to use. A spiritual shield of faith can surround or envelop us so that we are protected from all directions at the same time, twenty-four hours a day, even while we sleep. How do we obtain such a magnificent shield? We must create it. No one can give another person the faith it takes to create a spiritual shield. Many are discouraged and lament that they don't have enough faith, but the shield of faith is not dependent upon the *amount* of faith one has, only on where the faith is *focused*. No matter how tiny or weak our faith is, when we learn to focus it on the power of Jesus Christ, that beginning, tentative faith will grow strong and powerful, drawing strength from the Savior until it is sufficient for every need. In Chapter 20, "Putting on the Armor," we will explain how to develop faith sufficient to win every battle. We will explain how even the weakest, most doubtful attitude can be changed into a powerful faith in Christ. But we will now examine seven ways to create or envision a shield of protection, wrapped around us, that can deflect Satan's attacks and temptations.

Deflector #1: Use Light as a Shield

The first image that is helpful in picturing this spiritual shield is to imagine ourselves surrounded by bright light. Satan works only in darkness and deception. He is repelled by light and slinks away in shame. "For we wrestle not against flesh and blood, but against principalities, against powers, against the rulers of the darkness of this world, against spiritual wickedness in high places" (Ephesians 6:12). When Satan attacked Joseph Smith in the sacred grove, he nearly prevented that world-changing prayer with a suffocating, "thick darkness" (see Joseph Smith—History 1:15). When he attacks us it is also with darkness. "The mists of darkness are the temptations of the devil" (1 Nephi 12:17). For "that wicked one cometh and taketh away light and truth . . . from the children of men" (D&C 93:39). Satan can only take away a person's light when they are deliberately disobedient and unrepentant, and he is ever watchful for those opportunities (see D&C 1:33).

Christ, on the other hand, is "the true Light, which lighteth every man that cometh into the world" (John 1:9). Disciples of the Savior shun spiritual darkness and work to surround themselves with light because "light and truth forsake that evil one" (D&C 93:37). Darkness cannot exist in the presence of light, "let us therefore cast off the works of darkness, and let us *put on the armour of light*" (Romans 13:12), "that you may chase darkness from among you" (D&C 50:25). What a thrilling revelation, to know that we can actually drive Satan away by surrounding ourselves with a shield of light.

DEFLECTOR #2: USE PRAYER AS A SHIELD

Because "the effectual fervent prayer of a righteous man availeth much" (James 5:16), prayer is a shield mentioned frequently in the scriptures. Prayer can be used both as a defensive and an offensive weapon. President Benson promised, "If you will earnestly seek guidance from your Heavenly Father, morning and evening, you will be given the strength to shun any temptation" (*Ensign*, November 1977, 32).

> Be watchful unto prayer continually, that ye may not be led away by the temptations of the devil, that he may not overpower you, that ye may not become his subjects at the last day. (Alma 34:39)
>
> Therefore let the church take heed and pray always, lest they fall into temptation. (D&C 20:33)

Pride causes many of us to resist praying about our temptations because we are ashamed to admit we are being tempted. We want to be perfect. We want to be above temptation and we have trouble accepting that, as long as we are human, we are going to need the Lord's help in overcoming our temptations.

> Be wise in the days of your probation . . . ask with a firmness unshaken, that ye will yield to no temptation, but that ye will serve the true and living God. (Mormon 9:28)

If we humble ourselves and sincerely ask for strength to resist temptations *before* we enter our personal battlegrounds, our resolves will be strengthened and we will be shielded when Satan attacks.

We also need to pray *during* the time of temptation. Peter saw the Savior walking on the surface of the stormy sea. Exercising incredible faith, he got out of the boat and walked on the water toward the Savior. But when he took his attention off the Lord and looked at the reality of wind and waves, he was afraid and began to sink into the depths of the sea, demonstrating the truth that **what gets your attention gets you.** "Beginning to sink, he cried, saying, *Lord save me.* And immediately Jesus stretched forth his hand, and caught him." (Matthew 14:30–31) Peter did not allow embarrassment over his wavering faith to get in the way of his cry for help. His pride could have plunged him into the depths of the sea, but he was humble enough to cry for help at the very moment of defeat and was wise enough to recognize the Savior as the source of help he needed to compensate for the inadequacy of his wavering faith. Peter did not wait until he was "up to his neck" before he cried for help. He prayed the instant he began to fail and so should we.

"Lord, save me," is a magnificent prayer. Heavenly Father loves to respond to that kind of prayer. He loves to reach down, as Christ reached to Peter, and lift us out of the darkness of desire into the light of victory. Allowing pride to prevent our prayers at the time of temptation will block divine assistance and lead to failure, while timely, honest prayers will shield us from danger.

Deflector #3: Use Music as a Shield

Sacred music has a way of slipping past our mental blockades and nourishing the heart in spite of our intellectual doubts or wicked desires. Elder Boyd K. Packer has advised that one effective way to deflect temptation is to sing or hum a hymn at the time of battle. This is an effective defense because our minds can only focus on one thing at a time, and if we are thinking about the words and melody of the hymn, we won't be thinking about the pleasures of the sin. One hymn that is helpful is "I Need Thee Every Hour" (see *Hymns*, 98). One need not memorize the entire song. Consider the power of these two lines:

"I need thee every hour, stay thou nearby;
"Temptations lose their power when thou art nigh."

Another powerful hymn is "How Firm a Foundation" (see *Hymns*, 85):

"Fear not, I am with thee, O be not dismayed,
"For I am thy God and will still give thee aid;
"I'll strengthen thee, help thee, and cause thee to stand,
"Upheld by my righteous, omnipotent hand."

There are many inspiring hymns. If we will select several that we like and then practice them when we are not under fire, it will be natural to recall the words and melody when we are beset by temptation. The Lord has declared, "My soul delighteth in the song of the heart; yea, the song of the righteous is a prayer unto me, and it shall be answered with a blessing upon their heads" (D&C 25:12). One of those promised blessings will be an increased resolve and power to say "no" to the temptations that try to come between us and our God. How could we possibly give in to temptation while singing or humming the words of our favorite hymn?

DEFLECTOR #4: USE SCRIPTURE AS A SHIELD

Diverting our thoughts away from the pull of temptation can also be achieved by quoting scriptures. When Christ was faced with temptations he responded by saying, "It is written" and then he quoted the appropriate scripture to counter the temptation Lucifer offered. By using this method to reject his own temptations, he set the example of how we should respond to ours. It is logical to assume that Satan's demons hate the scriptures and that it is not likely they will stay around to listen to you quote them. Like the repelling force of a powerful magnet, quoting scriptures in response to temptation will drive the demons away. Some examples of effective scriptures to use as a shield during one's battles with temptation follow:

The Lord will help me, therefore shall I not be confounded. (2 Nephi 7:7)

Inasmuch as ye are humble and faithful and call upon my name, I will give you the victory. (D&C 104:82)

If ye will have faith in me ye shall have power to do whatsoever thing is expedient in me. (Moroni 7:33)

He has all power to save every man that believeth on his name. (Alma 12:15)

In Appendix B, we will provide a list of several hundred of these powerful references.

Every time we quote a scripture we are throwing up a shield that will deflect temptation. Such scriptures may be printed on 3 x 5 cards and carried with us to refer to frequently throughout the day. The more times we read them, the more firmly they will be planted within our brain cells and the more quickly they will come to our rescue when we are faced with temptation. We will discuss this principle in more detail in Appendix B and Chapter 20, "Putting on the Armor."

DEFLECTOR #5: USE COMMITMENT TO CHRIST AS A SHIELD

People would not deliberately succumb to temptation if they could remember their commitments to the Lord at the moment of desire. We give in to temptation because we forget our commitments and covenants. Every time we remind ourselves of our commitments we throw up a shield of protection that can deflect temptations. Let me suggest two methods of reminding ourselves to think of Christ and remember our commitments of discipleship at the moment of temptation. The first is to place your favorite picture of him where you will see it often. Looking at his picture frequently not only reminds us to think about him, but is also a way of inviting him to join us in our battles. It helps to remind us that he is watching our conflicts and hoping we will remember him and resist.

The second suggestion is to print six words on a 3 x 5 card: "**I am disciple of Christ**." Keeping this card with you and referring to it frequently throughout the day can change the focus of your life. We need to do this because we get preoccupied with the affairs of daily life and forget who we are and the sacred covenants we have made with our God. How many times during the last week did you consciously reaffirm to yourself, **I am a disciple of Christ**? We just get busy and involved with the affairs of day-to-day life and we forget.

I am a disciple of Christ is a powerful affirmation. It is quite unlikely that a person could read that commitment several times a day and then deliberately do things that a disciple would not do. After using this affirmation for several weeks a person's thought process will begin to change. This affirmation will change the way a person thinks about himself, the way he thinks about Christ, and the way he thinks about temptation. Remember the principle of thought: **What holds your attention holds you.** Remember the promise of the sacrament prayer, that by remembering the Savior always, we will "always have his spirit to be with us." When faced with temptation that a part of our nature wants to give in to, our minds will warn us: "Wait a minute. A disciple of Christ wouldn't do that." Instead of automatically responding to temptation with the old habits, the mind will begin to work for us, helping to resist instead of acting out the old sins. When we are faced with difficult decisions and wonder what choice to make, the thoughts will arise: "What would a disciple of Christ do? What would Jesus do?" President David O. McKay said, "I never make a decision without asking myself, How will I explain this to the Savior when I meet him?" (see *Ensign*, August 1984, 38). By training our minds to focus on our commitments of discipleship, we will receive strength, inspiration and protection from the Lord we are worshipping and placing first in our lives.

DEFLECTOR #6: USE LOVE FOR GOD AS A SHIELD

There are many motives for obedience. One, for example, is fear of punishment. Another is fear of embarrassment. We want the respect of our peers. We don't want the shame of not respecting ourselves. But these kinds of motives are shallow and often succumb to the passions of temptation. The spiritual warrior determined to conquer the enemy seeks a better foundation. When Potiphar's wife enticed Joseph to commit adultery he replied, "How then can I do this great wickedness, *and sin against God?*" (Genesis 39:9) One of the greatest shields against evil is the love we feel for God. When we feel greater love for him than we do for ourselves, we will *want* to resist our temptations and honor the blessings he has made available to us through the Atonement. The real triumph over temptation comes when we love God so much that we will make any sacrifice, pay any price to return his love and show him how much we appreciate the gospel, the Atonement, and the opportunities he has made available to us. Elder Hartman Rector Jr. taught:

> I believe this is the greatest lesson that can be learned by the youth of Zion—to do the right thing because you love the Lord. It is so vitally important that, I feel, if you do anything in righteousness for any other reason than you love the Lord, you are wrong—at least you are on very shaky ground.
>
> And, somewhere your reasons for acting in righteousness will not be strong enough to see you through. You will give way to expediency, or peer group pressure, or honor, or fame, or applause, or the thrill of the moment, or same other worldly reason. Unless your motives are built upon the firm foundation of love of the Lord, you will not be able to stand. (*Ensign*, January 1973, 130)

One effective way to use love for God as a shield against temptation is to picture Christ on the cross, remembering that it was our sins that put him there, and then realize that deliberately giving in to our temptations would be the same as picking up the Roman hammer and pounding another nail through his flesh. Once a person learns to visualize the pain and disappointment in the Savior's eyes, he will not give in so quickly the next time he is tempted.

Another way to train ourselves to love God more than the pleasures of sin is to add to our 3 x 5 disciple card these seven words: **"I will do nothing to disappoint Him."** When we make this affirmation to ourselves several times a day we gain strength for the times of temptation. When we are attacked by unworthy desires, we will hear an inner voice say, "Wait a minute. You don't want to do that. You are a disciple of Christ. You wouldn't want to disappoint the Lord after all he has done for you." Every time people reaffirm their love for God they are throwing up a shield of defense that will protect them from Satan's attacks.

DEFLECTOR #7: ALLOW THE SAVIOR TO BE YOUR SHIELD

We have considered the protective shields of light, prayer, music, scripture, commitment, and love. All these shields are powerful and effective, but the most important of all is Jesus Christ himself, who promised "I will be their shield" (D&C 35:14). Indeed, the most frequent scriptural references to spiritual shields are of the Savior standing between us and evil demons. For example, "The Lord is my strength and my shield" (Psalms 28:7). "But thou, O Lord, art a shield for me" (Psalms 3:3; see also Genesis 15:1; Psalms 59:11; 84:9; 115:9–11; 119:114). How foolish and unnecessary to fight the battles with temptation by ourselves when the Savior has promised to fight the battles with us (see 1 Samuel 17:46–47; D&C 105:14). The mind has great powers of imagination and we can use these powers to deflect the blows of Satan's temptations by visualizing the Savior protecting us like a shield. Imagine him standing by your side when Satan approaches and offers the temptation. Picture Christ lovingly placing his arm on your shoulder, offering encouragement and strength. How could we possibly give in to temptation with the Savior at our side?

Another scene that is helpful to visualize is a small child needing protection from a schoolyard bully. Picture that young boy, eager and willing, but too weak to defend himself, hiding behind the older brother who puts himself between the bully and the object of attack. There will always be times of peril when the forces of evil combine against us with such intensity that we are in danger of being overcome in spite of our best resolves and defenses. This is when we need Christ himself to come to the rescue and step between us and Satan's demons as a personal shield. A person can rely upon the Savior to come to his rescue when his shield is in danger of being penetrated because he knows the Savior has promised to be "our help and our shield" (Psalms 33:20).

If Christ is our shield, what does it matter if Satan's hosts attack with all their fury? "Ye shall not fear them: for the Lord your God he shall fight for you" (Deuteronomy 3:22). Christ is faithful and fulfills his promises. When our shields are inadequate he comes to the rescue, adding his strength to ours, shielding us where we are willing but weak. The confrontation ends. For now the battle has been won. The demons will be back, but so will our shield. We are safe.

The God of my rock; in him will I trust: he is my shield, and

the horn of my salvation, my high tower, and my refuge.
(2 Samuel 22:3)

KEEPING SCORE

A major part of military score-keeping is a daily body count. If Side A killed or wounded more soldiers than Side B did, then Side A is winning. There will also be daily scores on the number of tanks, planes, and ships damaged or destroyed on each side. If the score shows a general that he took out 20 tanks, planes, or soldiers for each one he lost, then he knows he is winning. Keeping score is the only way of measuring the effectiveness of each side's strategy and power. And so it is in our spiritual battles with Satan. If we do not have an accurate measurement of the number, frequency and intensity of the enemy's attacks, we will usually feel inadequate and overwhelmed by Satan's opposition. Keeping score of the battles, personal victories, and failures can have a dramatic effect on our confidence and progress, because even if we conquer the enemy in only 51 percent of the battles, we are winning and will eventually be victorious.

Most people keep score of the wrong thing—their failures. They can tell you exactly how many days, weeks, or months they were able to go without giving in and indulging their weakness. This is a very dangerous method of keeping score, because **what holds your attention holds you**. Focusing on the *failures* instead of the victories can keep us chained to the mistakes of the past. And besides, even if we gave in and indulged our bad habit 20 times last week, how do we know if that was a victory or a loss? Only by measuring the number of attacks. For example, at one point I recorded ninety-four confrontations with a specific temptation within a twenty-eight day period. I was astonished. I had no idea I was being tempted that much. No wonder I was having trouble overcoming my habit. This was not mere temptation, it was war. During those four weeks, I was able to record eighty victories over the temptations, Eighty successes out of ninety-four battles. Of course I regretted the fourteen failures. But I gained such strength, joy, and confidence from this simple score-keeping that during the next month I was able to resist temptations that previously would have brought certain failure.

So the first thing to keep track of is the number of temptations we face each day. This means the real confrontations with desire, where that carnal, addicted part of us is screaming and begging us to stand tall and resist. Each time throughout the day (and night) that we have to fight a battle and decide whether or not to give in, we can make a slash mark on a 3 x 5 score card. The benefit of keeping score in this way is discovering just how real and powerful the enemy is. If we are to win these battles we must realize that it is more than just a weakness or bad habit we are struggling with. We must learn that it is not only *ourselves* we are fighting, but also *the enemy*. It is all-out war with our Satanic enemies who are determined to destroy us and will use every cunning device they know to pull us down to their level.

The second thing to keep score of is the number of our daily victories; not the number of days we have resisted, but the number of temptations we have conquered each day. This is crucial to winning our battles with Satan because if we focus only on the failure, we unwittingly chain ourselves to our defeats. Measuring the opposition and discovering we are winning more than half the battles will increase our enthusiasm and confidence. Here's how it works. Every time we successfully resist a temptation we place a slash mark in the victory column on that 3 x 5 card. Suppose we average ten temptation-battles a day where part of us wants to give in to the temptation. Then in one week we would have faced the enemy and done battle with temptation seventy times. Suppose we gave in and indulged the desire on the last day. If we only kept score of the number of days between failures, we would only have six victories and this could be very discouraging. But this kind of scoring does not give ourselves proper credit. Seven days times ten temptations a day equals seventy confrontations with the enemy in one week. And if we only gave in once then we have achieved sixty-nine victories. If we gave in twice we still have sixty-eight victories. Even if we gave in once a day, there would still be sixty-three victories out of seventy battles. Satan tries to make us think we are losing when we are actually winning.

Many people have testified that this simple method of keeping score has made dramatic changes in their spiritual progress. It immediately increases hope and enthusiasm and it gives us more confidence and self-respect. It also endows us with more power to resist, because if we come to that seventh day with nothing but six days of restraint, it is not hard to rationalize that we are only breaking a small score of six days abstinence. That's not so much to give up before starting over, Satan whispers. But if we have sixty-nine victories on the score card for that week, *that* is really something to hang on to. It is not so easy to throw away sixty-nine victories for one quick indulgence. We probably paid dearly for that many victories, so we find ourselves resisting with greater determination. Think of the power of the accumulating score after several weeks or months of keeping track this way. It gives an unexpected military strength far beyond one's normal will power.

There is something else we can do to increase the effectiveness of this score-keeping: Find a partner who will join us in the record-keeping. It might be a bishop or spouse, a parent, a supportive brother or sister, or just a friend. Reporting to a partner on a daily or weekly basis will give an even greater determination to make those scores as high as possible. As President Spencer W. Kimball advised:

> Continued contact seems to be helpful. To have the man return to report success in his efforts, or even to tell of partial failure is helpful, and to these continuing visits much credit is due for recoveries. An additional strength comes from the realization that they will be making reports, and people thus control themselves and their thoughts a day at a time, a week at a time; and soon the months have passed and their thoughts are under control and their actions are above reproach. (*The Miracle of Forgiveness*, 84)

The last part of keeping score is to report each day's total to Heavenly Father before going to bed. Confide in him the number of temptations that part of you wanted to indulge. He already knew about it anyway, so go ahead and admit it, reassuring him that you don't want to be that vulnerable and expressing your willingness and desire to overcome those temptations. And then report to him the number of victories you scored. Thank him for the strength to win those battles, acknowledging that it came from him. And then ask him, plead with him to remove the evil desires from you, to change your heart and nature so that the carnal, fallen part of you will no longer be attracted by these temptations. Then, over the days, weeks, and months, as you see your score cards changing, with fewer and fewer temptations that you wanted to give in to, you will know, because you have measured it, that the new birth is unfolding in your life. You will find yourself filling your prayers with praise and thanksgiving instead of hopeless begging, because you can see that the miracle of divine grace is transforming you into his image. Keeping score can make the difference between victory and defeat in your battles with Satan.

> Wherefore take unto you the whole armour of God, that ye may be able to withstand in the evil day, and having done all, to stand. (Ephesians 6:13)

13

The Battleground of Repentance

WE HAVE DISCUSSED THE LINE THAT DIVIDES GOOD AND EVIL. IF we remain on the Lord's side, we are entitled to his help in our battles. When we give in to temptation, however, we have chosen to cross the line into the devil's territory and we become subject to his power. If we are to win our battles with Satan, we must learn to recognize this line and do all we can to stay on the Lord's side.

Once the devil has lured us into his territory, he fights desperately to keep us there. He opposes the effort to repent with every temptation and discouragement he can devise. It will hurt too much to deal with this now, he whispers. You will be far more comfortable if you put it off awhile. But God did not send us to this earthly battleground to be comfortable. He sent us here to grow.

> Repentance is not easy or painless or convenient. Only [Satan] would say, "You can't change. You won't change. It's too long and too hard to change. Give up. Give in. Don't repent. You are just the way you are." That, my friends, is a lie born of desperation. Don't fall for it. (Jeffrey R. Holland, *New Era,* October 1980, 12)

President Kimball taught that when a person sets about to repent and abandon former sins, "Satan will not readily let go. Rather, he will probably send a host of new temptations to weaken the resolve of the repentant one" (*The Miracle of Forgiveness,* 86). Since all of us sin from time to time, the best strategy is to decide ahead of time that when we do make a mistake and cross that line, we will admit the error and return as quickly as possible. Repentance is admitting our mistakes, turning around, and crossing back to the Lord's side. "Repent, and *turn* yourselves from all your transgressions; so iniquity shall not be your ruin" (Ezekiel 18:30). "The Father . . . sent me to bless you in *turning away* every one of you from his iniquities" (3 Nephi 20:26). Therefore, "*turn ye* even to me with all your heart" (Joel 2:12). And the wonderful promise is that "when the wicked man *turneth* away from his wickedness that he hath committed, and doeth that which is lawful and right, he shall save his soul" (Ezekiel 18:27). In this chapter we will explore some of the strategies Satan uses on this battleground, strategies which always include these elements:

> Don't repent.
> Don't repent yet. Just wait awhile. Enjoy yourself.
> You've gone too far. It's too late to repent.
> Repent if you must, but keep it to yourself. Don't tell anyone.
> Don't pray about this. God will just get angry and punish you.
> How awful you are. Don't expect any mercy or forgiveness from God just because you change now.

REPENTANCE APPLIES TO EVERYONE

Satan would have us believe that we are worse than everyone else because we need to repent. But needing repentance does not mean we are inferior—it only shows we are mortal. To win our battles with Satan, we must understand that except for Jesus Christ, *every person* who has ever lived upon this earth needed repentance, including the apostles and prophets. Jesus did not bring the gospel and establish his church to find a few superstars who are so righteous they can earn their way into God's presence without repentance. He came to establish a system by which every person, no matter how weak, can be strengthened, purified, and prepared to return to Father's presence. His invitation is: "I am not come to call the righteous, but sinners to repentance" (Matthew 9:13).

Because every mortal person sins and needs the cleansing of repentance, the Savior "suffered the pain of *all* men, that *all* men might repent and come unto him" (D&C 18:11). It would not have been necessary for Christ to suffer for "all men" if there were some who could live perfect lives and needed no repentance. "Behold, I, God, have suffered these things *for all,* that they might not suffer if they would repent; But if they would not repent they must suffer even as I" (D&C 19:16–17). When Satan tries to discourage people from repenting and improving their behavior, they should shun his mocking ridicule and remember that "*all men,* everywhere, must repent, or they can in nowise inherit the kingdom of God, for no unclean thing can dwell there, or dwell in his presence" (Moses 6:57).

BLESSED ARE THE REPENTANT

When Satan sees us determined to repent, he also tries to make us ashamed for needing repentance. Always, always he is trying to put barriers between us and God's love. But repentance is not something to be ashamed of. It is simply proof that we are progressing and learning a better way, and that is why we came here. The Lord emphasized this when he said, *"Blessed* are they who will repent" (Helaman 13:13). *"Blessed* are they who will repent and hearken unto the voice of the Lord their God" (Helaman 12:23). Nowhere do the scriptures say or even hint, "Blessed is he who never needs repentance," for there is no such person. One of the strategies Satan uses to make people feel guilty about their repentance is to divert their sorrow and remorse into self-deprecation. What an awful person you are. Look what you have done. You are worthless. If people are not careful, Satan's cunning whispers can persuade them to cling to the guilt they feel as a *substitute* for repentance. In some clever way, Satan convinces them that the more guilty they feel, the more holy and repentant they are. What a terrible distortion of a divine gift. That is not repentance. It is a grievous error, for instead of drawing us closer to the Lord through repentance, over-emphasized guilt pulls us away from him.

The scriptures explain how the Lord feels about people who have made mistakes and corrected them through repentance. "What man of you, having an hundred sheep," he challenged, "if he lose one of them, doth not leave the ninety and nine in the wilderness, and go after that which is lost, until he find it?" (Luke 15:4) And when he finds that careless sheep which wandered from the flock, does he drive it home angrily? No, but "when he hath found it, he layeth it on his shoulders, rejoicing" (Luke 15:5). "And how great is his joy in the soul that repenteth!" (D&C 18:13).

The proper response to feelings of shame and worthlessness is to do all we can to put our lives in order. Then we must place the rest in the hands and grace of Jesus Christ, who has promised to show mercy as he removes the guilt from our repentant hearts (see D&C 38:14; Enos 1:5–8; Alma 24:10).

> People must somehow be made to realize that the true meaning of repentance is that we do not require people to be punished or to punish themselves, but to change their lives so they can escape eternal punishment. If they have this understanding, it will relieve their anxiety and fears and become a welcome and treasured word in our religious vocabulary. (Theodore M. Burton, *Speeches of the Year*, Provo, Utah: BYU Press, 1984–85, 97)

THE BEST MOTIVATION FOR REPENTANCE

There are at least two kinds of guilt which affect repentance: worldly and spiritual. *Worldly* guilt is merely the pain of being caught. It is the sorrow one feels when one cannot indulge in sin and get away with it. The higher, *spiritual* guilt is given to us by a loving Heavenly Father to help us correct our lives. "For godly sorrow worketh repentance to salvation, not to be repented of: but the sorrow of the world worketh death" (2 Corinthians 7:10). The sorrow of the world is certainly to be repented of, but the higher remorse, the "godly sorrow," motivates us to repent because, as true disciples, we do not want to do anything that would hurt the Lord. Alma counseled:

> Let your sins trouble you, with that trouble which shall bring you down to repentance . . . let the justice of God, and his mercy, and his long-suffering have full sway in your heart; and let it bring you down to the dust of humility. (Alma 42:29–30)

If we truly love the Lord, we will be *anxious* to repent as fast as we can. Don't you know, asked Paul, that "the goodness of God leadeth thee to repentance?" (Romans 2:4) If we truly appreciate the sacrifice Christ made so that we could repent and receive forgiveness, one of our greatest priorities will be to honor that sacrifice by refusing to do anything that would disappoint or hurt him. As Christians we do not repent so that God will forgive us and atone for our sins. It is the fact that Christ has *already* atoned and paid for our sins that prompts us to repent and justify his faith in us. It is awareness of his unconditional love, offered even while we were yet in our sins, that makes us respond and bring to fulfillment the forgiveness and changes that he *initiated* in Gethsemane, but which cannot be *fulfilled* without repentance. As President Spencer W. Kimball said:

> When we think of the great sacrifice of our Lord Jesus Christ and the sufferings he endured for us, we would be ingrates if we did not appreciate it so far as our power made it possible. He suffered and died for us, and yet if we do not repent, all his anguish and pain on our account are futile. (*The Miracle of Forgiveness*, 145)

REPENTANCE—STOPPING OR GOING?

Traditionally we have thought of repentance as the process of *stopping* rather than *going.* It is true that in order to "turn" from our wicked ways, we have to stop doing whatever we did that was wrong. But merely stopping the sin we committed does not constitute a complete repentance. If we would achieve victory on the battleground of repentance, it is helpful to think of repentance as a process of moving forward, rather than merely stopping and staying where we were. If we have crossed the line into the devil's territory, it would be foolish just to stop there. What we need is to turn around and move forward to the Lord's side as quickly as we can.

It is better "to do" something positive than to "not do" something negative. It is very difficult to stop a sinful habit unless we find something positive and spiritual with which to replace it. Remember, **what gets your attention gets you**. If you place all your attention on merely *not doing* the bad things, then your attention will be diverted from *doing* the right things which would remove the desire for wickedness and return you to fellowship with the Lord. By focusing our efforts on the *positive* things that bring us to Christ, we will find the strength to eliminate the things that were keeping us apart. "Bringing forth" implies movement, doing, growing, and progressing, which are far more beneficial and healing than merely restraining an inappropriate behavior. Raise the intent of your repentance from merely restraining a sinful habit to the goal of becoming more like Christ, and you can be certain of victory in every conflict on the battleground of repentance.

TOTAL ABANDONMENT

Making repentance a process of moving toward the Lord requires the willingness to leave behind everything associated with our past sins. "By this ye may know if a man repenteth of his sins," the Lord declared, "behold, he will confess them *and forsake them*" (D&C 58:43). Without a total "forsaking" of the sin and all its connections, there is no real repentance, no matter how sorry we feel. If Satan cannot break a person's determination to repent, he tries to persuade that person that he or she can cling to sinful indulgences and still be active in the church and gospel. Satan even whispers that all those good works entitle the person to a few sinful pleasures. But true repentance—repentance based on love of the Lord and the desire to repay the Savior for his sacrifice—involves a total abandonment of the sin and all entanglements associated with it.

A person, for example, who stops committing physical adultery but continues in mental imaginings, perhaps longing for an abandoned partner and wishing for a way to return to the sin, has not really repented, even though the physical act is being avoided. As President Kimball warned,

> The adulterer who still has desires toward the object of his sin, who still revels in the memories of his sin, has not forsaken it 'with all his heart' as required by holy scripture. (*The Miracle of Forgiveness*, 333)

He also said,

> The true spirit of repentance, which all should exhibit, embraces a desire to stay away from sin. One cannot simultaneously be repentant and flirt with transgression. (Ibid., 215)

If one is trying to repent of improper eating, junk food must be removed from the house and replaced with more nourishing food. If one is struggling to repent of immoralities, all pornographic magazines, inappropriate videos, and cable television channels must be abandoned and replaced with scriptures, good literature and music, and more wholesome forms of entertainment.

> In abandoning sin one cannot merely wish for better conditions. He must make them. He must be certain not only that he has abandoned the sin but that he has changed the situations surrounding the sin.
>
> He should avoid the places and conditions and circumstances where the sin occurred, for these could most readily breed it again. He may not hate the persons involved, but he must avoid them and everything associated with the sin.
>
> He must dispose of all letters, trinkets, and things which will remind him of the "old days" and the "old times." He must forget addresses, telephone numbers, people, places and situations from the sinful past, and build a new life. He must eliminate anything which would stir the old memories. (Ibid., 171–72)

Do It Now

When Satan realizes he cannot *prevent* a person's repentance, his backup plan is to *delay* it. Repent if you must, but not right now. Wait awhile. Since you've already sinned, go ahead and enjoy it for awhile. Satan knows that the longer we wait and the longer we continue in sin, the more difficult it will be to admit and abandon our errors. Once we are on his side, it is much easier to slide deeper and deeper into sinful indulgence, developing strong habits and even addictions that chain us to our sins. As Elder James E. Talmage taught, "As the time of repentance is procrastinated, the ability to repent grows weaker" (*Articles of Faith*, 1952, 114). And the longer we indulge sin without repentance, the more desensitized we become, losing our perspective in the onslaught of Satan's constant whisperings that "it mattereth not." Therefore, "we ought to repent as quickly as possible from our every sinful act before we lose the ability to repent" (ElRay L. Christiansen,

New Era, September 1975, 6). If we slipped and broke an arm, we would be at the hospital having it fixed within minutes. When we slip and break one of the commandments, we must not compound the problem by leaving it dangling, unresolved. Procrastination is equivalent to spiritual suicide.

> Don't put your eternal life at risk. Keep the commandments of God. If you have sinned, the sooner you begin to make your way back, the sooner you will find the sweet peace and joy that comes with the miracle of forgiveness. (Thomas S. Monson, *Ensign,* November 1990, 47)

If we would triumph on the battleground of repentance, we must ask ourselves continually, "If not now, when?" As we face the need for repentance, we must remind ourselves that "later" usually means "never." "If men would only let their sins trouble them early, when the sins are small and few, how much anguish would be saved them" (Kimball, *The Miracle of Forgiveness,* 142).

> I beseech of you that ye do not procrastinate the day of your repentance until the end; . . . [for] ye cannot say, when ye are brought to that awful crisis, that I will repent, that I will return to my God. Nay, ye cannot say this: for that same spirit which doth possess your bodies at the time ye go out of this life, that same spirit will have power to possess your body in that eternal world.
>
> For behold, if ye have procrastinated the day of your repentance even until death, behold, ye have become subjected to the spirit of the devil, and he doth seal you his; therefore, the Spirit of the Lord hath withdrawn from you, and hath no place in you, and the devil hath all power over you; and this is the final state of the wicked. (Alma 34:33–35)

The real issue on the battleground of repentance is simply this: Where do you wish to spend eternity? In joy with your loved ones in the presence of Jesus Christ and Heavenly Father? In the light and glory of the celestial kingdom, or in everlasting cold darkness and misery, with the devil and those he has captured? We make that choice every time we move toward repentance or delay it.

REPENTANCE IS INCOMPLETE WITHOUT CONFESSION

When a soldier is sent on a mission into enemy territory, the first thing that happens upon his return is a debriefing by his officers in charge. Likewise, when we sin and wander into the devil's territory we, too, need debriefing. In the gospel this process is called confession. We cannot complete a successful repentance as long as we hide our sins and refuse to confess them. "By this ye may know if a man repenteth of his sins—behold, he will confess them and forsake them" (D&C 58:43). If Satan finds us determined to do the *forsaking* part of repentance, he works hard to keep us from the *confessing* part, because he knows that without this part of repentance we cannot be healed or cleansed. "He that covereth his sins shall not prosper: but whoso confesseth and forsaketh them shall have mercy" (Proverbs 28:13).

When we try to repent deceptively, without confession to the Lord and his priesthood representatives, the unrevealed sin and the unresolved guilt rots and festers inside us like a spiritual cancer, spreading poison throughout our entire being and pulling us down into the darkness of spiritual death. "And wo unto them that seek deep to hide their counsel from the Lord! And their works are in the dark and they say: Who seeth us, and who knoweth us?" (2 Nephi 27:27)

> *It is confession that starts the process of forgiving.* It is a healthy, healing thing to drop all evasions and say that you have failed, sinned, blundered, hurt someone, disappointed yourself. This is the place to start. Admit it. All else comes later. *Until you get over this hurdle, you have not [even] started the race.* Until you open this door, the fresh air and sunshine that awaits you will be locked out. (Don Baker, *Forgiving Yourself,* Portland, Oregon: Multnomah Press, 1985, 23)

John said, "If we confess our sins, he is faithful and just to forgive us our sins, and to cleanse us from all unrighteousness" (1 John 1:9). How can we expect the Atonement to apply to our efforts to repent if we avoid confession and attempt to alter the divinely prescribed procedure?

> The Lord suffered and died so that your sins could be paid for by *him,* rather than by you. *But it can only work if you do your*

part—by confessing and forsaking your sin. And the sooner this is done, the sooner the sweetness and joy of that forgiveness can surround you. (Editorial, *New Era,* October 1989, 18)

When we break a law in the civil world, the usual legal advice is to deny everything and admit to nothing. Confession to authorities of the law can and will be used to convict and punish the offender. In contrast, when we break one of God's commandments, the best advice is full confession, which leads to forgiveness, healing, and the transfer of our debt to the Atonement of Jesus Christ.

> Confession is a necessary requirement for complete forgiveness. It is an indication of true "godly sorrow." It is part of the cleansing process. *Starting anew requires a clean page in the diary of our conscience.* Those transgressions requiring confession to a bishop are adultery, fornication, other sexual transgressions and deviances; and sins of a comparable seriousness. (J. Richard Clarke, *New Era,* November 1980, 4)

Sometimes, talking to the bishop, the family members or the friends we have betrayed can be embarrassing, and Satan will use those feelings to tempt us not to confess. There is no point in discussing this with anyone. They won't understand, he whispers. They will look down on you. Your reputation will be destroyed. They will reject you. You will lose everything if you confess this. Keep it to yourself. We can overcome such fears by remembering that one of the most vital of all commandments has to do with placing Christ and Heavenly Father at the center of our lives and putting them first above all else, regardless of the consequences or inconvenience. When the commandment was given, "Thou shalt have no other Gods before me" (Exodus 20:3), it included the gods of pride and reputation. Let us remember that when we doubt or question the compassion and understanding of priesthood leaders, we are actually doubting the Lord, who said, "Whether by mine own voice or by the voice of my servants, it is the same" (D&C 1:38). And even if we do encounter some negative response, whose opinion matters most in the eternal view of things: our fellow man's or the Lord's?

> Our Father in Heaven knows how hard it is for you, and if you overcome your fear and take this action, he will bless you accordingly. Satan, of course, would love to have you postpone your

> confession indefinitely. He'll whisper all manner of nonsense in your ear about how the bishop may be shocked by your confession—or that the bishop would not be understanding—or that the bishop might not keep our confession confidential. (Editorial, *New Era*, October 1989, 17)
>
> I, the Lord, forgive sins, and am merciful unto those who confess their sins with humble hearts. (D&C 61 :2)

When we are honestly ready to repent, confession is a wonderful experience. It removes heavy burdens from our shoulders. It feels wonderful to know we are at last being honest.

> The truth is that your bishop has been called of God because he is a compassionate and godly man who wants to help. He is God's agent on earth to hear your confession. He can help you get on the road to repentance and forgiveness and the unspeakable joy which comes from knowing your sins have been forgiven. (Editorial, *New Era*, October 1989, 17)

If Satan finds us not only determined to *forsake* our sins, but also to *confess* them, his next plan is to *delay* the confession. Wait until after you've repented and it's all behind you, he suggests. It won't be so embarrassing if you confess later, when you're all cleaned up. This cunning suggestion seeks to trade confession for admission. There is a vast difference between merely *admitting* your mistake long after the fact and honestly *confessing* your need for help and forgiveness while you are in the process of repenting. Don't try to do it all alone when the Lord is so anxious to be a part of the healing process. Stand tall on the battleground of repentance and let the Lord become a partner in your repentance by including timely confession when it is appropriate.

> Confession places you in a position to receive all the Lord's vast resources to rescue you from the sin confessed. There is substantial psychological strength in confession. Confession is not only the revealing of errors to proper authorities, but the sharing of burdens to lighten them. One lifts at least part of his burden and places it on other shoulders which are able and willing to help carry the load. Then there comes satisfaction in having taken another step in doing all that is possible to rid oneself of the

burden of transgression. (Kimball, *The Miracle of Forgiveness*, 187–88)

YOUR REPENTANCE WILL BE ACCEPTED

Finally, Satan tries to persuade us that repentance is a foolish waste of effort because God could not possibly accept you after what you have done. Things will never be the same. He lies. When the Savior said, "Draw near unto me and I will draw near unto you" (D&C 88:63), he was giving a divine promise to respond to each person's repentance, no matter how imperfect or flawed the present conduct has been. This promise is based on the *desire* to repent and the *direction* we are moving, not on the immediate worthiness. There is nothing in that promise about being perfect or good enough before he will respond to us. Yet Satan will taunt, It doesn't apply to you because you have not been drawing near. You have deliberately been going in the opposite direction. Again, he lies. The Savior said, "Return unto me and I will return unto you" (3 Nephi 24:7). Inviting us to "return" to him simply acknowledges that we have made mistakes which we need to correct through repentance. Who is typical of the celestial kingdom? Repentant sinners who recognized their mistakes and accepted the Lord's invitation to turn around and "return" to him.

> Behold, he sendeth an invitation unto all men, for the arms of mercy are extended towards them, and he saith: Repent and I *will* receive you. (Alma 5:33)

Christ has invited and promised to receive every person who comes to him in sincere repentance. Because he already suffered and died as a substitute for our punishment, he is now authorized to welcome us with arms of mercy and forgiveness when we acknowledge and change our unworthy behavior. (see D&C 19:15–19.) The Savior is perfectly willing to take our unworthy hands, as long as they are offered to him with a submissive and repentant attitude. Never let Satan talk you out of the Savior's eager mercy that follows every act of repentance.

Let the wicked forsake his way, and the unrighteous man his

thoughts: and let him return unto the Lord, and *he will have mercy* upon him; and to our God, for *he will abundantly pardon.* (Isaiah 55:7)

But if they will repent and return unto the Lord your God *I will turn away mine anger,* saith the Lord; yea, thus saith the Lord, blessed are they who will repent and turn unto me, but wo unto him that repenteth not. (Helaman 13:11)

14

The Battleground of Change

MANY PEOPLE BECOME SO ACCUSTOMED TO LOSING THEIR BATTLES with sin, bad habits, and temptations, that they really believe they cannot win—so why even try? The issues on this battleground are simple: God says we can change every imperfection, no matter how long they have held us in captivity, and Satan says we can't. The story is told of a scorpion who wanted to cross a river. He asked a turtle to swim across, allowing him to ride on his back. The turtle replied, "No way. As soon as I let you on my back you will sting me and I will die." The scorpion replied, "No I won't. That doesn't make sense. If I sting you, you would die and I would drown." The turtle said, "Well, that makes sense. Climb on." Halfway across the river the turtle felt the scorpion's stinger strike into his neck. In amazement he cried, "Why did you do that? Now we're both going to die." The scorpion's reply was, "I don't know. *I can't help myself, that's just the way I am."* To defeat Satan on the battleground of change we must never say "That's just the way I am." To win our battles with Satan we must accept the fact that there is no desire, no habit, no addiction so deeply ingrained and permanent that it is inescapable. To believe that we cannot change and escape our inappropriate behavior is to accept Satan's "no win" lies, denying everything God has done in the lives of countless thousands who have changed carnal thoughts and behaviors to spiritual ones. As BYU President Jeffrey R. Holland said:

> Here your most crucial challenge, once recognizing the seriousness of your mistakes, will be to believe that you *can*

change, that there can be a different you. To *disbelieve* that, is clearly a Satanic device designed to discourage and defeat you.

> Only he would say, "You can't change. You won't change. It's too long and too hard to change. Give up. Give in. Don't repent. You are just the way you are." That, my friends, is a lie born of desperation. Don't fall for it. (*New Era,* October 1980, 11–12)

As President Benson has said, "When you choose to follow Christ, you choose to be changed" (*Ensign,* November 1985, 5). He also promised that "attaining a righteous and virtuous life is within the capability of any one of us if we will earnestly seek for it" (*Ensign,* November 1983, 43).

> We must realize that, in spite of our weaknesses, our idiosyncrasies, and perhaps even our unfortunate backgrounds, a message of the gospel is that you and I can become changed—totally and completely changed! (George Pace, *Ensign,* September 1974, 48)

CONTROL VERSUS CHANGE

I was once involved in an automobile accident which resulted in severe neck and shoulder pains. Massaging with a strong vibrator was the only relief I could find. As the weeks passed and the pain grew worse, I found myself resorting to the vibrator more frequently until I required the treatment every couple of hours. My difficulty persisted and grew worse because I was only dealing with the outward *symptoms* and ignoring the *cause* of the pain. I finally obtained X-rays and the cause of my pain became obvious: three vertebrae in the neck had been twisted out of place and were causing stress on the surrounding nerves and muscles. When the vertebrae were placed back into position, the pain disappeared. As we reach for the changes required to experience the divine nature, we must understand the difference between merely *controlling* our bad habits and allowing Christ to change our hearts and natures so that we no longer *want* the habits.

When Satan sees that we are determined to change, he tries to detour us into merely *controlling* the outward behavior so that we won't seek the inward *transformation* of the new birth Christ means for us to have. But going to the celestial kingdom is not based upon suppressing our evil desires with superhuman restraint and will power, for then the evil is only caged and locked inside us like a ticking time bomb, just waiting for the right temptation to light the fuse. Controlling inappropriate behavior is an important element in change, but we must never let Satan hold us at that point. Focusing only on "outward conformity" prevents us from receiving the inward cleansing and new birth. Jesus came to save us *from* our sins, but he cannot save us *in* our sins, which is right where we are if we are merely *restraining* them with will power. What is required is a complete transformation of the heart, desires, and fallen human nature, so that we no longer *want* the sinful behavior. Nothing but the blood, Atonement, and grace of Jesus Christ can do that.

Satan also tries to hold us in captivity by persuading us to focus on *man's* solutions instead of *God's*. That is why scripture teaches that "it is better to trust in the Lord than to put confidence in man" (Psalms 118:8). And that "your faith should not stand in the wisdom of men, but in the power of God" (1 Corinthians 2:5). As Richard Chidester lamented:

> The world suggests that we can manufacture our own change by goal-setting, behavioral objectives, behavior change techniques, positive mental attitudes, and various other forms of self-improvement programs.
>
> Although these approaches may be useful in bringing about a measure of desired behavioral change, they are only partial because they are terrestrial. They are the best man can produce by himself. (*Ensign*, February 1984, 8)

No one can change the carnal nature of his own heart and disposition by "iron-jawed will power," or with man-made behavioral techniques and self-improvement programs alone—and the Lord doesn't expect it. We may, by applying will power and the wisdom of man, do much good in *controlling* our behavior, but until we allow Jesus Christ to alter our hearts and desires, we will continue to suffer a struggle between the desires of the flesh and the will of the spirit.

I am not suggesting that Christ will do everything for us, because he won't. He does nothing for us that we are capable of doing ourselves. But when we do our best, he will do everything else that needs to be done, which we are incapable of doing by ourselves. When we give him our *willingness* to change, he gives us the *ability* and *power* to change. The miracle of his grace is his ability to reach inside us and remove all the restrictions of the carnal nature, to make it possible for us to achieve the changes we always wanted, but were unable to accomplish by ourselves.

It is not necessary to understand how the Savior does this in order to receive the blessing. But it is necessary that we reject Satan's lies that the Savior *won't* perform this transformation, or that he *can't* do it, and then place our faith in the Savior's promises that he *will* do it. We will then be able to add our own testimonies to those of Ammon's converts, "that their hearts had been changed; that they had no more desire to do evil" (Alma 19:33).

THE STARTING POINT

To win our conflicts on the battleground of change we must learn how to get the promises of deliverance off the pages of scripture and into the deeds of our everyday lives. To do this we must understand that the *starting point* of all change is not the *ability* to achieve instant, perfect obedience, but to "show unto your God that ye are *willing* to repent of your sins and enter into a covenant with him to keep his commandments" (Alma 7:15). Christ is far more concerned with one's *willingness* and *desire* to change than he is with the inability to make those changes immediately. He can work around our inadequacies, but there is little that even he can do for us when we are not *willing* to change. No matter how deeply entrenched our bad habits may be, each of us can start the process of change with a willing mind.

One of the ways Satan tries to hold us in defeat is by confusing the difference between a *willingness* to do what is right and the imperfect ability to *live* that intent immediately. Many of us are defeated on the battleground of change by a very serious misconception. We think there is something wrong with us because, in spite of our sincere desire and intent to change, our emotions do not immediately follow our mental choices and commitments. *Mentally* we commit ourselves to repent and turn to the Lord with all our hearts, but *emotionally* we find ourselves being pulled back toward the old desires by a lifetime of improper habits. We judge ourselves harshly because we do not understand this to be a natural part of spiritual progress. *Mentally* we do not want to go back to our sins, yet we feel certain that God will reject our efforts to change because our *feelings* and *desires* are not immediately in harmony with our intentions.

To defeat Satan's discouragements on this issue, we have to understand that changes in our feelings come only after changes in our actions. It is only reasonable that at the beginning of our efforts to change we may not have the ability to *feel* repentant, or to *feel* forgiving, or humble, or spiritual, or to *feel* whatever it is we are trying to achieve. But no matter how discouraged or hopeless we are in spite of our *feelings,* we can always express a mental *willingness* to our Heavenly Father. Once we voice that choice, once we covenant through an act of the will that we are truly *willing* to change, even though we may not be *able* to overcome the fault by our efforts alone, then Christ will come into our lives and add to our limited ability all the power we need to make the changes the proper emotions will follow in good time.

> We think we must climb to a certain height of goodness before we can reach God. But he says not "at the end of the way you may find me;" He says "I am the way; I am the road under your feet, the road that begins just as low down as you happen to be."
>
> If we are in a hole then the Way begins in the hole. The moment we set our face in the same direction as his, we are walking with God. (William R. Parker & Elaine St. Johns, *Prayer Can Change Your Life,* 17th Ed., Englewood Cliffs, New Jersey: Prentice-Hall, 1965, 244–45)

Perhaps we stumble as we take those first faltering steps toward the Lord. Satan immediately fills our minds with reminders of past failures as he mocks, I told you it was no use. You'll never change. You'll always be like this. Give up now, before you make a fool of yourself. But the Lord understands our struggles and has promised to accept us, even with our temporary limitations. He has promised not to reject our efforts to change, even if we do not yet have the perfected feelings and habits of obedience that can only be produced with time.

> For if there be first a willing mind, it is accepted according to that a man hath, and not according to that he hath not. (2 Corinthians 8:12)

When we find ourselves wavering in our efforts to change, we could pray for help in this manner: "Father, I *want* to repent of this sin but I can't seem to do it by myself. I keep falling back into the old ways in spite of my intentions. Father, I know thou hast all power in heaven and on earth, so I'm asking thee to give me the strength to live my commitments to thee." We know he will respond to such prayers because he has given this assurance:

> Verily I say unto you, all among them who know their hearts are honest, and are broken, and their spirits contrite, and are willing to observe their covenants by sacrifice—yea, every sacrifice which I, the Lord, shall command—they are accepted of me. (D&C 97:8)

At the beginning of the change process it is difficult to break the tyranny of bad habits and addictions, simply because we are in the *habit* of making wrong choices. We have trained the brain to act out inappropriate behaviors each time we are tempted or stressed. However, as the Lord helps us to change, the brain's response will become just as conditioned to say "no" to temptation as it now is to say "yes." Because God changes people from the inside, with a total transformation of spirit and character, we won't always have the terrible battles between unworthy desires and will power. Of course there will still be temptations. As long as we live in this world we will be required to face and overcome temptations. But once we experience the "mighty change" in our hearts, our battles will be different. We will no longer feel like we are hanging on by our fingernails, trying not to fall over the cliff of desire. Temptations will no longer fill us with feelings of fear or self-condemnation, but will actually draw us closer to Christ.

CHANGE TAKES TIME

We live in a society that expects instant change. While it is unreasonable to expect a habit that grew over months or years to disappear the instant we resolve to set it aside, we often feel discouraged and even doubt the scripture's principles and promises when we do not receive a miraculous, instant healing. God will keep his promises and help every person who sincerely desires to change, but in most cases the changes come slowly, step by step, progressively undoing the long process by which the addict became a slave. Satan is an expert in using delays to discourage us. See, I told you, he whispers. You trusted in those scriptures and it didn't work. You are still just the same. Perhaps it works for some people, but it will never work for you. You will be happier when you give in and be your real self. One can overcome Satan's discouragements by focusing, not on the distant future, but on each battle, moment by moment. As Elder Marvin J. Ashton said, "One day at a time, the price of change can be paid. The cost will then not be overwhelming." (*Ensign*, May 1979, 68)

One reason change takes longer than we want it to is that once we place ourselves in the Lord's hands, he is going to do a lot more changing than to simply remove our outward symptoms. We are anxious to stop doing this or that, but his goal is larger: to make us *whole*, to turn our weaknesses into strengths, to remove every character defect, to achieve a total transformation of heart and nature. Change always produces withdrawal pains and we must be willing to endure the struggle and pain for months, if not for years. Just as a *physical* birth is the result of many months of preparation within the body, even so a *spiritual* birth is the result of much development and maturing within the personality. Instant change is the exception, not the rule.

> Each one who resolves to climb that steep road to recovery must gird up for the fight of a lifetime. Healing doesn't come after the first dose of any medicine. So the prescription must be followed firmly, bearing in mind that it often takes as long to recover as it did to become ill. But if made consistently and persistently, correct choices can cure. (Russell M. Nelson, *Ensign*, November 1988, 6–7)

Progress will come as we learn to give up things we want today for things we want more tomorrow. Remember, if we are not willing to pay the price *today*, then six months or a year from now we will be in the same captivity—or worse.

> These things remain to overcome through patience, that such may receive a more exceeding and eternal weight of glory, otherwise, a greater condemnation. (D&C 63:66)

IT IS NEVER TOO LATE TO CHANGE

One characteristic of the Savior's mission was his immediate response to pleas for help—except in the case of Lazarus, whose sisters sent messengers to ask Christ to return to Bethany and heal him. He did not go, but delayed until word came that Lazarus had died. Intending to show his power to raise the dead, Christ deliberately waited until four days had passed. It was Jewish belief that a dead person's spirit might be allowed to tarry near the corpse for a few days in case there was a chance for the life to be restored. But they believed that by the fourth day the body's decomposition had progressed so far that there was no longer any chance of the person coming back to life. (see *Jesus The Christ,* 500–501.)

Thus, by waiting four days to restore Lazarus' life, the Savior was demonstrating that he not only had power over death and seemingly impossible circumstances, but even over time itself.

When he arrived in Bethany, both Mary and Martha declared their faith in the Lord's power but expressed alarm when Jesus asked that the grave be opened, saying, "Lord, by this time he stinketh: for he hath been dead four days" (John 11:39). However, rotting flesh was no barrier to Christ's infinite power. Jesus "cried with a loud voice, Lazarus, come forth. And he that was dead came forth, bound hand and foot with graveclothes: and his face was bound about with a napkin. Jesus saith unto them, Loose him, and let him go." (John 11:43–44)

Perhaps one purpose of this miracle was to teach us of Christ's power over the *spiritual death* which results from the weaknesses, bad habits, and addictions that hold us in captivity. As we awaken to Christ's power to change us, Satan would have us believe that we have been "dead," or caught in the captivity of our helplessness too long for the power of Christ to help. The promises do not apply to you, he sneers every time we seek to change. Not after all those years of addiction. Be real. If Christ could have changed this, why didn't he do it before? It's because he can't. Think of all the hours you've wasted in prayer and scripture study. And where did it get you? You can't change now. It's too late for you. You've gone too far. You are mine forever. But if a person is *willing* to change, it doesn't matter how long he has been in bondage to sin because Christ's power is both infinite and sufficient for every need. He can restore our lives *spiritually* as easily as he restored Lazarus' life *physically*.

Because of our past failures we may feel restricted, bound in the grave clothes of sin and addiction, unable to move forward or to free ourselves. Christ's instruction was "loose him, and let him go," and that will be his instruction to the powers of evil which hold us in bondage, once we are ready to surrender the foul stink of sin and accept the new birth he has waiting for us. Listen for his call, for surely he is saying to each one of us, "Come forth."

> Those who make one serious mistake tend to add another by assuming that it is then too late for them. It is never too late. The discouraging idea that a mistake makes it everlastingly too late, does not come from the Lord . . . You must never give up! It is never too late! (Boyd K. Packer, *Ensign*, May 1989, 59)

The Choice Is Ours

The battle lines are drawn. The enemies face each other across the line. On one side Satan and his army chant the lies that we are trapped and cannot change. On the other side the Lord encourages us with the promise that we can change any defect and that he will personally help us make those changes. We must each choose whom to believe. It makes little difference whether our present captivity is the result of deliberate sin, or simply the result of unwise choices, because Christ can help us change either situation. The God who can transform water into wine and a few loaves and fishes into a satisfying feast for thousands, this God of the impossible, is certainly capable of transforming a sincerely repentant person into a victorious, valiant disciple.

> Roadblocks to eternal progress are cast aside when resolves are made that no man needs to walk alone. It is a happy day when we come to know that with God's help, nothing is impossible for us. (Marvin J. Ashton, *Ensign*, May 1979, 68)

15

The Battleground of Memory

MANY VALIANT WARRIORS HAVE BEEN DEFEATED ON THE BATTLE-ground of memory. One of the devil's favorite weapons could be symbolized by a rear-view mirror. Though necessary for any driver wanting to stay aware of traffic behind his moving car, the rear-view mirror would be disastrous if most of that driver's attention was focused there. Satan works hard to keep us looking in our spiritual rear-view mirrors, looking back at our past mistakes so he can destroy our confidence in the future. I doubt if anyone endures more misery and unnecessary suffering than the person who won't take his attention off the past, who insists on going through life with that mental rear-view mirror stuck in front of his eyes, always looking back, always digging up the mistakes of the past, continually criticizing and condemning himself for his failures. Surely this does not please the Lord. Elder Marvin J. Ashton said, "Where you've been is not nearly as important as where you are and where you're going" (*This People*, March 1984, 27). The past can never hurt us once we decide to let it go and allow it to truly be the past.

Perhaps you have tried to conquer a weakness and have failed over and over. Perhaps you have even failed a thousand times. The devil would have you believe that because you have *failed* in the past, you *are* a failure. Believing that lie places us in his power instead of Christ's. No matter how many times we have failed, we are not actually failures until we give up and quit trying.

Whenever a person resolves to accept the invitation to draw closer to the Lord, Satan invades and floods his or her mind with memories of past mistakes and present imperfections in an attempt to discourage the effort to change. He knows that a person cannot fix *today* as long as *yesterday* remains the focus of attention. When Satan gets us to focus too much on the mistakes of the past, that negative focus unwittingly perpetuates the very thing we are trying to overcome. Realize that **what holds your attention holds you.** The daily thoughts we focus attention on are like blueprints of our future reality. If we constantly look back at the past, we are assuredly perpetuating it into the future. In a sense, we become our own worst enemy because the very act of dwelling on, analyzing, regretting, pondering, and forcing our whole life to revolve around a problem increases its strength and gives it power to dominate our lives. As Dr. Lloyd Ogilvie said, "We mortgage the future based upon what happened in the past" (Quoted by H. Norman Wright, *Making Peace With Your Past,* Old Tappan, New Jersey: Fleming H. Revell, 1985, 40).

> The sure sign that we have an authentic relationship with God is that we believe more in the future than in the past. The past can be neither a source of confidence nor a condemnation. God graciously divided our life into days and years so that we could let go of yesterdays and anticipate our tomorrows. For the past mistakes, he offers forgiveness and an ability to forget. For our tomorrows, he gives us the gift of expectation and excitement. (Lloyd Ogilvie, *God's Best For My Life,* Eugene, Oregon: Harvest House, 1981, 1)

No one ever made a mistake in the future. Therefore, no matter what mistakes lie in your past, your future is just as spotless as the prophet's. And with the Lord's help, you can put anything there that you choose. It is true that a necessary part of repentance is to look at the past and acknowledge our mistakes. But let's not confuse repentance with self-deprecation. There comes a time when we must take our eyes off the past and look forward to the redemption of Christ which erases the past. It is only when we let go of the past that we can move forward into the newness of life Christ intends for us. "Therefore if any man be in Christ, *he is a new creature:* old things are passed away; behold, all things are become new" (2 Corinthians 5:17).

Because of Satan's whisperings, some of us get so trapped by the guilt and shame we feel for past mistakes that we just can't let go of the memories and believe in the forgiveness Christ is trying to give us when we repent. Many times this preoccupation with the past is like setting up a mental video that never stops. Over and over it replays painful memories and the person sinks lower and lower into despair and self-loathing. Elder Neal A. Maxwell has counseled:

> Some of us who would not chastise a neighbor for his frailties have a field day with our own. We should, of course, learn from our mistakes, but without forever studying the instant replays as if these were the game of life itself. (*Ensign*, November 1976, 13–14)

The loving forgiveness of our Savior can turn that video replay off. The Savior's incredible sacrifice can stop the cycle of self-condemnation if we will only accept it and stop punishing ourselves. The Savior is anxious to forgive, but he will not force it upon us. We must open our hearts and accept it. Elder Richard G. Scott said:

> Yet there are others who cannot forgive themselves for past transgressions, even knowing the Lord has forgiven them. Somehow they feel compelled to continually condemn themselves and to suffer by frequently recalling the details of past mistakes.
>
> Can't you see that to continue to suffer for sins, when there has been proper repentance and forgiveness of the Lord, is not prompted by the Savior, but by the master of deceit, whose goal has always been to bind and enslave the children of our Father in Heaven? Satan would encourage you to continue to relive the details of past mistakes knowing that such thoughts make progress, growth, and service difficult to attain.
>
> When memory of prior mistakes encroaches upon your mind, turn your thoughts to Jesus Christ, to the miracle of forgiveness and renewal that comes through him. Then your suffering will be replaced by joy, gratitude, and thanksgiving for his love. (*Ensign*, May 1986, 11–12)

As Moses set about to deliver the Israelites out of Egyptian bondage, he faced the challenge of bitter memories. He faced a people who only knew Jehovah as the God of the past and the God of the future. For centuries they had treasured the knowledge that Jehovah had been real to Abraham, Isaac, and Jacob—the God of the past. And they dreamed of some day in the future when Jehovah would once again act on their behalf in fulfillment of his promises and covenants with the three patriarchs—the God of future. When Jehovah appeared to Moses at the burning bush on Mount Horeb and commissioned him to deliver the Israelites, Moses asked:

> When I come unto the children of Israel, and shall say unto them, The God of your fathers hath sent me unto you; and they shall say to me, What is his name? what shall I say unto them? And God said unto Moses, I AM THAT I AM: and he said, Thus shalt thou say unto the children of Israel, I AM hath sent me unto you. (Exodus 3:13–14)

The Lord sent Moses to teach Israel (and us) that Jesus Christ is the God I AM—the God of right now; the God who will intervene on our behalf in our present needs, our present circumstances and situations, in our day-to-day lives. When we focus on Christ as the Great I AM, the God of today, we can let go of the past and endure whatever is required as we wait for the glories of tomorrow.

The past is to be learned from, not lived in, and the future is to be planned for, not for us to be paralyzed by. God has declared himself in the present tense, I am the Great I AM. (Jeffrey R. Holland, *Ensign*, September 1974, 7) If we are being defeated by memories from the past, we must look to the God of the present for healing. We must grant him permission to enter our memory banks and remove the pains which we cannot remove by ourselves. Alma suffered terrible memories of his past. He said, "And now, for three days and for three nights was I racked, even with the pains of a damned soul. I was harrowed up by the memory of my many sins" (Alma 36:16–17). Most of us can relate to those feelings. It is the very point of defeat at which Satan seeks to keep us chained. But Alma's conversion illustrates the path to freedom from painful memories and guilt. He said that as he placed his faith in Jesus Christ and his atoning blood:

> I could remember my pains no more; yea, I was harrowed up by the memory of my sins no more. And oh, what joy, and what marvelous light I did behold; yea, my soul was filled with joy as exceeding as was my pain! (Alma 36:19–20)

True holiness requires surrendering one's past to the Lord's divine healing as Alma did, and then pressing forward to make the future what God would wish it to be. While realizing he had not yet attained the perfection the Lord commanded us to seek, Paul said that he had learned to let go of his past mistakes and focus on the goals of the future.

> Brethren, I count not myself to have apprehended: but this one thing I do, forgetting those things which are behind, and reaching forth unto those things which are before, I press toward the mark for the prize of the high calling of God in Christ Jesus. (Philippians 3:13–14)

If we would win our battles on the battleground of memory, we must do the same. "Wherefore, ye must press forward with a steadfastness in Christ, having a perfect brightness of hope" (2 Nephi 31:20).

> Brethren, shall we not go on in so great a cause? Go forward and not backward. Courage, brethren; and on, on to the victory! Let your hearts rejoice, and be exceedingly glad. (D&C 128:22)

16

The Battleground of Perfectionism

SATAN HAS A BACKUP PLAN FOR EVERY STRATEGY THAT FAILS. HE IS the master of contradictory attacks. For example, to the world the devil can say, Do whatever you want. Have fun. If it feels good, do it. Don't worry, it mattereth not. But to sincere disciples who recognize and reject those lies, he reverses the strategy and tells them that every imperfection matters so much that there is no hope of attaining the celestial kingdom. This exaggerated lie is one of his major strategies because he knows that expecting too much of ourselves too soon will defeat us as surely as deliberate sin. I am convinced that an overemphasized, fanatical perfectionism will keep more Latter-day Saints in defeat and discouragement than will deliberate sin. Let us now consider some of the lies Satan presents on this battleground.

1. "You Have to Be Perfect Right Now"

The word "perfect" and its derivatives appear in scripture more than 200 times. Yet in all those verses there is not one place that a timetable or deadline is given for the attainment of perfection. It is true that the more perfect and Christlike we become, the more joy we will have. That is one of God's reasons for creating man and sending him to this earth-school (see 2 Nephi 2:25). But if we are not careful, Satan can take our good intentions in seeking to perfect ourselves, and twist and distort them so they become a major stumbling block, one of our worst defeats. For example, when Satan sees that we are committed to reaching for perfection and that he cannot pull us from our determination, he reverses his strategy and urges us on faster and faster, trying to wear us out by over-exertion and breaking our wills. You've got to try harder, he whispers, You're not doing enough. Push, push. You'll never make it unless you do better than this. Then, when we do try harder, he floods our minds with memories of past and present failures, whispering continual doubts about our ability to make it.

A common feeling shared by people who are struggling to overcome various spiritual defeats is that their duty is to punish themselves because of their imperfections. This is most unfortunate. As Elder Bruce C. Hafen said:

> The person most in need of understanding the Savior's mercy is probably one who has worked himself to exhaustion in a sincere effort to repent, but who still believes his estrangement from God is permanent and hopeless. (*The Broken Heart*, Salt Lake City. Utah: Deseret Book, 1989, 5)

Sometimes, in their zeal to please God, people become so fixed on the eternal goal of attaining perfection that they lose their perspective and allow their inadequacies to create barriers between themselves and the God they are trying so hard to please. Feelings of inadequacy create barriers when we demand more of ourselves than God does. As Bishop Victor L. Brown Jr. said, "Narrow, self-centered obsession with perfection can become an emotional disability" (*Ensign*, August 1985, 36). Elder Marvin J. Ashton warned, "When we take it upon ourselves to pass self-judgment and simply declare, 'I am not worthy,' we build a barrier to progress and erect blockades that prevent our moving forward. We are not being fair when we judge ourselves" (*Ensign*, May 1989, 20–21).

To achieve victory on this battleground, we must realize there is an important difference between feeling godly sorrow and remorse for our mistakes and being caught in Satan's twisted distortions that make us feel ashamed to have a mortal weakness or imperfection. As we reach for higher spirituality, we do the best we can, but we never condemn ourselves for the inability to achieve instant perfection. As Relief Society President Barbara Smith said, "Goals are stars to steer by, not sticks to beat yourself with" (*Sunstone*, May 1985, 21). The Lord has never said that the celestial kingdom is reserved for people who had no imperfections to overcome. But he did say, "To him that overcometh will I grant to sit with me in my throne, even as I also overcame, and am set down with my Father in his throne" (Revelation 3:21). No one is condemned or considered less in the Lord's eye for having to overcome mortal flaws as he progressively moves toward the gospel ideals. President Gordon B. Hinckley explained:

> I do not ask that you reach beyond your capacity. Please don't nag yourself with thoughts of failure. Do not set goals far beyond your capacity to achieve. Simply do what you can do, in the best way you know, and the Lord will accept of your effort. (*Ensign*, November 1989, 96)

God did not create the world in one session, but divided his labors into progressive steps. We are expected to do the same. The Lord knows our weaknesses. He knows how hard it is to obey when we are being pulled by the desires of the flesh and the whisperings of Satan. He does not expect us to arrive all at once. He understands that salvation and perfection are not achieved in a single event, but by a process of growth requiring lots and lots of practice. Jesus said: "And ye must practice virtue and holiness before me continually" (D&C 46:33). Even Christ himself had to grow and develop his perfection in progressive steps (see Luke 2:52; Hebrews 5:8–9).

In our eagerness to please the Lord, we must not expect too much of ourselves too soon and then fall into depression because we are not as perfect as we had hoped to be. It is not pleasing to him when we demand instant perfection of ourselves and then feel poorly because we do not obtain the impossible. The strength of one's commitment to "endure to the end" is often more important than the pace of his growth. "Ye are not able to abide the presence of God now . . . wherefore, continue in patience until ye are perfected" (D&C 67:13). Sometimes the hardest test of patience comes from expecting ourselves to grow toward perfection faster than our mortal limitations allow. As we attempt to "lengthen our stride," we must not confuse going fast with being valiant, for what is most needed is not speed but patient, steady growth.

> Wherefore seeing we also are compassed about with so great a cloud witnesses, let us lay aside every weight, and the sin which

doth so easily beset us, and let us run with patience the race that is set before us. Looking unto Jesus the author and finisher of our faith; who for the joy that was set before him endured the cross, despising the shame, and is set down on the right hand of the throne of God. (Hebrews 12:1–2)

2. "Nothing Less Than Perfection Is Acceptable to God"

What an ugly lie this is. We must recognize that there are two kinds of perfection we are striving for: one attainable in this life, the other reserved for the next. Elder Bruce R. McConkie explained:

> *Perfection* is of two kinds—*finite or mortal,* and *infinite or eternal. Finite perfection* may be gained by the righteous saints in this life. It consists in living a godfearing life of devotion to the truth, of walking complete submission to the will of the Lord, and of putting first in one's life the things of the kingdom of God. *Infinite perfection* is reserved for those who overcome all things and inherit the fullness of the Father in the mansions hereafter. It consists in gaining eternal life, the kind of life which God has in the highest heaven within the celestial world. (*Mormon Doctrine,* Salt Lake City, Utah, Bookcraft. 1966, 567; emphasis in original)

It will be centuries, or probably millennia, before we gain enough experience and spiritual maturity to achieve the ultimate, eternal perfection spoken of, but that should not discourage us as we progress through mortality. "We have to become perfect to be saved in the celestial kingdom, but nobody becomes perfect in this life," Elder McConkie cautioned, for "only the Lord Jesus attained that state, and he had an advantage that none of us has. He was the Son of God. Becoming perfect in Christ is a process." (*Ensign*, June 1989, 43)

> We don't need to get a complex or get the feeling that you have to be perfect to be saved. You don't . . . have to live a life that's truer than true. You don't have to have an excessive zeal that becomes fanatical and becomes unbalancing. What you have to do is stay in the mainstream of the Church and live as upright and decent

people live in the Church—keeping the commandments, paying your tithing, serving in the organizations of the Church, loving the Lord, staying on the straight and narrow path. (Bruce R. McConkie, "The Probationary Test of Mortality," an address to the institute of religion students, University of Utah, 10 January, 1982)

It is significant that two of the last three verses of the Book of Mormon close that magnificent testimony of Christ by explaining that the only path to perfection is through the enabling, quickening grace of Jesus Christ, which always comes to compensate for the inadequacies of those who do the best they can within their limitations.

Yea, come unto Christ, and be perfected in him, and deny yourselves of all ungodliness; and if ye shall deny yourselves of all ungodliness, and love God with all your might, mind and strength, then is his grace sufficient for you, that by his grace ye may be perfect in Christ; and if by the grace of God ye are perfect in Christ, ye can in nowise deny the power of God. (Moroni 10:32)

Here is an intriguing analogy: "But now, O Lord, thou art our Father; we are the clay, and thou our potter; and we are all the work of thy hand" (Isaiah 64:8). What a strange analogy this would be if we did not understand how much we need the Lord in our struggles toward perfection. "Behold, as the clay is in the potter's hand, so are ye in mine hand, O house of Israel" (Jeremiah 18:6). When we let Satan trick us into judging ourselves in comparison to a finished vessel, we feel inferior and unworthy because we know we are so far from perfection. But when we see ourselves as unfinished clay in the hands of the Master Potter, we have the confident assurance that he will make of us a far more beautiful vessel than we could ever imagine or make of ourselves. And because we know that he will never stop working with us until he has molded us to our perfect capacity, we can have the patience to love and accept ourselves as he continues to fashion us (see Philippians 1:6; 2:13).

I think that the Lord will not be particularly comfortable dwelling with a person who ponders continually on his or her problems, who is obsessed and finally immobilized by them, who hasn't learned to bear those limitations serenely. That isn't humility, it is near-blasphemy.

When you dwell on your limitations excessively, to the point that they affect your inner view and strength, you mock God in his very creation. You deny the divinity within you. You resist the gift of Christ on the cross. So be patient in your pursuit of perfection. (Patricia T. Holland, *Devotional Speeches of the Year*, Provo, Utah: BYU Press, 1988–89, 25)

If Satan does not succeed in urging us to go too fast and expecting more of ourselves than is reasonably possible, he will adapt the strategy of trying to overwhelm us with the size of the task. Perfection is beyond your reach, he whispers. You have so many faults. Look how far you have to go. It is hopeless. You may as well give up and be your real self. We must not believe these lies. What is important to God is not how perfect we are right at this moment, but where our hearts and commitments lie. Elder Marvin J. Ashton explained:

We need to come to terms with our desire to reach perfection and our frustration when our accomplishments or our behaviors are less than perfect. I feel that one of the great myths we would do well to dispel is that we've come to earth to perfect ourselves, and nothing short of that will do. If I understand the teachings of the prophets of this dispensation correctly, we will not become perfect in this life, though we can make significant strides toward that goal.

I am also convinced of the fact that the speed with which we head along the straight and narrow path isn't as important as the direction in which we are traveling. That direction, if it is leading toward eternal goals, is the all-important factor. (*Ensign*, May 1989, 20–21)

3. "GOD CANNOT LOVE YOU BECAUSE YOU ARE IMPERFECT"

If Satan cannot overwhelm us with the enormity of the effort to achieve perfection, if we demonstrate the determination to press forward toward that goal patiently, day by day, in spite of his whispered discouragements, the devil has yet another strategy. And this is the place where many faithful, devoted Latter-day Saints are defeated. One of Satan's favorite perfectionism lies is: Since you are not yet perfect, God (who commanded your perfection) could not possibly love you as you are, with all your faults and imperfections. He will never love you or accept you until after you achieve perfection. Nothing could be further from the truth. The Lord loves each one of us just as we are this very moment, no matter what our faults are, but he loves us too much to leave us that way. He doesn't demand we change before he loves us, because he knows that if we need changing, discovering the reality of his love will change us. "God loves us, not because we are good, but because we need his love in order to be good" (David A. Seamands, *Healing For Damaged Emotions,* Wheaton, Ill., Victor Books, 1985, 137).

> A legitimate way to increase your self-esteem is to become aware that God loves you as you are at this moment. What you have done in the past in no way diminishes his love for you. It is unconditional love. There are no ifs or buts attached. If your feelings about yourself are largely negative, you can change them by realizing that your Heavenly Father loves you unconditionally. (Joseph C. Bentley, *The Instructor,* November 1969, 399)

It is true that God has very strict standards, and that he "cannot look upon sin with the least degree of allowance" (D&C 1:31). But it is also true that he has infinite allowance, infinite tolerance, compassion, and mercy, infinite patience and forgiveness, for every repentant person, no matter how imperfect they remain. How the Savior longs to assure us that we are not condemned simply because we have unconquered weaknesses. "Some of you are guilty before me," he said, "but I will be merciful unto your weaknesses" (D&C 38:14). He also said, "Verily I say unto you, notwithstanding their sins, my bowels are filled with compassion towards them. I will not utterly cast them off; and in the day of wrath I will remember mercy." (D&C 101:9)

> I am convinced that much of the discouragement that exists in the hearts and minds of some Latter-day Saints may be traced to their inability to rely on the Lord and trust in his mercies. We need to do all we can to prove ourselves worthy of the Lord's goodness, to seek to live the life of a true Saint. But we must also come to know that when we have done all we can—when we have stretched to the limit, have placed our offerings upon the

altar of faith, no matter how meager they may seem to us at the time—we then have done what was asked of us and we will come to know that the Lord is pleased with us. (Robert L. Millet, *By Grace Are We Saved,* Salt Lake City, Utah: Bookcraft, 1989, 109)

None of what we have said in this chapter should be construed to accommodate rationalizations or justification for mediocrity. The purpose is to find a reasonable compassion and tolerance for our present limitations so that Satan cannot use our yearning to be better than we are against us. One of the Lord's most encouraging revelations is that his gifts and blessings are given not just for the perfect, but also "for the benefit of those who love me and keep all my commandments, and him that seeketh so to do" (D&C 46:9). That leaves room for every sincere person who is earnestly striving toward righteousness. It tells us that the gospel is not for the perfectly obedient superstars, but for the weakest of Saints who sincerely desire to be obedient and in fellowship with the Lord. "Does it matter if at this moment I am less than perfect?" asked Elder Francis M. Gibbons. "What does matter is that I am trying hard to keep the commandments, which is the sure road to perfection" (*New Era,* January 1989, 6). As C. S. Lewis said:

> This Helper who will, in the long run, be satisfied with nothing less than absolute perfection, will also be delighted with the first feeble, stumbling effort you make tomorrow to do the simplest duty. (*Mere Christianity,* 29th ed., New York: Macmillan Publishing, 1979, 172)

Since God allows us an entire span of mortality in which to grow, and since he does not reject or condemn us for having unconquered weaknesses, what right do we have to condemn ourselves? Of course we are disappointed when we fail to do as well as we hoped to do, but we can fail without being a failure. There is an important difference between being disappointed in one's performance and being derailed by feelings of disapproval. We must be humble enough to stop condemning ourselves and not allow our unwanted imperfections to distort our self-images and form barriers between us and the Lord.

> When we have done all that we can, our desires will carry us the rest of the way. If our desires are right, we can be forgiven for the unintended errors or mistakes we will inevitably make as we try

to carry those desires into effect. What a comfort for our feelings of inadequacy! (Dallin H. Oaks, *Pure in Heart,* Salt Lake City, Utah: Bookcraft, 1988, 79)

PART THREE

Victory through Christ

17

A Strong Foundation

Ultimately, in every war, the generals must decide where to draw the line, make a stand and fight it out. It may be on a hill, in a line of concrete bunkers, or simply in dug-out trenches. Against that "front line" the enemy wages war with all his power, seeking to destroy the opposing forces or drive them into retreat. There will be tank fire, bombardment from naval and ground artillery, missiles, bombs, and strafing from the air. The strength of that "front line" determines who prevails in the battle. Similarly, Satan directs his army of evil spirits to weaken or destroy our front line and foundation of resistance, which is either reliance upon ourselves, or reliance upon Christ.

SELF-CENTERED OR CHRIST-CENTERED?

As we battle on this front line of spiritual foundation, Satan would have the Lord's soldiers center their attention on their individual defenses rather than standing firm in the Lord's resources. The devil knows that only those whose lives are built upon the foundation of Jesus Christ will have the protection and stamina necessary to weather his powerful, unceasing attacks. Choosing Christ as the center and foundation of our spiritual lives is compared to building upon a rock. As Helaman emphasized, "And now, my sons, remember, remember, that it is upon the rock of our Redeemer, who is Christ, the Son of God, that ye must build your foundation" (Helaman 5:12).

Therefore, whoso heareth these sayings of mine and doeth them,

> I will liken him unto a wise man, who built his house upon a rock—And the rain descended, and the floods came, and the winds blew, and beat upon that house; and it fell not, for it was founded upon a rock.
>
> And every one that heareth these sayings of mine and doeth them not shall be likened unto a foolish man, who built his house upon the sand—And the rain descended, and the floods came, and the winds blew, and beat upon that house; and it fell, and great was the fall of it. (3 Nephi 14:24–27)

The comparison between the safety and strength of building upon rock instead of sand is obvious. What we do not always realize, however, is that this analogy shows the contrast between relying upon Christ, who is the rock, and the substitute plan of Satan which would have us rely upon our strength alone. Self-sufficiency seems a noble goal and worthy of pursuit, but it can also be deceptively destructive if it prevents us from developing the proper dependence upon Christ, which he has declared essential to winning our battles.

> I am the true vine, and my Father is the husbandman . . . Abide in me, and I in you. As the branch cannot bear fruit of itself, except it abide in the vine; no more can ye, except ye abide in me.
>
> I am the vine, ye are the branches: He that abideth in me, and I in him, the same bringeth forth much fruit: for without me ye can do nothing. (John 15:1, 4–5)

As we strive for success in living the gospel it is natural to center our thoughts, confidence, and reliance upon ourselves. After all, it is our duty to do right and it is our duty to do well. We should realize, however that this self-centered philosophy was one of the main points of the antichrist doctrine preached by Korihor and others like him. As Satan's messenger Korihor taught that reliance upon Jesus Christ's remission of their sins was "the effect of a frenzied mind; and this derangement of your minds comes because of the traditions of your fathers, which lead you away into a belief of things which are not so" (Alma 30:16).

As he went about teaching people to rely solely upon themselves rather than upon Christ, Satan, through Korihor, taught the popular and appealing humanistic doctrine that to rely upon Christ was to rely upon "a foolish and vain hope" (Alma 30:13). His rationalization was that independent of any divine assistance, "every man fared in this life according to the management of the creature; therefore every man prospered according to his genius, and that every man conquered according to his [own] strength" (Alma 30:17).

Today, as he attacks our front lines of spiritual foundation, Satan might say, Certainly there was a man named Christ who lived 2,000 years ago, but he can't have any effect on your life today. You must make your own way. Don't waste your time asking God for help. Show him how independent you are. Show him you can do it on your own. Make him proud of you. Of course it is our duty to do the best we can and to use all our personal strengths and abilities in obeying the commandments and serving each other. But Satan's philosophy of exaggerated self-reliance will lead one directly into the arms of defeat because, by ourselves, no matter how sincerely we strive, none of us is capable of resisting every attack of Satan and standing firm in the face of every temptation and weakness.

> Only Jesus Christ is qualified to provide that hope, that confidence, and that strength to overcome the world and rise above our human failings . . . Faith in Him is more than mere acknowledgment that He lives. It is more than professing belief. Faith in Jesus Christ consists of complete reliance on Him. (Ezra Taft Benson, *Ensign*, November 1983, 6, 8)
>
> Only in him can any man find the strength, the power and ability to live a godly life. Only in Christ is there power to transform the human mind and the human heart. Only in Jesus Christ can any man learn the truth of what he is and how he can be changed from what he is to do the good for which he hopes. (*1969 Gospel Doctrine Manual*, "In His Footsteps Today," Salt Lake City, Utah: Deseret Sunday School Union, 4)

The Book of Mormon speaks of people who followed Korihor's self-reliance philosophy. "And because of this their great wickedness, and their boastings in their own strength, they were left in their own strength; therefore they did not prosper, but were afflicted and smitten" (Helaman 4:13). Elder Eldred G. Smith warned, "As soon as you think you can lick the devil alone, on your own, without the Lord's help, you have lost the battle before you start" (*Ensign*, December 1971, 46).

Robert J. Matthews, dean of Religious Education at Brigham Young University, explained the need to build our spiritual lives on the foundation of our relationships with Christ when he said, "A person cannot lift himself or herself by individual effort alone but must be lifted by the power of the Atonement of Jesus Christ" (*Ensign*, December 1980, 35). And Elder Hugh W. Pinnock said, "We function best in an environment of freedom. We are free when we are independent, and we are totally independent only when we are completely dependent upon the Savior." (*Speeches of the Year*, Provo, Utah: BYU Press, 1979, 116) Ultimately then, nothing in our lives is going to be right until we are right with the Savior. As President Howard W. Hunter said:

> Please remember this one thing. If our lives and our faith are centered upon Jesus Christ and his restored gospel, nothing can ever go permanently wrong. On the other hand, if our lives are not centered on the Savior and his teachings, no other success can ever be permanently right. (*Speeches of the Year*, Provo, Utah: BYU Press, 1988–89, 112)

SUBSTITUTES

When we feel vulnerable to Satan's attacks, do we look to the Lord for the strength to resist and conquer, or do we look to worldly substitutes? The Lord challenged, "Hearken unto me, ye that follow after righteousness, ye that seek the Lord: look unto the rock whence ye are hewn" (Isaiah 51:1). This is a difficult lesson for some because we are surrounded by so many other worthwhile sources to which we can look for guidance, strength, and resource in our struggles. The world is filled with inspiring self-help books, self-improvement and behavioral modification programs, and counselors of every kind to whom we may look for help in our struggles. These resources are fine as far as they go, but it is only when we look to Jesus Christ for the true light and resources we need that we will achieve the peace, success, and abundance in life that he meant for us to have. Isaiah warned that trouble would befall those who look elsewhere, substituting trust in the more obvious "arm of flesh" resources for reliance upon Jesus Christ. Referring to worldly might, Isaiah said, "Wo to them that go down to Egypt for help; and stay on horses, and trust in chariots, because they are many; and in horsemen, because they are strong; but they look not unto the Holy One of Israel, neither seek the Lord!" (Isaiah 31:1)

Satan knows that the truth which flows from Christ through the scriptures and the prophets can win us freedom from his evil influence. Thus, he works hard to divert our attention to other resources. I know the importance of learning to rely upon Christ's grace and power, because I wasted thirty-two years trying to cure myself of addiction without drawing upon his power. I used every tool I could think of. I set goals, used positive affirmations, made promises to myself and to the Lord. I read dozens of psychology, motivational, and self-improvement books and tried to apply their principles to controlling my behavior. There was nothing wrong or evil in using those resources, except that it was all based on the wisdom of men and no mortal resource can cure spiritual illness. That is why "your faith should not stand in the wisdom of men, but in the power of God" (1 Corinthians 2:5). That is why "It is better to trust in the Lord than to put confidence in man" (Psalms 118:8).

> Cursed is he that putteth his trust in man, or maketh flesh his arm, or shall hearken unto the precepts of men, save their precepts shall be given by the power of the Holy Ghost. (2 Nephi 28:31)

My preoccupation with man's wisdom allowed Satan to take my desire for righteousness and detour it into paths that kept me from discovering the power and grace available through Jesus Christ. He kept me preoccupied with trying to control my evil behaviors when I could have come to Jesus Christ and had my nature transformed so that I no longer desired the evil. My front line of defense was weak because I had built my foundation on nothing but my limited will power and the substitutes of man's wisdom. Consequently, I suffered endless cycles of defeat and Satan held me in bondage for more than half my life.

It was only when I learned to build my foundation upon Christ that I gained the spiritual strength to withstand Satan's powerful attacks. After the Lord freed me from my compulsive addictions, I was obsessed with the question, "Why?" Why now? After all those years of fasting and praying and trying so hard, why didn't it work before? What I learned was that because of his respect for our sacred agency, the Lord will never force himself upon us. Even though I had been trying hard to overcome my faults, even though I had fasted and prayed for help, I had actually shut him out with my ignorance and stubborn, prideful determination to do it all by myself. I had built my life on the wrong foundation. Do not misunderstand. It is both desirable and necessary to use our own strengths and abilities to do as much as we can. But it is also imperative to recognize that no one, by his own efforts alone, can ever do enough to live the obedient life that will result in exaltation. It is Satan's lie that we must do it all on our own, that we must not expect help from the same God who gave the commandments.

> We must do all that we can do. We must extend ourselves to the limit, we must stretch and bend the soul to its extremities. In the final analysis, however—at least when dealing with matters pertaining to spiritual growth and progression—it is not possible to "pull ourselves up by our own bootstraps," nor is it healthy to presume we can. (Robert L. Millet, *By Grace Are We Saved,* Salt Lake City, Utah: Bookcraft, 1989, 100)

PARTNERSHIP WITH CHRIST

A single soldier is easy for an army to defeat. A battalion is not. As a person defends his front lines, the strength of his defense and offense is dependent upon his relationship with the Savior. Either we fight alone or we fight in partnership with Christ. John said, "He that hath the Son hath life; and he that hath not the Son of God hath not life" (1 John 5:12). In this short, concise statement he clarified the seeming complexities we find in the difficulties of life. All success and failure, all problems and all solutions are rooted in the simple truth that everything we attempt to do in life is inseparably connected to our relationship with Jesus Christ. "For other foundation can no man lay than that is laid, which is Jesus Christ" (1 Corinthians 3:11).

In today's economic turmoil we are familiar with corporate mergers. Companies of strength eliminate competition by purchasing similar companies. Companies that are faltering seek survival by merging with larger, more successful companies. Lawyers for the weak companies face great challenges in advocating their cause to the healthy companies. They have to think of reasons it would be to the advantage of the successful company to merge with the loser. But when we find ourselves overwhelmed by adversity, weaknesses, or sins that are driving us into spiritual bankruptcy, we don't have to beg in order to persuade the Savior to merge his divine perfection with our imperfections. He is anxious to do so. "Come unto me all ye that labour and are heavy laden, and I will give you rest" (Matthew 11:28).

Many times we come to Christ with nothing but liabilities. We are captive to bad habits and sins. Our spiritual bank accounts are overdrawn. We are burdened with sin and spiritual debts we cannot pay by ourselves. We are poor, needy, and essentially helpless. We have nothing to bargain with. As we give ourselves to Christ in sincere repentance, however, our liabilities and his assets flow together. The debts are canceled, erased by the Savior's Atonement. We stand clean before God. Christ is not diminished by our desperate needs, for his resources are unlimited. We do all that we can do, we do the best we can do, and he either does the rest or enables us to do it.

The barrier that prevents this merger with divinity is not our liabilities, but our lack of faith and trust in God's willingness to help us in every difficulty. One of Satan's major efforts is to make us feel alone, to make us feel that we have to measure up to the overwhelming mountain of commandments all by ourselves. God won't accept you in your present condition, he jeers. You must correct your faults before he will be part of your life. The Lord counters these attacks by assuring us that the path to exaltation is supposed to be a partnership between our best efforts and his grace, which compensates for any deficiencies in our abilities.

It is important to know that "whosoever shall put their trust in God shall be supported in their trials, and their troubles, and their afflictions" (Alma 36:3). And that "God will support, and keep, and preserve us, so long as we are faithful unto him, and unto our faith, and our religion" (Alma 44:4).

As we face difficulties in our battles with Satan, we tend to either ignore the Lord's help and rely solely upon ourselves, or to "come boldly unto the throne of grace, that we may obtain mercy, and find grace to help in time of need" (Hebrews 4:16). The confidence to "come boldly" for help in overcoming our inadequacies is based on our personal testimonies of the God who promised, "I am with the faithful always"

(D&C 62:9), and who is "our refuge and strength, a very present help in trouble" (Psalms 46:1). We must realize that the hesitancy we feel toward asking for God's help comes from the pride of mortal self-sufficiency and from Satan who tries to place barriers between us and God. The commandment is to "Pray always, that you may come off conqueror: yea, that you may conquer Satan, and that you may escape the hands of the servants of Satan that do uphold his work" (D&C 10:5). Scripture does not say or even hint, "Blessed is the person who can do it all by himself and never needs to pray for help," for there is no such person. Praying for the Lord's help in our daily battles is a form of worship. For example, "Then came she and worshipped him saying, Lord, help me" (Matthew 15:25). Asking for divine help is not only a way of humbly acknowledging our weaknesses, but also a way of expressing faith in his divine power and love, and inviting his assistance in our efforts to obey.

> The Savior and his love are as near and as real as we permit. If we are open and humble, his presence and that of the Holy Spirit will carry us through the darkest of hours. At the same time he will respect our free agency and will stay away if we reject him. I fear that many of us, even in the Church, do not accept the Savior as a practical source of help. (Victor L. Brown Jr., *New Era,* November 1973, 36–37)

Many things God asks of us seem impossible. And they probably are impossible if we rely solely upon ourselves. But they are not impossible if we allow Christ to be our partner in the endeavor, because "the Lord giveth no commandments unto the children of men, save he shall prepare a way for them that they may accomplish the thing which he commandeth them" (1 Nephi 3:7). The way "prepared" is the flow of his grace. It may seem a strange doctrine for God to give us commandments and challenges and then say, in effect, "Don't worry if this commandment or opposition is too hard for you, because if you will give me your willingness to do it, I will give you the strength and ability to do it," but that is the kind of God we have.

We must never allow Satan to deceive us into believing that we can outgrow our need for the Lord. And we must never be deceived by the devil into believing that God is not ready, willing, and anxious to be our partner and provide whatever help we need to fulfill our righteous desires. "Be not thou far from me, O Lord: O my strengths, haste thee to help me" (Psalms 22:19).

> If you ask the Lord for help, he will give you strength, power, and ability to overcome Lucifer and withstand his efforts, and thus you will be strengthened and made more perfect . . . The Lord has made no promise to those who try to go it alone. (Eldred. G. Smith, *Ensign*, December 1971, 46)

RISKS AND GUARANTEES

In the premortal council, each of us was required to choose between Lucifer's plan, which supposedly guaranteed salvation without agency or risk, and the plan of our Heavenly Father, which involved both. Lucifer's plan appealed to the weaker third of our brothers and sisters because of its supposed guarantees. While Father's plan does involve risk, it is not without guarantees of its own. We are promised that all who choose Jesus as the center and foundation of their life and then live according to their covenants and endure to the end are guaranteed exaltation. Elder Bruce R. McConkie said:

> As members of the Church, if we chart a course leading to eternal life; if we begin the processes of spiritual rebirth, and are going in the right direction; if we chart a course of sanctifying our souls, and degree by degree are going in that direction; and if we chart a course of becoming perfect, and, step by step and phase by phase, are perfecting our souls by overcoming the world, then it is absolutely guaranteed—there is no question whatever about it—we shall gain eternal life. (*Speeches of the Year,* Provo, Utah: BYU Press, 1976–77, 399–400)

Of course, if the saints deliberately choose to sin, if they deliberately "keep not my commandments, and hearken not to observe all my words, the kingdoms of the world shall prevail against them" (D&C 103:8). But as long as we are sincerely striving to obey, as long as we sincerely "observe to do whatsoever I command you, I, the Lord, will turn away all wrath and indignation from you, and the gates of hell shall not prevail against you" (D&C 98:22). If we are living in cycles of defeat and failure it is probably because we are trying to fight our battles without the aid of the Savior.

> And if ye do these last commandments of mine, which I have given you, the gates of hell shall not prevail against you; for my grace is sufficient for you, and you shall be lifted up at the last day." (D&C 17:8)
>
> And now, behold, whosoever is of my church, and endureth of my church to the end, him will I establish upon my rock, and the gates of hell shall not prevail against them. (D&C 10:69)
>
> Therefore, fear not, little flock; do good; let earth and hell combine against you, for if ye are built upon my rock, they cannot prevail. (D&C 6:34)

We need to remember these promises when temptations are pulling at us. As long as we know that Satan cannot prevail over our righteous desires without our permission, then he will not prevail. As Helaman explained, the reason Satan cannot prevail over one whose life is founded upon the rock-like foundation of Jesus Christ is because of the divine protection that person is given against Satan's attacks.

> And now, my sons, remember, remember that it is upon the rock of our Redeemer, who is Christ, the Son of God, that ye must build your foundation; that when the devil shall send forth his mighty winds, yea, his shafts in the whirlwind, yea, when all his hail and his mighty storm shall beat upon you, it shall have no power over you to drag you down to the gulf of misery and endless wo, because of the rock upon which ye are built, which is a sure foundation, a foundation whereon if men build they cannot fall. (Helaman 5:12)

Imagine being so effectively shielded from Satan's attacks that he can "have no power over you to drag you down." These scriptures do not indicate that we might not fall, or that we probably won't fall, but that we cannot fall. Of course we could deliberately sin, we could always choose to fall, but the promise is that Satan cannot pull us down against our will when our lives are centered and founded upon a strong relationship with Jesus Christ.

Because of the power of deliverance Jesus Christ obtained through his Atonement, he is now "able to keep you from falling, and to present you faultless before the presence of his glory with exceeding joy" (Jude

1:24). No matter how earnestly we strive, with our own limited abilities we are not able to keep ourselves from falling in all situations. But our Savior has promised that "whoso cometh in at the gate and climbeth up by me shall never fall" (Moses 7:53).

> I am in your midst, and I am the good shepherd, and the stone of Israel. He that buildeth upon this rock shall never fall. (D&C 50:44)

18
Rescued

MY FAMILY RECENTLY SUFFERED A HEART-WRENCHING EVENT THAT increased our awareness of the Lord's desire to rescue people from their difficulties. We have several pets: two birds, a dog, and cat. But our favorite, most-loved pet is Tiffany, a little bunny rabbit. This animal is one of the most loving, responsive pets we've ever had. Unlike Savario, our haughty cat, Tiffany will sit in our laps for hours at a time without trying to escape. She loves to be petted and responds with affection by licking our fingers and crawling up our laps to gaze into our eyes.

Surprisingly, Tiffany doesn't care much for carrots, but she loves to snack on apples, grapes, cookies, Pop-Tarts, and Fruit Loops. She is a very curious animal. She enjoys romping through the house, exploring the closets and under the beds, but most of the time we leave her in the backyard to run freely. We have carefully plugged all holes, even built special fences so she can't get out of the yard, so we were astonished one Sunday morning when we went out to bring her in from the pouring rain and she was nowhere to be found. We searched every nook and cranny but it was as if she had vanished into thin air. We concluded that the only explanation was that she must have slipped into the house without us noticing. When a thorough search did not find her, we just smiled at her cleverness and waited for her to finish her explorations and come hopping down the hall as she does so often. But she never appeared. After we got back from church we once again searched the house and then the yard, where we finally heard a faint scratching noise coming from the outdoor laundry room. We were perplexed because we had already searched behind the washer and dryer.

What we eventually discovered was that this curious little rabbit had hopped up on the washer and from there to the top of the water heater and then slipped head first into the three- or four-inch triangle formed in the corner. A flashlight revealed her little white tail wiggling frantically in the light beam. Panic ensued. We quickly estimated that she must have been crammed in that tight triangular crevice, upside down, for over eight hours. What sorrow and pain we felt because of the fright and helplessness Tiffany was suffering, with no hope of escape during those long, lonely hours.

The one hundred gallon water heater is five feet tall. We could think of no way to lift her vertically in that tight, narrow space. Of course the pipes prevented us from moving the water heater which pressed hard against each wall. There was only one solution—to cut a hole through the wall from the outside. Do you think we hesitated for one second? No. This was Tiffany. We loved her. What was a mere hole in the wall compared to that? Hastily I grabbed a drill, hammer and chisel and set to work. Our eleven-year-old daughter's tears were flowing in anguish for her bunny's fright and discomfort as we chiseled, hammered, and drilled, calling to Tiffany that we knew her problem, that we loved her, and help was coming. Finally I got a hole of sufficient size through the outer wall, only to discover, to our dismay, that there was yet the inner wall to penetrate. In our panic we had forgotten about that. Work began anew as we continued calling our assurances to her. What great relief and rejoicing we felt when she was successfully removed with no damage. Imagine how much greater anguish we would have felt if it were a child, brother or sister, a wife or husband trapped in a similar situation.

Many of us have reached a point where, because of repeated evil choices, our habits are so firmly entrenched that in spite of an intense desire to repent and free ourselves, we are trapped by the accumulated power of past mistakes and cannot break free by ourselves. Like Tiffany, we are frightened and desperate for freedom, but we are just as unable to escape our captivity alone as was the bunny. We might be in bondage to drugs, tobacco or alcohol, compulsive addictions to lust or overeating, fits of temper, or other weaknesses and habits we can't seem to conquer by ourselves. Or we might be held captive by feelings of depression, discouragement, unresolved guilt, inferiority, or hopelessness which trap us and prevent us from enjoying the fruits of the Spirit.

Book of Mormon prophets frequently warned the people of the dangers of becoming trapped by the spiritual negligence which allows the devil to "grasp them with his everlasting chains," even "with his awful chains, from whence there is no deliverance." (2 Nephi 28:19, 22) When we are trapped in a situation requiring outside assistance, Satan whispers suggestions of defeat and hopelessness. There is no way out of these chains. You are stuck. It is your own fault that you are in this situation and there is no help. You have no right to receive help. There is no chance of escape. When judged by our own limited powers, Satan's lies can seem very reasonable, but there is no situation beyond the reach of Christ's power of deliverance. If we would win our battles with Satan, we must never abandon our faith in Christ's power to rescue us because to do so is to surrender to the enemy and accept defeat. To the ancient, doubting Israelites the Lord demanded, "Is my hand shortened at all, that it cannot redeem? or have I no power to deliver?" (Isaiah 50:2) The answer is no. "Behold, the Lord's hand is not shortened, that it cannot save; neither his ear heavy, that it cannot hear" (Isaiah 59:1). Not only does Christ have the power to rescue us from our captivity, but also to break the chains of habit by reaching inside and giving us a new heart and nature so that we no longer desire the pleasures of the old ways.

All the remorse and regret possible could not undo Tiffany's misfortune without a rescue from outside help. Nor can remorse remove the consequences of our unwise choices, which often lead us into the enslaving bondage of sin. Like Tiffany, we sometimes need outside help, a rescue, if you will, by a higher power. That source of deliverance is Jesus Christ, who "is mighty to save" (Alma 34:18), and who promised, "I am with you to bless you and deliver you forever" (D&C 108:8).

> The spirit of the Lord is upon me, because . . . he hath sent me to heal the brokenhearted, to preach deliverance to the captives, and recovering of sight to the blind, to set at liberty them that are bruised. (Luke 4:18)

Modern Israel has been assured of the same divine rescuing power, "For ye are the children of Israel, and of the seed of Abraham, and ye must be led out of bondage by power, and with a stretched-out arm" (D&C 103:17). The Lord would not have described the necessity for his power in leading us out of our captivities if he felt we could do it by ourselves. While we are certainly expected to discipline our passions and to use our agency to choose the right, nowhere do the scriptures say, or even imply, that God expects us to save ourselves from the consequences of our own sinfulness and bondage. Rather, it is Jesus who "shall save his people from their sins" as they come to him in repentance and humility, asking for his help to live worthily (Matthew 1:21).

The tender, loving concern of our Heavenly Father and Savior for those in trouble is infinitely greater than that which we felt for Tiffany. They love with a perfect love and are ready, even anxious, to rescue every person who recognizes his need for divine assistance and calls to them in a repentant attitude. Nothing is more important to the Lord than saving the sinner who is ready to return to him. There is no obstacle that cannot be removed, there is no cost too high. Jesus proved that when he stretched out his arms on the cross and "gave himself for our sins, that he might deliver us from this present evil world" (Galatians 1:4). To further encourage our trust he said, "I prepare a way for their deliverance in all things out of temptation" (D&C 95:1).

It is important to understand that Christ will not intervene in a person's life unless he is invited to do so. Indeed, he cannot change a person who is unwilling to be changed or who is not ready to honor that rescue with faithful obedience and service in helping other captives.

> But if ye will turn to the Lord with full purpose of heart, and put your trust in him, and serve him with all diligence of mind, if ye do this, he will, according to his own will and pleasure, deliver you out of bondage. (Mosiah 7:33)

When the Savior taught his disciples how to pray, one of the things they were commanded to include was a request to "deliver us from evil" (see Matthew 6:13). When we are in bondage to sinful habits it is urgent that we pray: "Deliver me from all my transgressions" (Psalms 39:8). For those prayers to be effective it is necessary that we "have faith on the Lamb of God, who taketh away the sins of the world, who is mighty to save and to cleanse from all unrighteousness" (Alma 7:14). In Chapter 8, "The Battleground of Prayer," we discussed how Satan schemes to destroy faith in prayer. The reason he concentrates his attacks on this vital source of divine power is that he knows "whosoever shall call on the name of the Lord shall be delivered" (Joel 2:32). The Book of Mormon testifies of the power of prayer in delivering those who were held captive by powers beyond their ability to conquer:

> But behold, he did deliver them because they did humble themselves before him; and because they cried mightily unto him he did deliver them out of bondage; and thus doth the Lord work with his power in all cases among the children of men, extending the arm of mercy towards them that put their trust in him. (Mosiah 29:20)

"Who could have supposed that our God would have been so merciful as to have snatched us from our awful, sinful, and polluted state?" (Alma 26:17) No joy is quite as precious as that experienced by a prisoner of war who is rescued, set free from the prison camp, bathed, clothed, fed, and returned to freedom. And so it is with the prisoners of spiritual warfare, for we "also shall be delivered from the bondage of corruption into the glorious liberty of the children of God" (Romans 8:21).

> They cry unto the Lord in their trouble, and he saveth them out of their distresses. (Psalms 107:19)
>
> He shall call upon me, and I will answer him: I will be with him in trouble; I will deliver him, and honour him. (Psalms 91:15)

19

The Power to Win

Whenever we encounter challenges which exceed our limited abilities, and recognize the need for divine assistance, we may be sure that Satan will attack us with whispered lies and discouragements. He might say, You have no right to expect help in this situation. God doesn't interfere with natural laws except in rare cases, and this is not one of them. Who do you think you are, anyway? What you are asking of God is too hard, even for him. But throughout the centuries Christ has demonstrated that he and Heavenly Father are both Gods of impossible circumstances and they are anxious to help us.

GOD HAS ALL POWER

The truth is that no matter how seriously a person has been wounded in the war with Satan, no matter how long the captivity, no one is beyond the reach of Christ's healing touch. No matter how desperate one's situation is, "He has all power to save every man that believeth on his name and bringeth forth fruit meet for repentance" (Alma 12:15). But how do we answer Satan's lies? How do we argue with the doubts he tries to place in our minds? We can challenge ourselves: "Do I believe this is too hard for God or not? Do I believe Satan or the Lord?" And then we can fight Satan's lies with the word of God. We place our faith and trust in what the Lord has said, not what Satan would have us believe.

Ah Lord God! behold, thou hast made the heaven and the earth

216

by thy great power and stretched out arm, and there is nothing too hard for thee. (Jeremiah 32:17)

Almost the last words Christ spoke before ascending into heaven and leaving his work in the hands of the apostles were, "All power is given unto me in heaven and in earth" (Matthew 28:18). Of all the things Jesus could have said at the time of his departure, why did he choose to speak of his power? All power. Unlimited power. Power to do the impossible. The Savior knew that we would encounter many difficult situations in building the kingdom and in perfecting our individual characters; situations that would often surpass our limitations and which we could not resolve without his help. He does not want us to think of him as an isolated, faraway God who is unable to affect our needs here on earth. He wanted us to know that even though he is now in heaven, he still governs the affairs of men and that he has unlimited power with which to influence our circumstances here on earth. "And he received all power, both in heaven and on earth" (D&C 93:17). King Benjamin challenged us to believe that Christ "has all wisdom, and all power, both in heaven and in earth" so that when we face seemingly impossible circumstances, we will have the faith to draw upon his power (Mosiah 4:9).

> Know ye not that ye are in the hands of God? Know ye not that he hath all power? (Mormon 5:23)
>
> But this much I do know, that the Lord God hath power to do all things which are according to his word. (Alma 7:8)

God Is Able

When King Nebuchadnezzar threatened to cast Shadrach, Meshach, and Abednego into the fiery furnace for refusing to worship his image of gold, they boldly declared their confidence in Jehovah to protect and deliver them from even that impossible situation. "Our God whom we serve is able to deliver us from the burning fiery furnace," they testified confidently (Daniel 3:17). And deliver them he did, demonstrating that there is absolutely no situation from which God cannot deliver us, whether it be a physical, financial, mental, emotional or spiritual problem. The Christ who controls nature can surely control the elements of our circumstances and environment when we need a seemingly impossible blessing, for "He is able even to subdue all things unto himself (Philippians 3:21).

We pray for help as we face great challenges. Satan whispers, God is not able to do what you are asking. But scripture says that "there is nothing that the Lord thy God shall take in his heart to do but what he will do it" (Abraham 3:17). As we struggle to overcome our imperfections we often grow weary and lose confidence. Satan taunts, God is not able to save you from these problems. He cannot save you from your weaknesses, bad habits, sins, or addictions. But God did not send us here to waste our mortal probations being overcome by difficult circumstances or living lives of defeat. Because of the triumph of Jesus Christ, there is no habit, no weakness, personality or character defect, no sin over which we cannot gain the victory. There is no reason to listen to Satan's lies or to waste our lives in misery and defeat.

> God is able to make all grace abound toward you; that ye, always having all sufficiency in all things, may abound to every good work. (2 Corinthians 9:8)

Beyond Any Circumstance

Saddened by the death of John the Baptist, Jesus went into the wilderness for solace, but was followed by a crowd of more than five thousand men plus an uncounted number of women and children. Forgetting his own sorrow, he "was moved with compassion toward them, and he healed their sick" (see Matthew 14:10–14). When evening arrived, the disciples asked Christ to send the people away into the villages to purchase food. Preparing to expand their minds to grasp that he was truly the God of the impossible, Jesus challenged the disciples to feed the people themselves. That would be impossible, they protested. "And they say unto him, We have here but five loaves and two fishes." (see Matthew 14:16–17.) We can understand their reasoning. To all apparent reality, it was impossible to provide food for such a vast crowd. But this was precisely what Christ wanted to demonstrate, that he is never limited by the circumstances that limit us. He said, "With men this is impossible; but with God all things are possible" (Matthew

19:26). After Christ's blessing on the few loaves and fishes they had among them, the food expanded sufficiently to not only satisfy the entire crowd, but to leave them with twelve baskets surplus (Matthew 14:19–21).

In the same manner, the Savior can provide for our needs even when there are no resources to start with but a willingness to change, or a willingness to accomplish a difficult assignment. He can even start when we can offer him nothing more than a hesitant, wavering desire to change, and then actually multiply that feeble offering into the power to do whatever we need to do.

Those situations which appear disadvantageous to us are only opportunities for the Lord to manifest his power in our behalf. But to enjoy the miracles of his great power we must shut out the discouraging whisperings of Satan that it cannot be done and then trust the Lord's power, no matter how detrimental our circumstances may seem. Consider this wonderful message by Steven R. Covey:

> To my understanding, the Lord is telling us that our attitude or frame of mind, heart, and spirit is of crucial importance in releasing the true power of prayer. While this seems obvious, I believe it not to be very common. Too often we place our faith in the seen realities rather than in the unseen God and his promises to us. We then call ourselves realistic, but with the Lord nothing is impossible: if the thing we request is right—that is, if it is wise from the Lord's point of view, even though all the seen realities might shout at us that it cannot be done—and if we pray in faith, believing that it can be done and that it is right, and then put ourselves in alliance with God in doing our part, the Lord will work his miracles.
>
> I have come to believe from my own experiences that many times faith in the Lord Jesus Christ just begins when "it cannot be done," when all of the seen realities combine together to hedge up the way, and people mock, and ridicule. (*Spiritual Roots of Human Relations*, Salt Lake City, Utah: Deseret Book, 1970, 173–74)

The problem with limiting our faith and trust to what we think God can or cannot do for us is that we do not fully comprehend the unlimited scope of his power and ability to affect our environment and circumstances. It is easy to trust him when our "seen realities" are favorable. For instance, once the Red Sea opened and half the camp of Israel had passed through safely, it would have been rather easy to trust God to allow us through also. But the real trust comes before God has revealed his means of deliverance. What he wants to know and what we must decide is, will we trust him in the dark as well as in the light? Will we trust him even when we haven't the slightest idea how he might fulfill our needs?

Paul said, "But my God shall supply all your need according to his riches in glory by Christ Jesus" (Philippians 4:19). When a person is facing circumstances that make it appear impossible for the Lord to keep that promise, his faith must be expanded beyond the lies of Satan that are shouted so loudly, There is no way to accomplish this. We think of Noah and Nephi facing ridicule for daring to construct a ship. What if they had looked only at their "seen realities" instead of placing faith in God? We think of how unlikely it was that a young shepherd boy could conquer the giant, Goliath. What if David had listened to the doubts Satan shouted at him through the fearful soldiers? How often are we defeated by our Goliaths because we are more in tune with Satan's whispered doubts than we are with the Lord and his encouragements?

> And I know, O Lord, that thou hast all power, and can do what-soever thou wilt for the benefit of man. (Ether 3:4)

A MODERN MIRACLE

Let us consider a situation in which the seen realities would quench all but the most fervent faith. During the early 1930s, Saints from Mexico and Guatemala were assigned to the Arizona Temple district. In December 1982, eighty-six Saints made the trip in two buses. The travelers were looking forward to performing endowments, baptisms and sealings. About halfway into the journey one of the buses broke down. Two days and nights were spent trying to fix the bus, but to no avail. They decided to finish the trip in the remaining bus. The children sat on laps or crowded into the aisles. Because the unexpected delay had exhausted their supplies, the remaining two-day trip would have to be made without food. Although they would be passing through several small towns, they had no money left for anything but gasoline.

During the next one hundred miles a tire blew out. They all got off the bus and fixed the tire. A hundred miles later a loud noise erupted from the engine. The driver stopped and lifted the hood. The water was boiling, sending forth clouds of steam. A radiator hose had ruptured. The driver said, "We might as well start walking. It's a hundred miles to the nearest town ahead and a hundred miles behind us, but I don't know what else we can do." Bishop Rodriques, who was in charge of the group, said, "I know what we can do. We will all get on our knees and pray to the Lord that he will send us a hose." As they knelt in the dirt Satan was surely shouting in their ears, Don't do this. Don't believe. A new hose in the middle of the desert? Impossible.

After the prayer they ran to the front of the bus and found their miracle lying on the ground. Under the engine was a brand new hose, just the right shape and size. They installed the miracle hose and completed their trip to the temple. (Related by Harold Wright, Mesa Arizona Temple President, in *The Latter-day Sentinel,* June, 1985, 6)

Never let Satan tell you that you cannot win every battle and overcome every adversity, for no matter how hopeless your "seen realities" may appear, our precious Savior has promised, "I will show unto the children of men that I am able to do mine own work" (2 Nephi 27:21).

> The foolish believer stares despondently at his or her circumstances. The present situation seems to the foolish to be hopeless, and the grim realities of life block every prospect of relief.
>
> But to the wise, the ultimate reality is God—not the present circumstance. The God of Gideon, who can put great armies to flight with a handful of men, is not limited by our circumstances. (Larry Richards, *When It Hurts Too Much To Wait,* Carmel, New York, Guidepost Books, 1985, 35)

20

Putting on the Armor

All scripture is given by inspiration of God, and is profitable for doctrine, for reproof, for correction, and for instruction in righteousness: *That the man of God may be perfect, thoroughly furnished unto all good works.* (2 Timothy 3:16–17)

I KNOW OF NOTHING MORE IMPORTANT OR EFFECTIVE IN CREATING spiritual change, protecting ourselves with the armor of God, and winning our battles with Satan than filling our minds with the word of God. This may be one of the things Paul had in mind when he said, "Be not overcome of evil, but overcome evil with good" (Romans 12:21). When the Lord commanded us to wear the armor of God, he was not referring to something physical that can be seen on the outside of our bodies. The armor of God is on the inside. *It is faith in the word of God.* Whether we are thinking of the helmet of salvation, the sword of the Spirit, the shield of faith, or the breastplate of righteousness, the strength and effectiveness of a person's armor is dependent upon his relationship with God and the scriptures. Some people are weakly protected while others wear armor that renders them almost invincible.

It has been said that wars are won or lost by the food supply to the soldiers. This is certainly true of our spiritual battles. Moroni spoke of new members of the church being *"nourished* by the good word of God, *to keep them in the right way,* to keep them continually watchful unto prayer, relying alone upon the merits of Christ" (Moroni 6:4). Nephi advised us to feed our hunger for spiritual knowledge and nourishment by *"feasting* upon the word of Christ" (2 Nephi 31:20).

"Wherefore, I said unto you, *feast upon the words of Christ:* for behold, the words of Christ will tell you all things what ye should do" (2 Nephi 32:3). The Savior promised that his disciples who literally *"hunger* and thirst after righteousness," would be blessed by having that yearning filled with the presence and strengthening influence of the Holy Ghost (see 3 Nephi 12:6).

Job so loved the words of God that he said, "I have esteemed the words of his mouth more than my necessary food" (Job 23:12). To indicate the urgency with which we should desire spiritual nourishment from the scriptures, Peter said that we should, "As newborn babes, desire the sincere milk of the word, that ye may grow thereby" (1 Peter 2:2). Everyone smiles at the eager enthusiasm which an infant shows for its feeding, but how many of us apply that kind of enthusiasm to the study of scripture? Nephi said, "Behold, my soul delighteth in the things of the Lord; *and my heart pondereth continually upon the things which I have seen and heard"* (2 Nephi 4:16). If we would protect ourselves with the armor of God it is essential that we follow these examples, for one of the signs of true discipleship is that we "enjoy the words of eternal life in this world" (Moses 6:59). Joshua taught that success in our spiritual lives can be enhanced by frequent meditation in the scriptures:

> This book of the law shall not depart out of thy mouth; but *thou shalt meditate therein day and night,* that thou mayest observe to do according to all that is written therein: *for then thou shalt make thy way prosperous, and then thou shalt have good success.* (Joshua 1:8)

Perhaps if we are not currently enjoying the success we desire in overcoming our weaknesses and faults, we need to spend more time internalizing the scriptures, so that we can change the nature of our thoughts to fit into the revealed patterns of spiritual power.

We deny ourselves so many blessings when we regard the study of the scriptures as a difficult or unpleasant task. If this has been a problem in the past, please know that you can change. At first a person may have to force himself to study, but before long the mind and spirit will recognize the value of the new input. It will begin to feel good. When we make ourselves study God's word consistently, whether we feel like it or not, we are taking control of our bad habits by taking control of the input to our minds. Not only do we lose the desire for wickedness, but we feel a desire, even a gnawing hunger to do what is right. We find ourselves craving time with the Lord instead of our sins.

Many warnings have been given to those who do not care to devote time to studying the scriptures. For example, instead of saying, "I command you to give diligent heed to the scriptures," the Lord commanded us to "beware" of indifference toward the scriptures:

> And now I give unto you a commandment to *beware concerning yourselves,* to give diligent heed to the words of eternal life. For you shall live by every word that proceedeth forth from the mouth of God. (D&C 84:43–44)

Speaking of the Church's neglect of the Book of Mormon, the Lord said:

> And your minds in times past have been darkened because of unbelief, and because you have treated lightly the things you have received—Which vanity and unbelief have brought the whole church under condemnation. (D&C 84:54–55; see also verses 56–57)

In spite of a sincere desire to live the gospel and win our battles with Satan, we handicap ourselves when we neglect the scriptures. If we "treat them lightly" and refuse to shape our thought patterns with the scriptural promises of deliverance, our minds will be "darkened" and confused by Satan's attacks. Our minds will tend to wallow in self-defeating thought patterns that perpetuate our weaknesses and failures because we are, by our neglect, "making the word of God of none effect" (Mark 7:13).

> However talented men may be in administrative matters; however eloquent they may be in expressing their views; however learned they may be in the worldly things—they will be denied the sweet whisperings of the Spirit that might have been theirs *unless they pay the price of studying, pondering, and praying about the scriptures.* (Bruce R. McConkie, as quoted by President Benson in *Ensign,* May 1986, 81)
>
> And all they who receive the oracles of God, *let them beware how they hold them lest they are accounted as a light thing,* and

are brought under condemnation thereby, and stumble and fall when the storms descend, and the winds blow, and the rains descend, and beat upon their house. (D&C 90:5)

Some people excuse their avoidance of scripture study by virtue of a busy schedule or because of difficulty in reading, but we must realize that the consequence of such excuses is the same as that suffered by those who ignore the scriptures because of indifference or unbelief.

> There are those who have seemed to forget that *the most powerful weapons the Lord has given us against all that is evil* are his own declarations, the plain simple doctrines of salvation as found in the scriptures. (Harold B. Lee, as quoted by President Benson in *Ensign*, May 1986, 81)

The intimacy of love we feel *for* and *from* our Savior and Heavenly Father will be increased or decreased as we study or neglect to study the scriptures. "For how knoweth a man the master whom he hath not served, and who is a stranger unto him, and is far from the thoughts and intents of his heart?" (Mosiah 5:13) We cannot fully know the Lord or his love if we do not know his word as revealed in scripture. "And whoso receiveth not my voice is not acquainted with my voice, and is not of me. And by this you may know the righteous from the wicked." (D&C 84:52–53) If we are not familiar with Christ's promises, how can we possibly use them to refute Satan's lies and rely upon the Lord in our times of battle?

> Our Church magazines, lesson manuals, and videotapes will never supply everything that a person needs to solve a problem, prepare a lesson, or find a new direction to life. These resources will remain helpful, but all of them together will never be as complete or as powerful as the scriptures. (Hugh W. Pinnock, *Ensign*, May 1989, 12)

SPIRITUAL FORMULAS

Alma taught that *"as much* as ye shall put your trust in God, *even so much* ye shall be delivered out of your trials, and your troubles, and your afflictions" (Alma 38:5). We could regard this scripture as an expression of a spiritual formula: The more trust we place in the Lord and his promises, the greater will be our victory over the attacks of Satan, while the less we know and trust his promises, the more vulnerable we will be. The Savior expanded and clarified this formula in our own time when he said, "and *inasmuch* as you *keep* my sayings you shall not be confounded in this world, nor in the world to come" (D&C 93:52). Throughout this book we have been exploring ways to put on the whole armor of God and win our battles with Satan. In this verse the Lord has explained that our power to do so is dependent upon the degree to which we "keep his sayings," which has at least two meanings. One, of course, is to follow his instructions and obey his commandments. But "keeping his sayings" also involves remembering and relying upon his promises as we defend ourselves from Satan's attacks. We previously discussed the concept of mental function: **What holds my attention holds me.** *"Inasmuch* as you keep my sayings" focused in your conscious mind can also mean *the degree* to which you keep them focused, or as much as you keep them focused. *It is the remembering, believing in, and applying of God's promises that envelops us in the armor of God and protects us from Satan.*

The Lord said, "I am a God of miracles; and I will show unto the world that . . . I work not among the children of men save it be according to their faith" (2 Nephi 27:23). The essential question is, *how* do we develop faith in Christ? Paul described the process when he said, "Faith cometh by hearing, and hearing by the word of God" (Romans 10:17). The key to protecting ourselves with the armor of God and the sword of the Spirit is realizing that one's faith is largely proportionate to the time invested in reading, studying, hearing, and internalizing Christ's promises. As Paul taught: "He which soweth sparingly shall reap also sparingly; and he which soweth bountifully shall reap also bountifully" (2 Corinthians 9:6). Therefore, the more often we implant the victory promises into our brain cells, so that we can really "keep his sayings" focused in our thoughts, the more victorious we will be because our faith and spiritual armor will be strong. On the other hand, the less effort we invest in studying and digesting his word, the more battles we will lose because our faith will be less than it needs to be.

Just as the strength and power of an electromagnet is dependent upon and proportionate to the amount of electrical current running through the metal, so the strength of our spiritual armor is dependent upon the amount and kinds of scripture we flow through our minds. Appendix B will explain a process by which everyone can use the scriptures to develop powerful faith, even if they have difficulty reading and understanding scripture.

THE SWORD OF THE SPIRIT

Even though the "rod of iron," which represents the word of God, will guide us safely through Satan's mists of darkness, we will not be able to complete that journey without spiritual hand-to-hand combat. Those mists of darkness are the temptations of the devil and we will encounter legions of evil spirits hiding there to prevent our progress if they can (see 1 Nephi 15:24; 12:17). The Lord has provided an effective weapon for these battles—"the sword of the Spirit."

Armor is *defensive,* designed to keep our enemies from wounding or killing us. No matter how complete one's armor is, however, no soldier would stand by passively while the enemy attacked him with blow after blow. He immediately throws up his shield to ward off the blows and then counterattacks with his own weapon. Thus, whenever the Lord has commanded us to clothe ourselves with the armor of God, he has included the instruction to protect ourselves with "the sword of the Spirit, *which is the word of God"* (Ephesians 6:17).

A sword is an *offensive* weapon which is used to wound, slay, or drive the enemy away from pursuing further combat. How can the "word of God" function as a sword in our spiritual battles with Satan? Our spiritual swords are not going to wound or slay Satan's demons, but they can drive the evil spirits away from us when we properly counterattack with the word of God. For example, at the end of Christ's forty-day fast in the wilderness, Satan attacked the Savior with three vicious temptations, seeking to lead him into spiritual detours that would nullify his sacred mission. Like the life-threatening thrust of a sword, Satan challenged, "If thou be the Son of God, command that these stones be made bread" (see Matthew 4:3). Jesus immediately thrust a counterattack with his "sword of the Spirit which is the word of God," by answering the temptation with a scripture: "It is written, Man shall not live by bread alone, but by every word that proceedeth out of the mouth of God" (Matthew 4:4). This response ended the first attack. There could be no debate, no struggle, no weighing of alternatives. The issue was quickly identified and settled by scriptural response as surely as if that mist of darkness had been sliced in two with a sharp sword.

> Behold, I am God; give heed unto my word, which is quick and powerful, sharper than a two-edged sword. (D&C 6:2)

Each time Lucifer lunged toward the Lord with another temptation, the blow was countered as the Savior struck back with his "sword of the Spirit" by quoting a scripture which exposed the flaws in the Satanic suggestions and defined the spiritual issues.

> Not only will the word of God lead us to the fruit which is desirable above all others, but in the word of God and through it we can find the power to resist temptation, *the power to thwart the word of Satan and his emissaries.* (Ezra Taft Benson, *Ensign*, May 1986, 80)

One reason it is so important to internalize Christ's promises of power and deliverance is the effectiveness of this method for adding the sword of the Spirit to our armor. If we do not study and treasure and internalize the Savior's promises, we will not be able to use them to defend ourselves against Satan's attacks because they will not be available in our mental arsenal of weapons. We cannot call to mind the exact scripture needed at the time of temptation (as the Savior did) if we have not been studying and depositing them in our memory banks ahead of time.

> However diligent we may be in other areas, certain blessings are to be found only in the scriptures, only in coming to the word of the Lord and holding fast to it as we make our way through the mists of darkness to the tree of life. (Ezra Taft Benson, *Ensign*, May 1986, 82)

When we ignore the "sword of the Spirit" and attempt to defend ourselves from Satan's attacks with nothing but will power, he surrounds us with even more tempters and intensifies the attack. It is not likely that these demons will stay nearby to listen to us quote scripture. When we respond to Satan's attacks with the word of God, as Jesus did, we can drive the demons away just as surely as Satan was driven away from the presence of the Savior. In Appendix B, we will explain a process for protecting ourselves with the sword of the Spirit as we learn to use the scriptures as spiritual weapons. The evil spirits may not be eager to obey our commands, but they cannot resist the authority of God's word, especially as found in the Book of Mormon. As President Benson promised:

> Young men, the Book of Mormon will change your life. It will fortify you against the evils of our day. It will bring a spirituality into your life that no other book will . . . A young man who knows and loves the Book of Mormon, who has read it several times, who has an abiding testimony of its truthfulness, and who applies its teachings will be able to stand against the wiles of the devil and will be a mighty tool in the hands of the Lord. (*Ensign*, May 1986, 43)

As the ancient Israelites prepared to inherit the land of promise, the Lord promised them power over their *physical* enemies. Considering the legions of evil spirits who are working to prevent us from receiving our inheritance in the celestial kingdom, we might apply the promise in the following scripture to the power wielded against Satan's army by our spiritual swords.

> And ye shall chase your enemies, and they shall fall before you by the sword. And five of you shall chase an hundred, and an hundred of you shall put ten thousand to flight: and your enemies shall fall before you by the sword. (Leviticus 26:7–8)

PERSONALIZING THE PROMISES

One of the ways Satan's spirits try to defeat us after we have studied and identified the power principles and promises is to persuade us that they do not apply to us personally. "These promises may work for others," they lie, "but they do not apply to you." This is a serious attack because it would defeat the purpose in studying the scriptures if we then doubted their application to our personal situations. To create a strong spiritual armor we must not only trust the Lord's promises, but also recognize their application to *our* personal battles.

> For whatsoever things were written aforetime were written for our learning, that *we* through patience and comfort of the scriptures might have hope. (Romans 15:4)

We know that the Lord desires to treat everyone equally and without partiality because "he inviteth them all to come unto him and partake of his goodness; and he denieth none that come unto him . . . and all are alike unto God" (2 Nephi 26:33). When the Lord places the record of his dealings with specific individuals or groups of people in the scriptures, he does so to show that we also have the right and privilege to lay claim on every promise or principle we find there. Scriptural promises apply to us just as much as if God had spoken them to us personally, because, in reality, he did. Nephi taught that we should *"liken all scriptures unto us,* that it might be for our profit and learning" (1 Nephi 19:23).

It is so vital to our spiritual progress that we believe in the universal application of his promises that Christ has made it a commandment to interpret them this way: "And now I give unto you a commandment that what I say unto one I say unto all" (D&C 61:18; see also 61:36; 82:5). Having been commanded to consider his promises applicable to our own situations, we have no excuse to dismiss or rationalize them away. As Victor L. Ludlow, director of Bible studies and associate professor of ancient scripture at Brigham Young University said:

> To unlock Old Testament prophecy, *readers first need to relate to the scriptures and assume that God is speaking forth personally to them* (see Romans 15:4). If readers think that prophecies, warnings, and promises apply only to others, the scriptures remain distant, foreign, and hidden, and their great power is never unlocked. Since all of us in the Church are inheritors of the promises made to the house of Israel, we can particularly identify with the history and messages of the scriptures, and *we can read them as if Isaiah, Moses, and other prophets were not only speaking about us, but to us. (Ensign,* October 1990, 60)

As we seek to apply the scriptures to our personal situations, we can personalize them by actually inserting our own name into the verse. As Robert J. Matthews, dean of Religious Education at Brigham Young University, said:

> There are hundreds of promises from the Lord that are so casually stated that unless one is alerted to them, they almost go unnoticed. It is in these quiet promises that we can substitute our own name for those given in the revelation. Put your name

in front of it and the promise is yours. (*Church News*, September 2, 1989, 5).

Here are some examples of personalized scripture:

"Bear with patience thine afflictions, and, *[insert your name]*, I will give unto you success." (Alma 26:27)

"Come now, *[insert your name]*, and let us reason together, saith the Lord: though your sins be as scarlet, they shall be white as snow." (Isaiah 1:18)

Personalizing the expression of the promises can increase our faith in the power they have to change our lives and to draw us even closer to the Lord who gave them to lead us into victory. (Note: this section was adapted from a previous presentation by Steven A. Cramer. See *In The Arms of His Love*, American Fork, Utah: Covenant Communications, 1991, 129–31.) Appendix B will explain how to select the appropriate promise scriptures and how to internalize them so that they will come to our defense as we fight our battles with Satan.

21

Trusting the Promises

IF WE ARE TO WIN OUR BATTLES WITH SATAN, IT IS VITAL TO BELIEVE that God is going to fulfill his promises exactly as he said: "For *I will fulfil my promises* which I have made unto the children of men" (2 Nephi 10:17). And "as the words have gone forth out of my mouth *even so shall they be fulfilled*" (D&C 29:30).

As we try to apply the Lord's scriptural promises to our lives, Satan will be shouting at us that they won't work, that God is a fraud, that he lies, that his principles and promises only lead to frustration and defeat rather than growth and happiness. If we listen to Satan's untruths and accusations, it may indeed appear impossible for God to fulfill his promises, especially when we consider all our mistakes and the limitations of our overwhelmingly negative circumstances. But God is not limited by circumstances and his principles and promises always work—if we apply them properly: "For the eternal purposes of the Lord shall roll on, until *all his promises shall be fulfilled*" (Mormon 8:22).

It is natural to experience times when we doubt the Lord's promises and feel they just won't work for us. But always, as experience grows, we inevitably learn that the fault never lies with the promise or principle, but in ourselves. We lacked either the faith or the understanding to lift the promise off the pages of scripture into our hearts and minds.

Let's consider a young neighbor as an example. Richard knew it was possible to ride a bicycle because he saw the other children riding theirs. He yearned to join them. His parents purchased a bike, which he quickly learned to ride—provided that someone was there to lift him on and give him a starting push. But Richard's legs were just too short for him to get on the bike and get going by himself—or so he thought. It seemed impossible to do this by himself and he shed tears of frustration and disappointment. He must have told himself dozens of times how utterly hopeless it was. But starting on the bike by himself wasn't impossible for Richard at all. He simply needed to apply the proper principle and then he was able to experience the joy of independent biking. When Richard learned to lean the bike over sideways where his foot could reach the pedal, he was able to give himself an initial push forward while he righted the bike. Suddenly he was free. What had seemed impossible became easy because he learned how to apply a principle that gave him success. So it is when we lay claim to Christ's promises of power, grace, and deliverance. We, too, can win seemingly impossible battles. If our present lives do not reflect the righteousness and happiness the Lord means us to have, it is not because his promises and principles do not work, but simply that we have not yet learned how to apply them correctly.

A person who is trained and skilled can take an ordinary camera and obtain stunningly beautiful photographs, while an untrained person may take an extraordinarily expensive camera and obtain disgustingly poor pictures. Obviously, it is not the fault of the camera but of the user. Anyone who learns and applies the principles of photography can obtain the desired results. And so it is with applying gospel principles to obtain scriptural promises of spiritual development. There is only one power strong enough to prevent God from blessing us in fulfillment of his promises. It is not the power of Lucifer and his demons, for no evil spirit can thwart God's power. Only one person has the power to withhold God's blessings from you, and that person is *you*.

> Ye endeavored to believe that ye should receive the blessing which was offered unto you; but behold, verily I say unto you there were fears in your hearts, and verily this is the reason that ye did not receive. (D&C 67:3)

The scriptures make it clear that the responsibility for the flow of blessings from heaven rests upon *us* and not upon God. Only by failing to fulfill the requirements associated with God's blessings can we prevent his mercy and grace from flowing into our lives. "For all who will have a blessing at my hands shall abide the law which was appointed for that blessing, and the conditions thereof, as were instituted from before the foundation of the world" (D&C 132:5; see also 130:20–21). He has established the laws and conditions that govern our lives and made them plain to our understanding. "All truth is independent in that sphere in which God has placed it, *to act for itself*" (D&C 93:30). Hence, if we qualify through obedience and faith, the blessings will flow. If we disobey, our violation of the law restrains God's ability to bless us, for "I, the Lord, am bound when ye do what I say; but when ye do not what I say, ye have no promise" (D&C 82:10). Thus we read of ancient Israel preventing the Lord from blessing them because of their disobedience. "Yea, they turned back and tempted God, and *limited the Holy One of Israel*" (Psalms 78:41). Whenever we feel abandoned, or feel that his promises are not working for us, we must stop shaking our fists at the heavens and accusing God of defaulting on his promises, because it will always be inside our own hearts that we find the cause.

> I command and men obey not; I revoke and they receive not the blessing. Then they say in their hearts: This is not the work of the Lord, for his promises are not fulfilled. But wo unto such, for their reward lurketh beneath, and not from above. (D&C 58:32–33)
>
> What I the Lord have spoken, I have spoken, and I excuse not myself; and though the heavens and the earth pass away, *my word shall not pass away, but shall all be fulfilled.* (D&C 1:38)

The Lord declared the integrity of his promises when he said, "I have spoken it, I will also bring it to pass; I have purposed it, I will also do it" (Isaiah 46:11). He gave his promises to encourage us to come to him and to draw upon his power and love. He is prepared to deliver exactly as he has promised. "For as I, the Lord God, liveth, even so my words cannot return void, for as they go forth out of my mouth *they must be fulfilled*" Moses 4:30). Elder Glen L. Rudd said, "Faith is simply knowing that the Lord is there and that he will keep his promises to those who humbly approach him" (*Ensign*, January 1989, 71). "Now, the decrees of God are unalterable" (Alma 41:8). And "it is impossible for him to deny his word" (Alma 11:34). President N. Eldon Tanner said, "All I can do is take him at his word . . . he did not say anything he did not mean. He made no promise that he is not prepared to keep." (*Outstanding Stories by General Authorities,* comp. Leon R. Hartshorn, Salt Lake City, Utah: Deseret Book, 1970, 209) Every time we obey his law, every time we make claim upon a promise we find in his word, every time we allow his word to be fulfilled in our lives, we bring glory to the God who spoke it. And we add another defeat to Satan and his hosts who choose to believe that God's word and plan will not work, and who try constantly to dissuade our belief as well.

> For as the rain cometh down and the snow from heaven, and . . . watereth the earth, and maketh it bring forth and bud, that it may give seed to the sower, and bread to the eater:
> So shall my word be that goeth forth out of my mouth: *it shall not return unto me void, but it shall accomplish that which I please,* and it shall prosper in the thing whereto I sent it. (Isaiah 55:10–11)

The Savior sent his word to better our lives. If we accept the promises and claim them as ours, his words shall not return to him void, but will be fruitful in blessing us with the transformation he intended them to accomplish. If you have difficulty believing a promise you find in the scriptures, if the overwhelming circumstances of your present defeat make the promise seem impossible, try placing your faith in the Savior who made the promise and testified, "I cannot deny my word" (D&C 39:16). For "Who am I, saith the Lord, that have promised and have not fulfilled?" (D&C 58:31)

Jesus Christ gave each revelation, each principle and promise for a specific purpose. When we come to believe them, when we program our minds with them, internalize them, cling to them, keep them in the focus of our attention and affirmation, when we put his words to the test, he will prove that he does not lie nor exaggerate, "for the word of God must be fulfilled" (Alma 5:58). And "he proveth all his words" (2 Nephi 11:3). Indeed, the Lord has invited and challenged us to test him and prove him if he will not fulfill his words exactly as promised, (see Malachi 3:10) "And whosoever shall believe in my name, doubting nothing, *unto him will I confirm all my words, even unto the ends of the earth"* (Mormon 9:25).

There will be times when, in spite of our obedience, faith, and trust, the blessings we seek will be delayed. When the Lord promised to fulfill every word of promise, he was not obligating himself to grant blessings before we are sufficiently prepared. The principle of fulfillment is explained in these two verses:

> No good thing will he withhold from them that walk uprightly. (Psalms 84:11)
>
> I will *order* all things for your good, as fast as ye are able to receive them. (D&C 111:11)

We can trust the Lord, even when blessings are delayed, because he has not only promised to *grant* the blessings, but to actually *order* or command their fulfillment—but not before we are prepared to receive them. Hence, if we feel that we qualify and yet do not receive the expected blessings, we know there is a divine purpose in the delay and we can humbly ask for an explanation. We might pray: "Heavenly Father, in *(cite the scripture reference)* you promised *(state the blessing you seek),* and I believe these words are true. Father, I feel worthy to receive this blessing and I'm asking thee to teach me what more I need to do to qualify."

> And behold, I, the Lord, declare unto you, and my words are sure and shall not fail, that they shall obtain it. But all things must come to pass in their time. (D&C 64:31–32)
>
> And thus we see how merciful and just are all the dealings of the Lord, to the fulfilling of all his words unto the children of men. (Alma 50:19)

———◆———

The world has changed drastically since this book was first published. Evil has increased unimaginably, but the principles for winning our battles with Satan remain the same, and are just as effective today as they were then.

The next chapter, about the power of Family History and Temple Work to bring us added protection and divine power in our battles, has been added to expand our theme from merely "winning our battles with Satan," to taking advantage of the higher powers Heavenly Father has made available to us through temple and family history work to truly arm ourselves with righteousness.

I am grateful to my son, Don Curtis, for preparing this important addition to the book.

PART FOUR

Temple and
Family History

22

Armed with Righteousness

This chapter was written by Don Curtis, at the request of Steven Cramer.

THE POWERFUL COMBINATION OF TEMPLE WORSHIP AND FAMILY history can eliminate the influence of the adversary in our lives, give us power to overcome our trials, temptations, and even addictions, and give us joy as we, together with deceased family members, "come unto Christ, and be perfected in him" (Moroni 10:32).

I. TEMPLE WORSHIP

The Brethren have encouraged us over and over to attend the temple. Elder Bednar taught, "A temple literally is the house of the Lord, a sacred space specifically set apart for worshipping God and for receiving and remembering His great and precious promises" (David A. Bednar, "Exceeding Great and Precious Promises," *Ensign*, Nov. 2017). Those promises make temple attendance exceptionally compelling and motivate us to make temple worship a top priority. Here are some of them:

1.   We are perfected.
2.   We are protected.
3.   We are piloted.
4.   We are given power.
5.   We are given a place.

As we receive temple ordinances and covenants and as we worship in the temple, we are armed with righteousness.

1. WE ARE PERFECTED

President Hinckley implored, "**I urge our people everywhere, with all of the persuasiveness of which I am capable,** to live worthy to hold a temple recommend, to secure one and regard it as a precious asset, and to make a greater effort to go to the house of the Lord and partake of the spirit and the blessings to be had therein. I am satisfied that every man or woman who goes to the temple in a spirit of sincerity and faith leaves the house of the Lord a better man or woman" (Gordon B. Hinckley, "Of Missions, Temples, and Stewardship," *Ensign*, Nov. 1995, emphasis added).

Later President Hinckley added, "And so, my brothers and sisters, I encourage you to take greater advantage of this blessed privilege [of temple attendance]. It will refine your natures. It will peel off the selfish shell in which most of us live. It will literally bring a sanctifying element into our lives and make us better men and better women" (Gordon B. Hinckley, "Closing Remarks," *Ensign*, Nov. 2004).

I was witness to a dramatic example of the sanctifying influence of the temple. (Story related with permission.) Every Wednesday evening for two years, I served in the temple baptistry, assisting the patrons with baptisms and confirmations in behalf of those who didn't have that opportunity in their lifetime. One Wednesday evening, a man came to perform this service. At the time, we had been instructed to discourage adults from being baptized unless they brought their own family names so that the names provided by the temple could be used by the youth. But this situation was different because this man had a limited use recommend (given to worthy members who are not yet endowed), which was a bit unusual. He stood out, not just because he was an adult, but also because he had a rough, somewhat worldly look about him. The following week, he came to do baptisms again. When he came the third consecutive week, I introduced myself, and he told me a bit of his story.

Matt told me that he had become inactive as a teen and didn't go to church for many years. Over time he made lots of money, collected expensive "toys," and visited many exotic places. But his worldly lifestyle, with all the material possessions and travel, did not make him truly happy, and he often felt empty, with a longing for something better. Matt began to feel the Lord calling after him. "The Spirit spoke to me plain as day," he said, "saying, 'You have always known the church is true, yet you choose not to follow.' A few moments later the Spirit spoke again, saying, 'Matthew, why hast thou forsaken me? I have not forgotten you!'" For the next three or four years, the Lord helped Matt return to a circumstance in which he could repent and come unto Him. Matt said, "I was sick of walking in darkness. . . . I felt I had to make a choice to completely change before it was too late."

Matt did change. He studied the scriptures, reading the entire standard works in four months, and read other books to gain a fuller understanding of the gospel. He began meeting with his bishop and going through the repentance process until he was worthy to receive a temple recommend. Feeling regret for not having served a mission, Matt set a goal to, in his words, "be baptized for the armies of Helaman," or in other words, to be baptized for at least 2,060 people.

So Matt came faithfully to the temple—not just on Wednesdays but on most days and sometimes twice a day. He kept careful track of how many baptisms he did. Often after doing his allotted five names, he would get in line again to have the opportunity to do baptisms for another five names in the same evening. Day after day, week after week, and month after month, Matt came to the temple. I was privileged to be there the night that Matt was baptized for the 2,060th person—and a few more for good measure. But the true miracle is not that Matt accomplished his goal, but it is how the temple changed him. As the weeks and months went by, the rough look melted away and was replaced with light. Matt's countenance began to shine with the light of the gospel. Far from looking out of place, Matt was at home in the temple and the temple became part of him. Later, he shared with me a talk he had given in his ward. In it he said:

"I was fortunate enough to receive my temple recommend and start doing baptisms for the dead. It had been twenty years since I had done this great work, and I was more than ready to get back doing it. . . . The spiritual blessings that I have received are phenomenal. I have never been so blessed in every aspect of my life and in such a short period of time. This work I was doing helped my testimony grow more than any single work I had done before. I became addicted to feeling the Spirit and doing the work of the Lord."

Later, Matt received his endowments and became a baptistry worker himself. The temple played a large part in refining and sanctifying Matt, as President Hinckley promised. And Matt's experience didn't just change him—it strengthened all of us who worked in the baptistry and witnessed this miracle. The temple can help perfect each one of us as we sacrifice to attend as frequently as we can. As Elder Bednar said, the temple helps us to partake of the divine nature.

> A principal purpose of the temple is to elevate our vision from the things of the world to the blessings of eternity. Removed for a short time from the worldly settings with which we are familiar, we can "look to God and live" by receiving and remembering the great and precious promises whereby we become partakers of the divine nature. (David A. Bednar, "Exceeding Great and Precious Promises," *Ensign*, Nov. 2017)

2. We Are Protected

There is no doubt that the adversary has stepped up his game. The good news is that the Lord is also hastening His work and is providing His children with opportunities for additional protection and power. It's no accident that the Church has accelerated temple-building in our time. The dedicatory prayer for the Kirtland temple says: "That no weapon formed against them [who worship in the temple] shall prosper; that he who diggeth a pit for them shall fall into the same himself; That no combination of wickedness shall have power to rise up and prevail over thy people upon whom thy name shall be put in this house" (D&C 109:25–26).

President George Q. Cannon (1827–1901), First Counselor in the First Presidency, said, "Every foundation stone that is laid for a Temple, and every Temple completed . . . lessens the power of Satan on the earth, and increases the power of God and Godliness" (George Q. Cannon, "The Logan Temple," *Millennial Star*, 1877, p. 743). Similarly, John A. Widtsoe of the Quorum of the Twelve said, "President Young thought . . . that they also would have, if temple work were undertaken, a corresponding increase in power to overcome all evil. Men grow mighty under the results of temple service; women grow strong under it; the community increases in power; until the devil has less influence than he ever had before. The opposition to truth is relatively smaller if the people are engaged actively in the ordinances of the temple" (John A. Widtsoe, "Temple Worship," *Utah Genealogical and Historical Quarterly*, Apr. 1921, p. 51).

Elder Boyd K. Packer said, "No work is more of a protection to this Church than temple work and the genealogical research which supports it. No work is more spiritually refining. No work we do gives us more power. . . . Our labors in the temple cover us with a shield and a protection, both individually and as a people" (Boyd K. Packer, *The Holy Temple*, 1980, p. 265).

And Ezra Taft Benson said, "Our families will be protected, our children will be safeguarded as we live the gospel, visit the temple, and live close to the Lord" (*Teachings of Ezra Taft Benson*, p. 256). I love that the promised protection is not just for me, but that it extends to my family.

What can we do to increase the protection we receive from the temple? Three answers are to worship in the temple frequently, to honor the temple garment, and to keep our temple covenants.

By Worshiping in the Temple

The Lord wants us to receive the power and protection that the temple gives us. In 1997 President Hinckley stated, "We are determined . . . to take the temples to the people and afford them every opportunity for the very precious blessings that come of temple worship" (Gordon B. Hinckley, "Some Thoughts on Temples, Retention of Converts, and Missionary Service," *Ensign*, Nov. 1997). Thirteen years later, President Monson reported: "Eighty-five percent of the membership of the Church now live within 200 miles (320 km) of a temple, and for a great many of us, that distance is much shorter." He went on to encourage us to "make whatever sacrifices are necessary to attend the temple and to have the spirit of the temple in our hearts and in our homes" (Thomas S. Monson, "The Holy Temple—A Beacon to the World," *Ensign*, May 2011).

Brother Michael Wilcox shared his experience with seeking protection. "I went to the temple one afternoon to seek guidance about my children. . . . I told the Lord I was willing to offer any sacrifice if he would protect my children from Satan's power and bless them with his Spirit until they could come to his house and receive their own endowment. . . . As I sat in the temple, an answer was given in which the required sacrifice was revealed to me. . . . The Spirit simply whispered: 'This is the sacrifice I ask of you. Be in this house frequently, constantly, and consistently, and the promised protection you seek, which this house has the power to bestow, will be extended to those you love.'" He went on to say that he came to know that this promise wasn't unique to him but is "extended to all the Saints in behalf of those they love" (S. Michael Wilcox, *House of Glory*, pp. 47–48).

President Hunter encouraged us to attend the temple to receive its safety. "Let us truly be a temple-attending and a temple-loving people. We should hasten to the temple as frequently, yet prudently, as our personal circumstances allow. We should go not only for our kindred dead but also for the personal blessing of temple worship, for the sanctity and safety that are within those hallowed and consecrated walls. As we attend the temple, we learn more richly and deeply the purpose of life and the significance of the atoning sacrifice of the Lord Jesus Christ. Let us make the temple, with temple worship and temple covenants and temple marriage, our ultimate earthly goal and the supreme mortal experience" (Howard W. Hunter, "A Temple-Motivated People," *Ensign*, Feb. 1995).

By Honoring the Temple Garment

Elder Russell M. Nelson recommended (Russell M. Nelson, "Prepare for the Blessings of the Temple," *Ensign*, March 2002) that we read the *Ensign* article "The Temple Garment" by Carlos E. Asay (*Ensign*, August 1997), and I second his recommendation.

Elder Asay compares wearing the garment to taking upon one the whole armor of God. He says, "We must also 'put on the armor of righteousness' (2 Nephi 1:23) symbolized by the temple garment. Otherwise, we may lose the war and perish. . . . The piece of armor called the temple garment not only provides the comfort and warmth of a cloth covering, it also strengthens the wearer to resist temptation, fend off evil influences, and stand firmly for the right."

Receiving the protection of the garment requires that we keep our covenant to wear it. Elder Asay quotes a letter from the First Presidency that says, "The fundamental principle ought to be to wear the garment and not to find occasions to remove it. Thus, members should not remove either all or part of the garment to work in the yard or to lounge around the home in swimwear or immodest clothing. Nor should they remove it to participate in recreational activities that can reasonably be done with the garment worn properly beneath regular clothing. When the garment must be removed, such as for swimming, it should be restored as soon as possible."

A few years ago, in a training meeting in the temple, the temple president reminded us (ordinance workers) of the importance of wearing the garment and encouraged us to increase our devotion to wearing it and to find appropriate ways to wear it more.

I was feeling good about my commitment to always wear the garment, but as I prayerfully considered the challenge of the temple president, I was impressed that there was something more I could do—I could wear the garment during my exercising. So I put away my old exercise clothes—my tank tops and short shorts—and purchased some knee-length exercise shorts and some modest exercise shirts. From then on, I have worn the garment during my daily exercise. Yes, I sweat more, but that's not a problem if I keep myself hydrated, and I have felt an increased connection with my temple covenants and a greater protection from Heavenly Father.

I have thought about the battle of the Lamanites, who were led by Zerahemnah, against the Nephites, who were led by Moroni. "Now the army of Zerahemnah . . . were naked, save it were a skin which was girded about their loins" (Alma 43:20). When they met the Nephites, they "saw that the people of Nephi, or that Moroni, had prepared his people with breastplates and with arm-shields, yea, and also shields to defend their heads, and also they were dressed with thick clothing" (Alma 43:19). How did that make the Lamanites feel? Did they think something like, "That armor must be really heavy. They must be hot and sweaty and uncomfortable. The Nephites won't be nearly as agile and unrestricted as we are. I'm glad I chose not to put on such cumbersome armor." On the contrary! "They were exceedingly afraid of the armies of the Nephites because of their armor, notwithstanding their number being so much greater than the Nephites" (Alma 43:21). They were afraid with good reason. "And the work of death commenced on both sides, but it was more dreadful on the part of the Lamanites, for their nakedness was exposed to the heavy blows of the Nephites with their swords and their cimeters, which brought death almost at every stroke" (Alma 43:37).

Every day we are at war with the forces of evil. If we casually remove the garment, our armor of righteousness, we will be more exposed, as the Lamanites were, to the heavy blows of the adversary. Rather than feeling uncomfortable or restricted in our armor, we should feel safe and protected!

The garment has much in common with the sacrament. Both are symbols of the Savior and His atoning sacrifice. Both are a reminder of our covenants. Both are accompanied by promises from Heavenly Father. But in one way they are very different. We are commanded to "partake not of the sacrament of Christ unworthily" (Mormon 9:29). If there is a temptation we are struggling with, we may not be worthy to partake of the sacrament, but we must continue to keep our covenant to wear the garment. When we are wounded in the heat of a battle is not the time to remove our spiritual armor. We need its protection then more than ever!

Elder Asay quotes the First Presidency, "How it is worn is an outward expression of an inward commitment to follow the Savior." To receive the promised protection, we must do more than wear the garment—we must wear it properly. Elder Asay began his *Ensign* article with this story:

> A few years ago, in a seminar for new temple presidents and matrons, Elder James E. Faust, then of the Quorum of the Twelve Apostles, told about his being called to serve as a General Authority. He was asked only one question by President Harold B. Lee: "Do you wear the garments properly?" to which he answered in the affirmative. He then asked if President Lee wasn't going to ask him about his worthiness. President Lee replied that he didn't need to, for he had learned from experience that how one wears the garment is the expression of how the individual feels about the Church and everything that relates to it. It is a measure of one's worthiness and devotion to the gospel.

The garment is rich with symbolism. In the temple we are taught much of what that symbolism means. Elder Asay gives some of the historical context for the garment and says:

> They received this clothing in a context of instruction on the Atonement, sacrifice, repentance, and forgiveness (see Moses 5:5–8). The temple garment given to Latter-day Saints is provided in a similar context. It is given to remind wearers of the continuing need for repentance, the need to honor binding covenants made in the house of the Lord, and the need to cherish and share virtue in our daily living so that promised blessings may be claimed.

As a member of a high council I was a participant in a number of disciplinary councils. Not surprisingly, many of those we met with had stopped wearing the garment, forfeiting its protection. But the statement of one brother left an indelible impression on me. This brother indicated that he had worn his garment faithfully. But when asked how he felt about the garment, he paused and then admitted that it meant nothing to him—it was just the underclothing that he always wore. That statement set alarm bells ringing, making me question if I was giving the garment sufficient meaning in my life. Too often I have fallen into the same trap of thoughtlessly wearing the garment without considering its sacredness or meaning. I vowed that day to be more diligent in never taking for granted the wearing of the garment.

By Keeping Our Temple Covenants

Keeping our temple covenants gives us protection and power. Nephi saw this in vision: "And it came to pass that I, Nephi, beheld the power of the Lamb of God, that it descended . . . upon the covenant people of the Lord, . . . and they were armed with righteousness and with the power of God in great glory" (1 Nephi 14:14).

Elder Hales taught, "The ordinances and covenants of the temple are the protection for us in our trials and tribulations in our day and for what we will face in the future" (Elder Robert D. Hales, "Temple Blessings," *New Era*, Feb. 2014).

Elder Nelson also talked about the protection and power of covenants: "With each ordinance is a covenant—a promise. A covenant made with God is not restrictive, but protective. . . . When we choose to deny ourselves of all ungodliness, we lose nothing of value and gain the glory of eternal life. Covenants do not hold us down; they elevate us beyond the limits of our own power and perspective" (Russell M. Nelson, "Personal Preparation for Temple Blessings," *Ensign*, May 2001).

President Bonnie D. Parkin affirmed, "Covenants also protect us from being 'tossed to and fro, carried about with every wind of doctrine, by the sleight of men, and cunning craftiness.' Women of covenant stand firm when evil is called good and good is called evil. . . . Remembering our covenants keeps us from being led astray. Covenants can keep us and those we love spiritually safe and spiritually prepared" (Bonnie D. Parkin, "With Holiness of Heart," *Ensign*, Nov. 2002).

After receiving her endowments, my daughter asked me about the sacrament. "When we partake of the sacrament, which covenants do we renew—only our baptismal covenants or our temple covenants as well?" I had always assumed it was our baptismal covenants that we renewed with the sacrament, but I told her I would research it and let her know what I found. It didn't take long to find the answer.

> According to our latter-day prophets and leaders, when you partake of the sacrament you renew whatever covenants you have made with the Lord. For example, if you have been baptized only, that is the covenant you renew. If you have received the Melchizedek Priesthood, you also renew that part of the oath and covenant related to your having received that priesthood. If you have received your endowment, you also renew the covenants associated with it. Further, if you have been sealed, you also renew that covenant. In other words, when you partake of the sacrament, you renew all the covenants you have made with the Lord. ("I Have a Question," *Ensign*, March 1995; see also "Understanding our Covenants with God," *Ensign*, July 2012)

Knowing that has made the ordinance of the sacrament much more meaningful to me. As I partake of the sacrament, remembering each covenant I have made and pondering how I can improve my keeping of the covenants, I am blessed with greater desire and commitment and strength. I'm so grateful she asked that question!

Sometimes when I feel overwhelmed by my weakness and all the covenants I've made, it helps me to remember what Elder Boyd K. Packer said:

> When you come to the temple and receive your endowment, and kneel at the altar and be sealed, you can live an ordinary life and be an ordinary soul—struggling against temptation, failing and repenting, and failing again and repenting, but always determined to keep your covenants. . . . Then the day will come when you will receive the benediction: "Well done, thou good and faithful servant: thou hast been faithful over a few things, I will make thee ruler over many things; enter thou into the joy of thy lord" (Matthew 25:21). (Boyd K. Packer, *Let Not Your Heart Be Troubled*, 1991, p. 257)

The Lord gives this promise to those who strive to keep their covenants: "Keep all the commandments and covenants by which ye are bound; and I will cause the heavens to shake for your good, and Satan shall tremble and Zion shall rejoice upon the hills and flourish" (D&C 35:24).

3. WE ARE PILOTED

I can relate to hymn 104, which starts, "Jesus, Savior, pilot me over life's tempestuous sea." Life, even in its calmest moments, often feels tempestuous. We all need the Savior at the helm, directing our path through life. President Hinckley taught that we can receive the Lord's direction in the temple.

> The temple is also a place of personal inspiration and revelation. Legion are those who in times of stress, when difficult decisions must be made and perplexing problems must be handled, have come to the temple in a spirit of fasting and prayer to seek divine direction. Many have testified that while voices of revelation were not heard, impressions concerning a course to follow were experienced at that time or later which became answers to their prayers. (Gordon B. Hinckley, "The Salt Lake Temple," *Ensign*, March 1993)

Mormon taught that "we have a labor to perform whilst in this tabernacle of clay, that we may conquer the enemy of all righteousness, and rest our souls in the kingdom of God" (Moroni 9:6). Elder Pingree noted that the labor the Lord wants from one person may be different from what he wants from someone else:

> To Moses, God declared, "I have a work for thee" (Moses 1:6). Have you ever wondered if Heavenly Father has a work for you? Are there important things He has prepared you—and specifically you—to accomplish? I testify the answer is yes! . . . President Spencer W. Kimball taught: 'Before we came [to earth, we] were given certain assignments. . . . While we do not now remember the particulars, this does not alter the glorious reality of what we once agreed to.'" (John C. Pingree Jr., "I Have a Work for Thee," *Ensign*, Nov. 2017)

Sister Wixom also affirmed that there is an individual plan for each of us: "I testify that life is a gift. God has a plan for each one of us, and our individual purpose began long before we came to this earth" (Rosemary M. Wixom, "Discovering the Divinity Within," *Ensign*, Nov. 2015).

We may ask, "If God has an individual plan for me, how do I find out what it is?" One way we can answer that question is by worshipping and seeking in the temple. In the temple, we are taught Heavenly Father's Plan of Salvation for His children. In the temple we can also be taught His individual plan for each of us.

Elder Packer wrote, "The teaching of the temples is done in symbolic fashion. . . . That is why the teachings have so many applications to so many facets of our lives (Boyd K. Packer, *The Holy Temple*, 1980, p. 38).

When I first received my endowment and began to learn the temple teachings, I was determined to learn what all the temple symbols were and what each meant. One by one, I began to attach meaning to the symbols and, in effect, crossed them off my mental list of things to learn. But over time, I realized what a fallacy it was to think that each symbol had one and only one specific meaning. The beauty of symbolic teaching is that the Spirit can use the symbols to teach us whatever it is that we need to know at any given time.

This was drilled home to me in a story I heard about a seminary student who was struggling with her testimony. Her seminary teacher committed her to read a chapter of the Book of Mormon each night and to discuss it with him the next day. He had her skip some chapters, such as the quotes of Isaiah, to keep her from getting discouraged. Eventually, her reading took her to Jacob chapter 5—the longest chapter in the Book of Mormon, a symbolic allegory of wild and tame olive trees. The seminary teacher realized too late that he had forgotten to have her skip that chapter and worried how she might react to it. When she came in to discuss the chapter, she shocked him by announcing that she'd had the most spiritual experience of her life reading Jacob 5:37.

> But behold, the wild branches have grown and have overrun the roots thereof; and because that the wild branches have overcome the roots thereof it hath brought forth much evil fruit; and because that it hath brought forth so much evil fruit thou beholdest that it beginneth to perish; and it will soon become ripened, that it may be cast into the fire, except we should do something for it to preserve it.

As she read that verse, the Spirit told her that she was the tree and her boyfriend was the wild branch causing her to begin to perish. She felt it was true and immediately called her boyfriend and told him that she was breaking up with him because he was a wild branch, and that was that. Jacob 5:37 changed her life!

When Zenos wrote that allegory, was he thinking about that seminary student? Surely not. But the Lord used those symbols to inspire her with what she needed to know and to do. Similarly, if we worship in the temple, prayerfully seeking to know the Lord's will, He can use the temple symbols to inspire each of us with what we need to know and to do.

President Benson taught, "In the peace of these lovely temples, sometimes we find solutions to the serious problems of life. Under the influence of the Spirit, sometimes pure knowledge flows to us there. Temples are places of personal revelation. When I have been weighed down by a problem or a difficulty, I have gone to the House of the Lord with a prayer in my heart for answers. These answers have come in clear and unmistakable ways" (Ezra Taft Benson, "What I Hope You Will Teach Your Children about the Temple," *Ensign*, Aug. 1985).

The key to receiving answers is to ask questions. As we prayerfully ask and seek and knock (see Matthew 7:7) in the temple and open our hearts to the Spirit, the answers will come. These are some of the many questions I've taken to the Lord in His house and received answers to:

Should we have another child?
Should I accept this job offer?
Who should be my counselors?
Will you heal my daughter?
How can I forgive this person?
Should we move to that city?
Will you prolong my life?
How can I improve my marriage?
And even, How can I solve this technical problem at work?

Not all answers have been what I wanted or expected, and some were preliminary answers about what I needed to do to get the answer. Other answers I'm still waiting for, but I trust that the Lord will provide them when the time is right.

Hymn 104 ends with, "May I hear thee say to me, 'Fear not; I will pilot thee.'" I testify that listening closely in the temple, we can hear the Savior's loving reply, "Yes, I am here, and I will pilot thee."

4. We Are Given Power

The Lord wants to share his power with us, and that's one reason He has asked us to build temples. "Yea, verily I say unto you, I gave unto you a commandment that you should build a house, in the which house I design to endow those whom I have chosen with power from on high" (D&C 95:8).

The dedicatory prayer of the Kirtland temple makes it clear that arming us with power is a primary purpose of temples. "And we ask thee, Holy Father, that thy servants may go forth from this house armed with thy power, and that thy name may be upon them, and thy glory be round about them, and thine angels have charge over them" (D&C 109:22).

Elder Hales explained why it was so important for the pioneers to receive their temple ordinances before leaving Nauvoo: they needed God's power for what lay ahead.

The Nauvoo Temple was the first latter-day temple in which endowments and sealings were performed, which proved a great strength to the pioneers as they endured the hardships crossing the plains to Zion in the Salt Lake Valley.

When Joseph Smith was taken to Carthage, it was clear why the completion of the temple had meant so much to him. He knew what was going to be required of the Saints and that to have the strength to endure what was ahead of them they had to be endowed with power—the power of the priesthood.

For these early Saints, their participation in the ordinances of the temple was essential to their testimonies as they faced the hardships, the angry mobs, being driven from comfortable homes in Nauvoo, and the long and difficult journey ahead. They had been endowed with power in the holy temple. (Robert D. Hales, "Temple Blessings," *New Era*, February 2014)

My sister, Janae, is a woman of faith who inspires me with the power she receives from the temple. (Story related with permission.) This past summer was an extremely difficult one for Janae and her husband, Jeff. Their daughter chose to be married outside the temple—a heartbreaking disappointment for them. Of her feelings, Janae said, "I struggled a lot and grieved because of her choice. I needed help and strength from Heavenly Father to be able to see past my own feelings of hurt and disappointment and continue to love her where she was at, to be able to maintain a good relationship with her and strive to develop a relationship with her fiancé." Janae related that she found that help and strength by going many times to the temple.

Janae and Jeff had agreed to host a family reunion for Jeff's side of the family. Their daughter wanted to have the wedding shortly after—just two days later—so that family would be there to attend.

Then Janae and Jeff were asked to host a family reunion for Janae's side of the family as well. Agreeing to that seemed out of the question, not just because of what was already happening but also because there were some deep wounds that Janae and Jeff were suffering from in sibling relationships in Janae's family. Janae said, "I did not have much desire to be around the family who had engendered so much pain in my heart." Janae explained that as she considered her answer, she took it to the Lord and "spent much time with Him in His house, seeking to know His will." The answer came that they should do it, and Janae expressed her faith saying, "I knew He would be there to support me and bless me with His love for my family that I was struggling to feel for them on my own."

That family reunion was to be immediately before the reunion for Jeff's side of the family, so in 10 days Janae and Jeff would host two reunions, a wedding, and a reception! She continued to go to the temple and said, "From long experience I have learned that without fail, whenever I have felt too stressed, too busy, or too lacking in anything, Heavenly Father would strengthen me, give me peace, revelation, guidance, protection or whatever I needed . . . . Because of this, I went forward with faith knowing that I was doing His will and that He would sustain and support me."

Janae said that the week before the reunions and wedding she was feeling stressed and overwhelmed by the long list of things that needed to be done. To obtain peace and clarity, she went to the temple three times that week! And then she said, "People came forward and offered their help in our preparations and I was able to get everything done much faster than I would have on my own. I had an increase of love for my daughter as well as for my other family members. . . . I knew I had received grace and power from the Savior's atoning sacrifice. I felt God's love and watched His miracles flow."

I know that as we exercise our faith, seeking for divine help and worshipping in the temple, each of us will be blessed with similar power to meet our challenges.

5. We Are Given a Place

The Lord said, "In my Father's house are many mansions. . . . I go to prepare a place for you" (John 14:2). What place is He preparing for you and for me? To Alma, the Lord said, "it is I that granteth unto him that believeth unto the end a place at my right hand" (Mosiah 26:23). That is the goal—to have a place at His right hand. And the Savior taught us how to get a place there:

> And he shall set the sheep on his right hand, but the goats on the left. Then shall the King say unto them on his right hand, Come, ye blessed of my Father, inherit the kingdom prepared

for you from the foundation of the world: For I was an hungred, and ye gave me meat: I was thirsty, and ye gave me drink: I was a stranger, and ye took me in: Naked, and ye clothed me: I was sick, and ye visited me: I was in prison, and ye came unto me.

Then shall the righteous answer him, saying, Lord, when saw we thee an hungred, and fed thee? or thirsty, and gave thee drink? When saw we thee a stranger, and took thee in? or naked, and clothed thee? Or when saw we thee sick, or in prison, and came unto thee?

And the King shall answer and say unto them, Verily I say unto you, Inasmuch as ye have done it unto one of the least of these my brethren, ye have done it unto me. (Matthew 25:33–40)

As I pondered this scripture one day, I came to realize that we meet all these criteria for a place at His right hand through temple service. In the temple, we feed those deceased persons who hunger after righteousness with the "bread of life" (John 6:35), and to those who thirst we give "living water" (John 4:10). In the baptistry, we bring the departed out of spirit prison and into the fold where they "are no more strangers and foreigners, but fellow citizens with the saints, and of the household of God" (Ephesians 2:19). And in the initiatory ordinances, we clothe the naked with the temple garment.

Temple service not only saves the dead—it saves us and our families, and, if we remain faithful, it secures for us a place at the right hand of The King.

II. Family History

Having learned of the great and precious promises of the temple, I was surprised when Elder Scott said that those blessings are only half what we can receive if we will also find our own family names and do the temple work for them:

There are some members who engage in temple work but fail to do family history research on their own family lines. Although they perform a divine service in assisting others, they lose a blessing by not seeking their own kindred dead as divinely directed by latter-day prophets. . . .

I have learned that those who engage in family history

research and then perform the temple ordinance work for those whose names they have found will know the additional joy of receiving both halves of the blessing.

Any work you do in the temple is time well spent, but receiving ordinances vicariously for one of your own ancestors will make the time in the temple more sacred, and even greater blessings will be received.

Father in Heaven wants each of us to receive both parts of the blessing of this vital vicarious work. . . . It is up to you and me to claim those blessings. (Richard G. Scott, "The Joy of Redeeming the Dead," General Conference, Oct. 2012)

For much of my life, genealogy was an interest but seemed out of reach. It required an incredible commitment both in terms of the learning curve of knowing what to do and how to do it and in terms of the time and money it took to do effective research. Thankfully, in the past few years that has dramatically changed. Now almost anyone with desire, basic computer skills, and a bit of training can find family names to submit for ordinance work.

Just as the Lord has hastened temple building, He has also provided new technologies and tools to make family history more accessible and easier to do, and he has asked us to hasten that work. "The First Presidency has encouraged members . . . to emphasize family history work and ordinances for their own family names or the names of ancestors of their ward and stake members. . . . Hastening family history and temple work in our day is essential for the salvation and exaltation of families" (Quentin L. Cook, "Roots and Branches," *Ensign*, May 2014).

Doctrine and Covenants 128:15 says, "And now, my dearly beloved brethren and sisters, let me assure you that these are principles in relation to the dead and the living that cannot be lightly passed over, as pertaining to our salvation. For their salvation is necessary and essential to our salvation, as Paul says concerning the fathers—that they without us cannot be made perfect—neither can we without our dead be made perfect."

It's always been clear to me why the dead cannot be made perfect without us—they need us to find their information and do their temple work. It's been less clear to me why we cannot be made perfect without them. But as I've pondered that question, I've come to under-stand that we need the blessings of family history and temple work to have the power and protection to make it through the challenges of our time and to become like Jesus. "Never forget that family history—and the temple ordinances enabled by it—is an essential part of the work of salvation and that participation in this sacred work for the dead blesses the lives of the living" (Quentin L. Cook, "The Joy of Family History Work," *Ensign*, Feb. 2016).

What are the "even greater blessings," referred to by Elder Scott, of doing family history? Here are a few that have been promised us:

1. *THE INFLUENCE OF THE ADVERSARY IS ELIMINATED.*

The adversary's influence on us isn't just decreased—it is eliminated!

> Do you . . . want a sure way to eliminate the influence of the adversary in your life? Immerse yourself in searching for your ancestors, prepare their names for the sacred vicarious ordi-nances available in the temple, and then go to the temple to stand as proxy for them to receive the ordinances . . . I can think of no greater protection from the influence of the adversary in your life. (Richard G. Scott, "The Joy of Redeeming the Dead," *Ensign*, Nov. 2012)

This blessing of protection from the influence of the adversary is one of the most frequently promised in recent years by the brethren, making family history an essential part of putting on the armor of righteousness.

2. *OUR CONVERSION TO THE SAVIOR BECOMES DEEP AND ABIDING.*

In addition to protecting us against the adversary's influence, family history also increases our conversion to the Savior. As Elder David A. Bednar taught:

> I encourage you to study, to search out your ancestors, and to prepare yourselves to perform proxy [ordinances] in the house

of the Lord for your kindred dead. And I urge you to help other people identify their family histories.

As you respond in faith to this invitation, . . . Your love and gratitude for your ancestors will increase. Your testimony of and conversion to the Savior will become deep and abiding. And I promise you will be protected against the intensifying influence of the adversary. As you participate in and love this holy work, you will be safeguarded in your youth and throughout your lives.

Brothers and sisters, family history is not simply an interesting program or activity sponsored by the Church; rather, it is a vital part of the work of salvation and exaltation. You have been prepared for this day and to build up the kingdom of God. You are here upon the earth now to assist in this glorious work. (David A. Bednar, "The Hearts of the Children Shall Turn," *Ensign*, Nov. 2011)

3. WE RECEIVE POWER TO CHANGE AND TO HEAL.

Family history will give us great personal power.

As you take this challenge, to "find as many names to take to the temple as ordinances you perform in the temple, and teach others to do the same" . . . You'll find not only protection from the temptation and ills of this world, but you'll also find personal power—power to change, power to repent, power to learn, power to be sanctified, and power to turn the hearts of your family together and heal that which needs healing. (Dale G. Renlund, "Opening General Session," Family Discovery Day, Rootstech 2016)

4. WE RECEIVE MORE CLOSENESS AND JOY IN OUR FAMILIES.

"As an Apostle of the Lord Jesus Christ, I promise that if you look beyond the bonds of time and mortality and help those who cannot help themselves [by doing family history], you will be blessed with more closeness and joy in your family and with the divine protection afforded those who are faithful in His service" (Quentin L. Cook, "The Joy of Family History Work," *Ensign*, Feb. 2016).

My son created a picture pedigree on a wall in his home of the ancestors of his children. He is teaching them the importance and value of their heritage. When I expressed admiration for his picture pedigree, he offered to do one for me for my birthday. Now in my home office on the wall above my desk is this pedigree (see picture below). On the bottom of each picture is the name of the person (grayed out here). This has been a source of many conversations and has been a joy to have. Not long ago, my eight-year-old granddaughter asked me, "Grandpa, who are all those people on your wall?" That led to a tender teaching moment with her. Family history truly can and does bring families closer together.

5. WE RECEIVE HELP IN ALL THE AREAS OF OUR LIFE.

Brother Widtsoe taught that those on the other side will help us as we do family history.

> Brother Widtsoe reaffirmed that "those who give themselves with all their might and main to [family history] work receive help from the other side. . . . Whoever seeks to help those on the other side receives help in return in all the affairs of life." (Boyd K. Packer, *The Holy Temple*, 1980, p. 252)

As my wife, Penny, and I have done the temple work for our family members, we have often felt strongly their presence with us, inside the temple and out. I have no doubt that many, if not all of them, are aware of our efforts and are blessing our lives in return.

Penny relates that she has often received special help from family members from the other side of the veil on the days she plans to attend the temple. She has felt their anxiousness to have their work done, and she has been given additional strength and received inspiration on how to get her own work done—and get it done more efficiently—so that she could go to the temple to do their work.

Sister Nelson shared that she has had similar experiences: "I realized that if I was working on an overwhelming project and I was out of time, energy, and ideas, if I would make a sacrifice of time by finding the ordinance-qualifying information for some ancestors or by going to the temple to be proxy for them, the heavens opened and the energy and ideas started flowing. Somehow I had enough time to meet my deadline. It was totally impossible, but it would happen every time" (Russell M. Nelson and Wendy W. Nelson, "Open the Heavens through Temple and Family History Work," *Ensign*, Oct. 2017).

This list of five of the promised blessings of family history makes it clear that adding this work to our temple worship can indeed double our blessings as promised by Elder Scott. As I have made family history a priority in my own life, I have received great blessings. One of those is the joy I feel in doing the temple work for my ancestors, a fulfillment of the Lord's promise when He said: "And now, if your joy will be great with one soul that you have brought unto me into the kingdom of my Father, how great will be your joy if you should bring many souls unto me!" (D&C 18:16).

III. Conclusion

Steven Cramer and his wife have served a temple mission in Panama and a family history mission at the Family History Center in Salt Lake City, Utah. They continue to be examples of and strong proponents for temple worship and family history. I conclude with some powerful words that Steven Cramer was inspired to write and send to me.

> As we seek to resist, overcome and conquer the bad habits and
> sinful addictions that Satan has helped us create, it is natural for
> us to focus our resistance to such weaknesses head-on. Because

of that natural man response, it is also common to feel baffled, perhaps even doubtful and skeptical of apostolic and prophetic promises that our efforts in family history and bringing temple ordinances to our ancestors can do more for our spirituality than it can do for them. And that is amazing to think about when we know that if they accept the ordinances, it will mean they will be freed from the spirit prison and enter paradise, where they will mingle with the righteous saints, even with deceased apostles and prophets in that realm.

But if we do that selfless work for them, promises from the prophets teach us that we too can be freed from our own spiritual prisons and enter a new, born-again realm of freedom from the unworthy desires, appetites and passions that have held us in captivity. And that we will experience joy and happiness unimaginable to those who choose to dwell in darkness.

So, while our first glance at family history and temple work may seem to be a detour in pursuing our struggles to overcome and rise above our past faults, the reality is that it can put us on a fast track that is only available to those who participate.

Epilogue

We have uncovered "the cunning and the snares and the wiles of the devil" (Helaman 3:29). Our blindfolds have been removed. If we are watchful, he will never again "get an advantage of us: for we are not ignorant of his devices" (2 Corinthians 2:11).

We have learned that one theme running throughout every strategy is Satan's vicious whispering that we are worthless and unworthy of the Lord's help in our battles. But he can never defeat us with that lie again because we now recognize its origin. Brigham Young said that regardless of what mistakes a person might have made, "the least, the most inferior person now upon the earth . . . is worth worlds" (*Journal of Discourses,* vol. 9:124). And Sister Mary Ellen Edmunds, of the Relief Society General Board, said:

> Our worth is not a result of circumstance, or even of our particular level of obedience or righteousness. It is part of our heritage as children of God. *No condition, no action, no attitude or thought can change or diminish the love he has for us or the worth of our souls in his sight or his plan.* Our worthiness may change, but our worth is eternal in the eyes of our all-knowing, all-loving Heavenly Father. (*Ensign*, August 1990, 51)

Because of our infinite worth in the eyes of God, Isaiah's prophetic description of Christ's mission contained these encouraging and comforting words, written as though the Savior were speaking:

> The Spirit of the Lord God is upon me; because the Lord hath anointed me to preach good tidings unto the meek; he hath sent

me to bind up the brokenhearted, to proclaim liberty to the captives, and the opening of the prison to them that are bound . . .
to comfort all that mourn;

To appoint unto them that mourn in Zion, to give unto them
beauty for ashes, the oil of joy for mourning, the garment of
praise for the spirit of heaviness. (Isaiah 61:1–3)

All this is ours for the taking when we shun Satan's influence
and turn fully to the Lord. As for Lucifer and his demons, there is a
terrible doom awaiting them. Their dismal destiny is to be "cast out
into outer darkness," where there will be endless "weeping and wailing, and gnashing of teeth" (Alma 40:13). Their eternity will be spent
in "everlasting fire, prepared for the devil and his angels" (Matthew
25:41), where "their torment is as a lake of fire and brimstone, whose
flame ascendeth up forever and ever and has no end" (2 Nephi 9:16).
Unfortunately, there will be many of Father's children who join them
in that hell of eternal darkness and endless torment, for ". . . the final
state of the souls of men is to dwell in the kingdom of God, or to
be cast out because of that justice of which I have spoken" (1 Nephi
15:35). As our time together comes to an end, I ask you to make a commitment right now, before you close this book, that no matter what
Satan and his demons try to do, you will never, never give up.

O my brethren, hearken unto my words; arouse the faculties of
your souls; *shake yourselves that ye may awake from the slumber of
death; and loose yourselves from the pains of hell* that ye may not
become angels to the devil, to be cast into that lake of fire and
brimstone which is the second death. (Jacob 3:11)

If you will make that resolve and keep it, the time will surely come
when you will stand tall before your Heavenly Father and report, with
honor and integrity, "I have fought a good fight, I have finished my
course, I have kept the faith" (2 Timothy 4:7). And in return, they will
say to you, "Well done, thou good and faithful servant . . . enter thou
into the joy of thy Lord" (Matthew 25:21).

We close this book with the experience of two families who were
spending a holiday in a house boat on Lake Powell. It was a happy
occasion until their twelve-year-old daughter fell over the side and
disappeared beneath the boat, which was under power. The father

immediately dove to the rescue. He found her in a frightening situation at the rear of the boat. Her clothing was twisted in the propeller and she hung there, trapped and helpless to get free. The frantic father surfaced and quickly told them to bring knives to cut her loose. Then he began a series of dives, giving her air from his own lungs. He would put his mouth on hers, force the air into her lungs and then struggle for breath himself as he fought his way to the surface, gulped more air and returned again and again until the others could dive below and cut her free.

As I have pondered this remarkable rescue, my mind has been drawn to consider the incredible situations into which Satan gets us tangled. Because of his cunning attacks, we fall from the straight and narrow path and plunge into the waters of sin and unworthy habits. Many of us are nearly strangled from the guilt and hopelessness we feel as we find ourselves entangled beyond our own ability to break free. We suffocate from self-loathing and gasp for a breath of forgiveness and freedom. But we no longer need to despair because now we know that our loving Savior has the power and the determination to rescue us from our captivities and lead us gently, step by step, while he works out the process of rescue and transformation, so that our victories will be complete and we are fully his.

One can easily imagine the anguish of the frantic mother, brothers, sisters, and friends on that boat as they watched, waiting anxiously to welcome their loved one back to safety. And we can also imagine the happy shouting and joyful hugging on that boat when they finally brought this girl up from the waters of death. To win our battles with Satan we need to think about the rejoicing that occurs in heaven when we are cut free from *our* entanglements with sin. And we need to project ourselves forward in time and space to that glorious reunion that will someday take place on the other side of the veil. We need to envision the future joy and rejoicing that we will experience as we receive the welcoming embrace and approval of our Father and Mother in Heaven, and the Savior, who made it all possible. Cling to that vision. Dream of it, long for it, keep it alive in your mind and your heart, and someday it will be yours.

> He that overcometh shall inherit all things; and I will be his God, and he shall be my son. (Revelation 21:7)

PART FIVE

Resource Materials

Appendix A

Breaking the Cycle of Masturbation

This appendix is presented here because of the prevalence of the habit of masturbation and because I have been asked by hundreds of men, women, bishops, and therapists for specific steps one can use to conquer this debilitating addiction. The following suggestions have proven effective with a wide variety of individuals—when applied in harmony with the other principles explained in this book.

For the majority of addicts, the two major battlegrounds with masturbation are encountered either in the bathroom or in the bedroom. We will discuss bedroom strategies first. Satan is aware that a person is vulnerable when tired, and he uses that vulnerability to attack him or her—not only as the person goes to sleep, but also during the sleep and again on awakening. If we are not living worthy of the Lord's protection, or if we do not know how to protect ourselves and shield our bedrooms from their presence, Satan's spirits of lust can invade our bedrooms during the night, whispering suggestions that cause lewd dreams and arouse desires even while we are asleep. The Lord has given us spiritual armor with which to protect ourselves so that we are not influenced by demons as we sleep. Let us consider a seven-point formula for putting on the armor of God so that we can win both our bathroom and our nighttime battles.

1. Hang your favorite picture of the Savior by your bed and look at it while you prepare for the night. Think about his promises to provide power and divine assistance in your battles. Realize that you are not going to face the night's conflicts with Satan all by yourself. As you dress for bed, renew your covenants to the Lord as if he were actually

there with you in the bedroom. Know that he will be watching while you sleep. "He that keepeth Israel shall neither slumber nor sleep" (Psalms 121:4). The Lord has promised, "mine eyes are upon you. I am in your midst and ye cannot see me." (D&C 38:7) Looking at the Savior's picture will remind you of his loving concern and desire to protect you through the night, and will also redirect your emotions from the carnal to the spiritual.

2. What the brain focuses on during the last moments before sleep has a profound effect upon the things that take place in the mind during sleep. Never go to sleep without first pondering some scriptures so that you carry that holy spirit into your slumber. You could read directly from the scriptures or you could review some of the 3 x 5 cards containing the "combat scriptures" listed in Appendix B. Be aware that Satan and his demons will always try to distract you from the scriptures. They will be chanting how tired you are, that it won't hurt to skip this one time, that you already know what they say anyhow or that it really has nothing to do with your problems, etc. Succumbing to these whisperings and going to bed without reading scripture allows the mind to wander into lustful thoughts, memories, and fantasies, and sets you up for failure. By filling your mind with scriptural promises of divine aid, your spirit will be prepared to be on guard and do battle against the enemy's lewd whisperings while your body is asleep. Each time you crawl into bed, promise the Savior, "I remember thee upon my bed, and meditate on thee in the night watches" (Psalms 63:6).

3. Never get into bed without having real communication with the Lord. Satan's spirits will be screaming all their tired old lies to keep you from prayer, but don't listen. As you struggle through Satan's urgings not to pray, commit yourself as the repentant David did, "I will not give sleep to mine eyes, or slumber to mine eyelids, until I find out a place for the Lord." (Psalms 132:4–5). If you don't really *feel* like praying you can say so and ask the Lord to change your feelings. If you fear being tempted by masturbation, admit that you are entering a battleground of desire and ask the Lord to be with you. Testify to him that you believe in his promises of protection and deliverance, and that you are asking him to honor them in your life, *tonight*.

4. Pray not only for help *getting* to sleep, but also for protection

while you sleep. "When thou liest down at night lie down unto the Lord, *that he may watch over you in your sleep"* (Alma 37:37). Make it a practice to remind the Lord that you are aware of the evil spirits who try to disturb your sleep and fill your mind with erotic dreams. Ask for his protection from them. The Lord told Abraham "I am thy shield." (Genesis 15:1). And Samuel recorded, "He is my shield, and the horn of my salvation, my high tower, and my refuge, my saviour" (2 Samuel 22:3). You will sleep calmly when you have faith that the Lord will shield you during the night. "For thou, Lord, wilt bless the righteous; with favour wilt thou compass him as with a shield" (Psalms 5:12). Don't let Satan talk you out of these promises of protection, for they make no demand on perfection and are available to every sincerely repentant person. The Savior is anxious to be invited to protect you from the demons. Ask him to place a spiritual shield around your bed so that the evil spirits cannot affect you.

5. When sleep is prevented because of lustful desires, or if you awaken during the night inflamed with desire, get out of bed and back on your knees. Pour out your heart. Cry if you need to. Tell the Lord that you, the eternal spirit self, his child, do not want to gratify those desires of your body. And ask him to remove them and give your spirit dominion over your flesh. The Lord can actually change your desires when you ask him to. He can even be the God of our wayward, addicted flesh if it is surrendered to him. "Behold," he said, "I am the Lord, the God of all flesh: is there any thing too hard for me?" (Jeremiah 32:27) As you struggle to conquer this compelling habit, don't defeat yourself by relying upon your limited will power alone, but put your faith in Christ's power to help you.

6. When you awake in the morning, victorious for one night, fall on your knees and give God the glory. Praise him for your deliverance. Express your gratitude and ask his help in restraining your lust throughout the coming day. "When thou risest in the morning let thy heart be full of thanks unto God; and if ye do these things, ye shall be lifted up at the last day" (Alma 37:37).

7. Many people who are struggling with the habit of masturbation experience difficulty in other locations, especially the bathroom. Knowing a person's vulnerability, evil spirits will accompany him into

the bathroom to whisper suggestions urging indulgence. If the bathroom is a danger spot for acting out your habit, say a prayer before entering.

Frankly admit your vulnerability and then pray for the strength to get in and get out without doing anything improper.

No warrior should go into a battle unarmed. Your success in resisting temptation will be greatly enhanced if you take some weapons with you, weapons such as cards with victory scriptures printed on them. (This principle of spiritual defense is explained in Appendix B.) If you pray honestly before entering your battleground and read your scripture cards while you are there, it will be almost impossible to fall, (see Jude 1:24; Helaman 5:12; D&C 50:44; Moses 7:53.)

By faithfully applying this seven-point formula a person is allowing the Savior to be a partner in the battle. The result will be that instead of personal weaknesses placing barriers between the person and Heavenly Father as they used to do, they will actually lead to a closer relationship to the Lord than ever before. There will be no fear in going to bed. You will enter your bedroom with a confidence based upon faith in the Savior. "When thou liest down, thou shalt not be afraid: yea, thou shalt lie down, and thy sleep shall be sweet . . . for the Lord shall be thy confidence." (Proverbs 3:24, 26; see also Psalms 4:8)

These seven steps have proven effective in breaking the *physical* cycles of masturbation when the *spiritual* principles taught in the body of this book are also applied. Experience has shown, however, that people are not able to implement these seven steps until they are willing to abandon their pride and self-sufficiency. It hurts to be this open and honest about our weaknesses. This is one of the reasons no one can be saved without offering the sacrifice of a "broken heart and contrite spirit" (2 Nephi 2:7). It does break the heart to have to rely on the Lord night after night to be delivered from our habits. We want so badly to do it all by ourselves. But he never promised to save the arrogant person who either denies the reality of his sin or who believes he can resist every temptation by himself. Thankfully, he did promise not to judge or condemn us for weaknesses we are trying to conquer, (see John 6:37; 1 Nephi 1:14; D&C 6:35; 38:14; 101:9.) And he did say, "my grace is sufficient for all men that humble themselves before me; for if they humble themselves before me, and have faith in me, *then will*

I make weak things become strong unto them" (Ether 12:27). As remarkable and unreachable as it may seem to the addicted person, conquering the habit of masturbation can, with the Lord's help, lead one into such a strong bond of faith and fellowship with Deity that overcoming this weakness will indeed lead the person into great spiritual strength.

It is important to one's self-confidence to realize that no matter how great the determination is to break free from compulsive masturbation, there are likely to be occasional relapses. You should not panic when this happens because it is a normal part of growth and change. The demons hope that when you slip you will sink into despair, condemn yourself, and doubt the principles of spiritual warfare. You must not let them defeat you with feelings of self-condemnation and guilt. An occasional mistake while one is healing is not the same as deliberately choosing the evil way. If you are determined to defeat Satan and persist in your efforts to apply the principles taught in this book, your relapses will grow further and further apart until total victory is achieved. As President Kimball counseled:

> Being a god in embryo with the seeds of godhood neatly tucked away in him, and with the power to become a god eventually, man need not despair. He should not give up. If he has had problems and slipped ... from the path of rectitude and right, he must stop in his headlong slipping and turn and transform himself. He must begin again. If he slips, he must regain his footing and protect himself from further slipping and return to the sin no more. *If in his weakness he fails time and time again, he still should not despair but should make each new effort stronger than the last.* (*The Miracle of Forgiveness*, 173–74)

Appendix B

The purpose of this appendix is to learn how to change theological principles into spiritual weapons. We will discuss one of many methods for obtaining the faith in Christ that will enable us to protect ourselves with a strong, tough armor that can withstand Satan's most intensive attacks. To do this we must learn how to *digest* and *apply* certain parts of the scriptures. This appendix will explain a simple, proven process by which any person can gain the benefits of the victory principles and promises necessary to successfully overcome Satan on the various battlegrounds we have discussed.

We have been asked to read the Book of Mormon at least once a year, in addition to reading the other books of scripture regularly. We are under commandment not only to *read* the scriptures, but also to *search* them, which implies the fact that there are nuggets of truth spread throughout the centuries of revelation which must be *found* and collected as spiritual treasures. Reading and searching are vital to spiritual growth but are insufficient, by themselves, to guarantee victory over the Satanic threats we must encounter throughout mortality. Before the scriptures can have a serious effect on our behavior patterns they must be *internalized*, so that our brains are trained to respond *instinctively* to challenges in terms of scriptural principles and promises. Scriptures describe the process of internalization as "laying hold" and "holding fast" to the word of God. In Lehi's vision of the Tree of Life he saw a rod of iron which represented the word of God. All those who clung to the rod were enabled to pass through the mists of darkness, or

273

deceiving temptations, of the devil, and reach their Heavenly Father's love. Nephi interpreted his father's dream to mean that:

> Whoso would hearken unto the word of God, and would *hold fast unto it,* they would never perish; neither could the temptations and the fiery darts of the adversary overpower them unto blindness, to lead them away to destruction. (1 Nephi 15:24)

"Holding fast" to the word of God means a lot more than occasional reading. It means *internalizing* it, making it a part of the very fiber of our beings. The blessings promised for "holding fast" are priceless: Satan will be unable to deceive us, unable to overpower us with temptation or to lead us into destruction. As the Savior said, "If ye abide in me, *and my words abide in you,* ye shall ask what ye will, *and it shall be done unto you*" (John 15:7). Mormon emphasized similar blessings:

> Yea, we see that whosoever will may *lay hold* upon the word of God, which is quick and powerful, which shall divide asunder all the cunning and the snares and the wiles of the devil, and lead the man of Christ in a strait and narrow course across that everlasting gulf of misery which is prepared to engulf the wicked—
>
> And land their souls, yea, their immortal souls, at the right hand of God in the kingdom of heaven, to sit down with Abraham, and Isaac, and with Jacob, and with all our holy fathers, to go no more out. (Helaman 3:29–30)

The words "hold fast" and "lay hold" present the key to protecting ourselves with the armor of God. We have in the promises of these two revelations both the *goal* of this book, to win every battle with Satan, and the *key* for winning that victory, *internalizing* the scriptural promises until they literally *abide* in our conscious focus of attention. This is the most direct route I know of to obtaining the faith and spiritual armor we need to protect ourselves and win our battles. Paul advised us to seek that state of spirituality wherein the words of God are "written not with ink, but with the Spirit of the living God; not in tables of stone, but *in the fleshy tables of the heart*" (2 Corinthians 3:3). To accomplish this requires repetition—frequent and continual repetition. Over and over we must run the promises through our minds until that spiritual current, as it were, reprograms or repolarizes our thought patterns so that the brain is prepared to accept a new way of thinking about our problems and our faith in Christ's power to solve those problems.

> Thy word have I hid in mine heart that I might not sin against thee. (Psalms 119:11)

One way to "lay hold" on the promises of deliverance is to *mark* them in our scriptures and then review them frequently. I strongly recommend this as a starting point in the process, but I admit that it has serious limitations, such as the time required in turning the pages and searching for the highlights we have previously marked, and the fact that this method can only be used at a time and location when we can sit down with the scriptures.

Another way to "hold fast" to the promises is to memorize them and then repeat the verses to ourselves frequently. This too is a valuable process, but most people find it difficult and slow. If we are to take the offensive in the war against Satan, we must move forward against him with speed and organized, channeled power. I have found that I am able to digest and internalize hundreds of victory promises by placing them on 3 x 5 cards which I can carry with me each day to review during spare moments, like waiting at a stoplight or while on hold on the telephone, walking down a hall at work or while eating lunch, etc. This way I am feeding my mind spiritual input throughout the day by internalizing the life-changing promises I need to win my battles with Satan. The Savior said, "I will put my laws into their hearts, *and in their minds will I write them*" (Hebrews 10:16). Using the 3 x 5 cards to internalize the promises is one way to make it possible for the Lord to accomplish this goal. And by helping the Savior to actually imprint his scriptural promises in the very fiber of our brains and hearts, we not only surround ourselves with protective armor, but gain the faith and power to win our battles as we digest his precious promises.

Some people make extra copies of their favorite scripture cards to post on bathroom mirrors, refrigerators, above their kitchen sinks, and so on. But the most effective way to use the cards is to take some with you to review throughout the day. It only takes a few seconds to review one scripture. Then shuffle it to the bottom of the stack so that a new verse is ready for the next opportunity to look at the cards. Try to review twenty or thirty cards several times a day. Then, when you get home, rotate those cards to the bottom of your collection and take new cards to review the next day. You will experience great change and progress if you will do this day after day, month after month, until these wonderful promises have worn a path in your brain, establishing new thought patterns, overcoming doubts and fears, and making you more receptive to the influence of the Holy Spirit.

It is essential to have a correct understanding of the kind of verses we need to search for, mark in our scriptures, and then memorize or put on 3 x 5 cards. Jesus said, "And ye shall know the truth, and the truth shall make you free" (John 8:32). Which truths will set us free from our individual bad habits and addictions? We must think about these words carefully because all scriptures are not of equal value. For example, while it is interesting and informative to study the scriptures which Moses recorded pertaining to animal sacrifices, we will probably achieve far greater progress by studying the revelations pertaining to the Savior's Atonement and our resulting responsibilities. Some scriptures present history or genealogy; some teach administrative procedures; some contain "do and don't" commandments. Thus, while all scripture is valuable, some revelations have greater relevance to winning our battles than others do.

There are two thousand, four hundred and seventy-six pages of revelation in the current edition of LDS scriptures. On which of those pages will we find the specific promises and principles we need to fight our individual battles with Satan? Is it any wonder that the Lord said: "A commandment I give unto you that ye search these things diligently" (3 Nephi 23:1). Paul said that one should "study to shew thyself approved unto God, a workman that needeth not to be ashamed, *rightly dividing the word of truth*" (2 Timothy 2:15). Of course there is wisdom in reading all books of scripture from cover to cover on a repeating, rotating basis. But I think that "rightly dividing the words of truth" means focusing the majority of attention on the scriptures which present the principles of Spiritual warfare and the promises of the grace and enabling power of Jesus Christ to liberate and change our lives.

As we search the scriptures, we ask Heavenly Father to send the Holy Ghost to inspire us to recognize the important verses. Every principle of power, liberation, grace, and divine intervention that we can find in the scriptures—and in the words of the prophets—can be put on 3 x 5 cards. Then, as we read them over and over, we are "laying hold" on them as we build a resource of spiritual ammunition through repetition. The following scriptures represent the *kind* of verses I feel we should be training our minds to focus on.

> Behold, I say unto you, that you must rely upon my word. (D&C 17:1)

> The Lord knoweth how to deliver the godly out of temptations. (2 Peter 2:9)

> I can do all things through Christ which strengtheneth me. (Philippians 4:13)

> But thanks be to God, which giveth us the victory through our Lord Jesus Christ. (1 Corinthians 15:57)

> For I am able to make you holy. (D&C 60:7)

> For verily, I say unto you, I will that ye should overcome the world; wherefore I will have compassion upon you. (D&C 64:2)

> The kingdom is given you of the Father, and power to overcome all things which are not ordained of him. (D&C 50:35)

> Yea, and how is it that ye have forgotten that the Lord is able to do all things according to his will, for the children of men, if it so be that they exercise faith in him? Wherefore, let us be faithful to him. (1 Nephi 7:12)

> Verily, verily, I say unto you, even as you desire of me so it shall be done unto you. (D&C 11:8)

> I will fight your battles. (D&C 105:14)

> For the Lord your God is he that goeth with you, to fight for you against your enemies, to save you. (Deuteronomy 20:4)

The scriptures contain hundreds of power verses like these. Each new verse we find and internalize is like another weapon for our battles with Satan. It is highly unlikely that a person could run these kinds of promises through his mind over and over, day after day and not be changed, because faith grows every time we "hear" the word of God (see Romans 10:17). Cycling the promises through the brain over and over will drive away the old failure programming. As we plant God's power promises in our conscious and subconscious minds, we find our behavioral responses to temptations and discouragements becoming almost instinctive in achieving victory instead of defeat. Because we have literally saturated our thoughts with Christ's promises of deliverance, when times of temptation or discouragement invade, instead of being pulled back into cycles of defeat (which years of struggle and failure have programmed our *old* thought patterns to act out), our spiritually polarized minds will be armed with truths of deliverance and will work *for* us instead of against us. Our temptations and old patterns of thought cannot withstand the accumulated power of these kinds of promises when we actually "lay hold" on them and keep them in the focus of our attention. If we are not presently gaining the victory over our temptations, weaknesses and bad habits, one of the likely reasons is that there is something lacking in our application of the appropriate gospel truths. At the end of this appendix, I will provide a list of some of the verses you could use to start your arsenal of scriptural weapons.

Some people feel that the daily, repetitive use of 3 x 5 cards is fanatical, extreme, and unnecessary. Certainly the use of these cards is not a mandatory requirement for admission to the celestial kingdom. But digesting and applying scripture is, and using 3 x 5 cards is one good way to accomplish this. It is my conviction that a person who thinks he can achieve holiness, spirituality, and spiritual strength without a close relationship with the scriptures is deceiving himself. And Satan will surely be pleased with that delusion. For some reason, many people cannot see the connection between the change of their self-defeating behavior patterns and teaching their minds to build a mighty faith in Jesus Christ. The Lord has warned, "Wo be unto him that shall say: We have received the word of God, and we need no more of the word of God, for we have enough!" (2 Nephi 28:29) Who could possibly remember and internalize "enough" of God's promises by merely reading them occasionally? Unfortunately, some people make twenty or thirty scripture cards, review them halfheartedly for a couple of weeks and then defeat their purpose by giving up. No one can coast his way into the celestial kingdom. It takes a lot of effort to become the kind of person who would enjoy living there. It is not reasonable to think that we can undo years of failure patterns with just a few simple repetitions of scripture. "Therefore we ought to give the more earnest heed to the things which we have heard, lest at any time we should let them slip" (Hebrews 2:1).

One way to think about these mental deposits of scripture is to compare them to making deposits in a bank account. The more financial resources we have on deposit, the more secure we feel. It is not a very pleasant experience to have a financial need and find the checkbook empty. If we want to have the money available when our bills come due, we have to make the deposits ahead of time. And so it is spiritually. If we use a small part of each day to nourish our spirits by making deposits of divine promises and principles, then when the times of discouragement, temptation, and adversity come, we will have the spiritual resources to draw upon and we will be victorious. Like a powerful spiritual data bank, our brains will actually bring scriptures to mind that will encourage and strengthen us. We will be conquering temptations with faith in Christ and his power. Our spiritually polarized brains will be *repelling* Satan's evil enticements and *attracting* the power of the Spirit into our lives. "Thy words have upholden him that was falling" (Job 4:4). Again we are reminded of the spiritual formulas from Chapter 20: The more we cling to the word of God, the more we hold fast and internalize it, the more intimately we will know and remember and be able to claim the promises as our own.

Now it would be wonderful to go to the bank tomorrow and deposit $10,000, but for most of us, the only way we will ever have that sum in the bank is to accumulate it through a lot of small deposits over time. It is the same spiritually. We can't say a couple of prayers and read a couple of pages of scripture and then feel that we have deposited all the resources we'll ever need. We have to do it steadily, daily, over weeks, months, and years.

If circumstances in your past have led you to surrender to temptations, if you have sometimes felt confused and blind to the way out of your failures, if you have tried hard to win your battles but seen your efforts destroyed by weakness, if you feel the need to develop a powerful faith in Christ, try the 3 x 5 card method of "laying hold" on the word of God. Please believe that no matter how weak you are at the present moment, you *do* have the strength to make some cards and read them several times each day. Each new card added to your arsenal, each new promise found and made yours by repetition will add to the strength of your spiritual armor. Test the Lord and his promises. Open the door to his power by internalizing the victory scriptures. Make your personal set of 3 x 5 weapons and then make them a part of your daily life.

The list of scriptures which follows on page 267 is the result of fourteen years of research. It is one of my most prized possessions. I hope you will find value in it as well. As you study the verses listed, analyze each one prayerfully. See if you can identify the principles or promises they contain that will increase your faith, protect you with the armor of God and increase your ability to draw upon the power of Jesus Christ as you fight your battles with Satan. Don't be overwhelmed by the size of the list. You will find that recording each verse, or the portion of the verse that means the most to you will be an exciting adventure. Your appreciation will grow even more as you then use the cards to nourish your mind and begin to feel the effects they have on your faith and confidence.

With practice and prayerful study, you will soon discover relationships between verses that supplement or reinforce each other. You will find additional joy by combining them on one card. For example, when we combine the following three extracts onto one card, we obtain an even greater reinforcement to faith in the Savior's acceptance than we would experience from each verse independently.

Draw near unto me and I will draw near unto you. (D&C 88:63)

Return unto me and I will return unto you, saith the Lord of hosts. (3 Nephi 24:7)

Him that cometh to me I will in no wise cast out. (John 6:37)

Don't worry if you have difficulty memorizing scriptures. At the beginning of this strategy you can internalize dozens and even hundreds of promises simply by reading them over and over as you affirm your faith in what they say.

The list is not meant to be a complete resource of promises and principles. It is only meant to provide a starting point for your own searching. If you will study the footnotes and cross references provided in the standard works for each of these verses, you can quickly expand your resources and have the joy of discovering your own spiritual treasures. And then, as you read and search the scriptures through the coming years, pray for inspiration to recognize the power verses. Every time you find a promise which the Holy Ghost whispers is important, put it on a 3 x 5 card and "lay hold" on it by frequent repetition.

START YOUR 3 X 5 ARSENAL WITH THESE VERSES

Gen. 15:1	Job 34:21	Ps. 118:8	Isa. 55:11
Gen. 18:14		Ps. 119:9	Isa. 56:2
	Ps. 3:3	Ps. 119:11	Isa. 59:1–2
Ex. 15:3	Ps. 5:12	Ps. 119:16	Isa. 66:13
	Ps. 10:4	Ps. 119:114	
Lev. 26:7–8	Ps. 18:35	Ps. 132:4–5	Jer. 1:8
	Ps. 22:19	Ps. 139:11–12	Jer. 3:22
Numb. 32:23	Ps. 23:1	Ps. 141:1	Jer. 15:20
	Ps. 23:3	Ps. 145:8	Jer. 32:17
Deut. 1:30	Ps. 28:7		Jer. 32:27
Deut. 3:22	Ps. 29:2	Prov. 1:10	
Deut. 4:29	Ps. 29:11	Prov. 3:24–26	Lam. 3:22
Deut. 8:11	Ps. 31:9	Prov. 5:21	
Deut. 20:4	Ps. 32:1	Prov. 6:25	Ezk. 11:5
Deut. 31:8	Ps. 33:13–14	Prov. 6:32	Ezk. 18:21–22
	Ps. 34:1	Prov. 10:29	Ezk. 18:27–28
Joshua 1:8	Ps. 34:7	Prov. 15:3	Ezk. 18:30–32
	Ps. 34:18	Prov. 20:9	Ezk. 33:13
1 Sam. 14:6	Ps. 37:5	Prov. 22:3	Ezk. 33:16
1 Sam. 17:47	Ps. 40:1	Prov. 23:7	Ezk. 34:12
	Ps. 46:1	Prov. 28:13	Ezk. 34:16
2 Sam 22:3	Ps. 55:17	Prov. 30:5	
	Ps. 55:22		Dan. 9:9
1 Chr. 28:9	Ps. 63:6	Isa. 1:18	
	Ps. 66:18–20	Isa. 30:19	Joel 3:32
2 Chr. 30:9	Ps. 69:14	Isa. 38:17	
2 Chr. 32:8	Ps. 70:5	Isa. 40:29	Matt. 5:29
	Ps. 84:11	Isa. 42:6	Matt. 10:26
Neh. 4:20	Ps. 86:15	Isa. 43:25	Matt. 11:28
Neh. 9:17	Ps. 91:4	Isa. 46:11	Matt. 11:38
	Ps. 91:15	Isa. 48:17	Matt. 26:41
Job 4:4	Ps. 103:8–11	Isa. 49:14–15	Matt. 28:18
Job 11:20	Ps. 103:13	Isa. 53:4–5	
Job 23:12	Ps. 107:19	Isa. 54:10	Mark 10:27
Job 31:1	Ps. 118:6	Isa. 55:7	Mark 11:23–24

Luke 1:37	1 Cor. 6:9–10	Titus 2:12	1 Ne. 3:7
Luke 4:18	1 Cor. 6:12–13		1 Ne. 7:12
Luke 8:17	1 Cor. 6:19	Heb. 2:1–2	1 Ne. 9:6
Luke 9:23	1 Cor. 9:27	Heb. 2:17–18	1 Ne. 14:14
Luke 15:7	1 Cor. 10:13	Heb. 4:13	1 Ne. 15:24
Luke 16:13	1 Cor. 15:57	Heb. 4:15–16	1 Ne. 17:3
Luke 18:13		Heb. 7:25	1 Ne. 19:7
Luke 19:10	2 Cor. 1:3–4	Heb. 8:12	1 Ne. 22:26
	2 Cor. 2:5	Heb. 12:1–2	
John 1:12	2 Cor. 2:14		2 Ne. 1:23
John 3:16–17	2 Cor. 5:17	James 1:2–4	2 Ne. 2:7–8
John 6:37	2 Cor. 8:12	James 1:8	2 Ne. 2:18
John 8:34	2 Cor. 9:6	James 1:12–14	2 Ne. 2:27
John 14:23–24	2 Cor. 9:8	James 4:1	2 Ne. 4:16
John 15:1	2 Cor. 10:3–5	James 4:3	2 Ne. 4:27
John 15:4–5	2 Cor. 12:9–10	James 4:7–8	2 Ne. 7:7
John 15:7			2 Ne. 9:21
	Gal. 1:4	1 Pet. 2:11	2 Ne. 9:39
Acts 15:29	Gal. 2:20	1 Pet. 3:18	2 Ne. 10:16–17
	Gal. 5:16–17	1 Pet. 5:7–8	2 Ne. 10:20
Rom. 4:7	Gal. 5:24		2 Ne. 10:24
Rom. 5:6	Gal. 6:7–9	2 Pet. 2:9	2 Ne. 25:23
Rom. 6:12–13		2 Pet. 3:9	2 Ne. 25:26
Rom. 6:16	Eph. 3:20		2 Ne. 26:24–28
Rom. 8:1	Eph. 6:12	1 Jn. 1:9	2 Ne. 26:33
Rom. 8:5–8	Eph. 6:16	1 Jn. 2:1	2 Ne. 27:23
Rom. 8:28		1 Jn. 2:15–17	2 Ne. 27:27
Rom. 8:35, 37	Phil. 2:5	1 Jn. 4:4	2 Ne. 28:21–22
Rom. 10:17	Phil. 4:6	1 Jn. 5:12	2 Ne. 28:32
Rom. 12:1–2	Phil. 4:13	1 Jn. 5:14	2 Ne. 31:16
Rom. 13:14	Phil. 4:19		2 Ne. 31:20
Rom. 14:22		Jude 1:8	
Rom. 15:4	1 Thes. 4:3–4	Jude 1:21	Jac. 1:7–8
		Jude 1:24	Jac. 3:1
1 Cor. 2:5	1 Tim. 1:15		Jac. 4:6–7
1 Cor. 3:11		1 Ne. 1:14	
1 Cor. 3:16–17	2 Tim. 3:17	1 Ne. 1:20	Omni 1:26

Mosiah 3:7	Alma 26:12	3 Ne. 14:24–25	D&C 11:19
Mosiah 3:19	Alma 26:16–17	3 Ne. 18:15	D&C 17:1
Mosiah 4:2	Alma 26:27	3 Ne. 18:18	D&C 17:8
Mosiah 4:11	Alma 26:35	3 Ne. 24:7	D&C 18:3
Mosiah 4:27	Alma 26:37	3 Ne. 24:16	
Mosiah 5:2	Alma 29:4	3 Ne. 27:18	D&C 20:33
Mosiah 5:12–13	Alma 33:8	3 Ne. 17:20	D&C 21:6
Mosiah 7:30	Alma 33:11	3 Ne. 27:27	D&C 24:8
Mosiah 7:33	Alma 33:16	3 Ne. 28:35	D&C 27:14
Mosiah 16:5	Alma 34:38		D&C 19:1
Mosiah 24:15	Alma 34:40–41	Morm. 9:3	D&C 19:30
Mosiah 26:22	Alma 36:3	Morm. 9:9	
Mosiah 26:30	Alma 37:33	Morm. 9:21	D&C 31:13
Mosiah 27:30	Alma 37:36–37	Morm. 9:25	D&C 32:3
Mosiah 29:20	Alma 37:44–45	Morm. 9:27–28	D&C 35:8
	Alma 38:5		D&C 35:14
Alma 5:7	Alma 39:8–9	Moro. 6:8	D&C 38:7
Alma 5:12–13	Alma 41:8–9	Moro. 7:9	D&C 38:14
Alma 5:19–20	Alma 42:29–30	Moro. 7:12	D&C 38:31
Alma 5:33	Alma 44:4	Moro. 7:33	
Alma 5:53	Alma 50:19	Moro. 9:6	D&C 43:34
Alma 5:57		Moro. 10:7	D&C 46:33
Alma 7:8	Hel. 3:27–28	Moro. 10:22	D&C 49:27
Alma 7:11–15	Hel. 3:29–30	Moro. 10:32–33	
Alma 7:21	Hel. 4:24–25		D&C 50: 2–3
Alma 7:23	Hel. 5:12	D&C 1:3	D&C 50:16
Alma 9:17	Hel. 7:16	D&C 1:31–32	D&C 50:35
Alma 9:26	Hel. 12:23	D&C 1:38	D&C 50:44
Alma 10:25	Hel. 13:11	D&C 3:4	D&C 58:42–43
Alma 12:5	Hel. 13:13	D&C 3:8	D&C 59:6
Alma 12:15	Hel. 13:37–38	D&C 6:20	
Alma 13:28	Hel. 14:13	D&C 6:34–37	D&C 60:7
Alma 18:31–32	Hel. 15:7		D&C 61:2
Alma 19:33		D&C 10:4–5	D&C 61:18
Alma 19:36	3 Ne. 2:2	D&C 10:27	D&C 61:36
Alma 22:14	3 Ne. 9:14	D&C 10:70	D&C 61:38
Alma 24:10	3 Ne. 9:22	D&C 11:8	D&C 62:1

D&C 62:9	D&C 82:10	D&C 100:15	D&C 121:45
D&C 63:16	D&C 84:43–44	D&C 101:7	D&C 123:17
D&C 63:66	D&C 84:88	D&C 101:9	D&C 128:22
D&C 64:2	D&C 88:63	D&C 101:37–38	
D&C 64:31–32	D&C 88:83	D&C 103:17	D&C 132:5
D&C 66:8	D&C 88:86	D&C 104:36	D&C 133:53
D&C 67:3	D&C 88:126	D&C 104:82	D&C 136:19
D&C 67:13–14		D&C 105:14	D&C 136:22
D&C 68:6	D&C 90:5	D&C 108:8	
	D&C 90:24	D&C 109:25–26	Moses 4:30
D&C 76:5	D&C 93:17	D&C 109:44	Moses 7:26
D&C 76:41	D&C 93:49	D&C 109:53	Moses 7:53
D&C 78:18	D&C 93:52		
	D&C 95:1	D&C 110:5	Abr. 3:17
D&C 82:5	D&C 97:8	D&C 111:11	
D&C 82:7	D&C 98:11		

Index

A

Accountability: 42–43

Addictions: Relationship to demon possession, 92–100; Result of mental "polarity" and focus of attention, 55, 59–61, 147, 180, 182; Through Christ all a. can be overcome, 175, 180–83; An additional path to overcoming is through family history and temple work, 240–262; Family history protects us from Satan, 258–60

Adultery: Flirting a prelude to a., 128; Mental a, see Pornography; No circumstance justifies a., 126; Progressive steps toward, 126–28; Second only to murder, 103–04, 122; Weapon against marriage and family, 125, 128

Agency: Can be forfeited to Satan, 97–100; Controlled by Satan like puppets and robots, 96; Satan seeks to destroy, 5–6, 42, 93–94; see also: Possession

Ancestors: Allowed to help us when we do temple and family history service, 260–61

Angels: Lord sends to help us, 24–25; Temple service activates angelic protections, 253

Armed with Divine Power: Through temple service, 240, 253–55

Armed with Righteousness: 237, 240–62; Temple covenants endow with divine power, 248; Foreseen by Nephi, 248

Armor: A. is internal, not physical or external, 222; Effectiveness dependent upon relationship to God and scriptures, 153–54, 222, 226–27; How to create strong, invincible a., 273–81; see also: Formulas, Spiritual; Armor of God; Armor of Righteousness

Armor of God: Symbolized and fortified by the temple garment, 245–48

Armor of Righteousness: Family history work an essential part of, 259; Symbolized and fortified by the temple garment, 245–48

Attention: "What holds my attention holds me," 53–54, 60, 122, 132, 139, 143, 152, 155, 158, 166, 185, 226; Our a. to family history and temple service provide "more of a protection" than any other work we can do, 243–44, 258–59; see also: Focus of Attention

Avoid Temptations: See Prevention

Aware: We need to be a. of Satan, xvii–xx, 14, 18, 21, 26, 28, 40–42, 92, 107, 143, 149, 263

B

Bank Deposits: Compared to building faith, 279

Barriers: Satan tries to place b. between us and God, 164; Self-imposed by unrealistic expectations, 190

Battles: Christ will help fight, 277; Most intense within our minds, 52–53; Win by changing thought patterns, 273–81; Power to overcome comes through faithful temple and family history service, 240, 243–44, 253–55; Temple and family history work provide "more of a protection" than any other work we can do, 243–44, 258–59

Behavior Modification: Contrasted with change of nature, 53–55, 99, 121–22, 131–32, 134–35, 166, 176–78, 203–05, 273, 278

Bicycle: Example of God's promises always work, 232–33

Blessings: "Even greater" b. given for temple and family history service, 257–61; Only half limitation, 256; Our personal temple and family history blessings extend to our families, 244–45, 256–58, 260

Blindfolded: xvii, 39, 45, 263

Blueprints: Our thoughts are b. of future reality, 53, 112, 185

Breastplate of Righteousness: 86–87, 149, 222; Christ himself used, 86; How to create a powerful b., 273–81

Bunny Rabbit Rescue: Symbol of God's desire to rescue us, 211–13

C

Camera, Example of promises always work, 233

Captives to Satan: See Possession by Demons

Change: God says we can, Satan says we can't, 162, 175–76, 179, 183, 213; Never too late to c., 180–81; Requires time, 180–81; The starting point of c. is willingness, 178–80

Change of Nature: Contrasted with behavior modification, 53–55, 99, 121–22, 131–32, 134–35, 166, 176–78, 203–05, 273, 278

Chastity: Defined, 104, 124–25; Laws of c. will never change, 107–08

Christ: Always "The Way" out of difficulty, 179, 202–03; Aware of our every thought, 57; God of the present, 186–87; God of the impossible, 216–17; His example of honest prayer in Gethsemane, 66–68; His mission to provide comfort and deliver the captives, 213, 264; His power not restricted by circumstances, 218–20; Is "able" to do anything required, 217–18; No human condition he does not understand, 89, 218; Partnership with C., 137, 149; Understands our temptations and weaknesses, 88–90: Used scripture to defeat temptation, 153; Will be our personal shield, 156–57

Circumstances: Never limit God's power, 218–20, 232

Confession: Contrasted with admission, 172; Lack of c. like spiritual cancer, 170; Repentance incomplete without, 170–73: Satan seeks to prevent, 172–73

Confirm: God wants to c. his promises, 236

Control: Outward c. contrasted with real change, 176–78

Conversion: Greater c. a reward for family history service, 258–59

Covenants: Blessings we receive for family history service and keeping our temple c. extend to our families, 244–45, 249, 256–58, 260; Keeping temple c. should be part of our ultimate earthly goal and supreme mortal experience, 245; Not restrictive but protective and empowering, 248–50; Renewed during the sacrament, 249

Cycles of Defeat: Evidence of faulty relationship with Christ, 31, 94, 97–100, 146–47, 204, 207–08, 278; Overcome by changing thought patterns, 273–81; A person can live an ordinary life and still be faithful to their covenants, 250; see also Relapses

D

Decisions: Deciding ahead of time, 144–45; see also: Prevention

Delay: One of Satan's strategies, 64, 70, 168–69, 172, 181; Procrastination diminishes ability, 168–69; Why answers to prayer are delayed, 71–74, 235–36

Demon Possession: 92–97, 106; Relationship to addictions, 92–100

Dependence: Divine d. only path to true Independence, 177, 202–204, 207

Desires: Can compensate for inadequacies, 196–97; Control our choices and priorities, 86, 144–45; Major target of Satan, 86

Divine Nature: Don't feel guilty about imperfections, 250; Temple service helps us attain, 243; see also Perfect, Perfectionism

Drowned: D. girl beneath houseboat illustrates divine rescues, 264–65; D. missionary illustrates "whispered" communication to our spirits, 26–28; see also: Whispering

E

Electromagnet: Compared to mental function, 59–61, 147, 226–27; How to repolarize the mind, 273–81

Emotions: Satan's power to manipulate, 30–31, 37–39

F

Failures: Failing does not make us f., 184

Faith: Developing f. compared to bank deposits, 279: Focus on Christ, 148–49, 150, 153, 177, 202–03, 213, 235; How to create powerful f., 273–81; How to use f. as a shield, 149–50; Our f. proportionate to our relationship with scriptures, 226; Rely upon shield of faith "above all," 149

Family: Increased temple service softens bad feelings toward f., 254–55, 259–60; Our personal temple and family history blessings extend to our f., 244–45, 249, 256–58, 260

Family History: 240, 256–62; Entitles and authorizes help from ancestors, 260–61; No longer requires being an expert, 257; Perfection impossible without family history service, 257–59; Protects us from Satan, 258–59; Provides access to greater blessings, 257; Strengthens and heals family relationships, 254–55, 259; Strengthens our conversion and testimony, 258–59; Temple and F.H. work provide "more of a protection" than any other work we can do, 243–44, 258–59

Father: Receives revelation for his family in the temple, 244–45

Flirting with Temptation: 174; Don't create unnecessary t., 142–44

Focus of Attention: Determines emotions, priorities, choices and actions, 52–53; "Hold fast" to victory scriptures, 273–77; In keeping score, 158–61; Like blueprints of our future realities, 53, 95, 112; More important than will power, 53–54; Needs to center on Christ, not failures, 54, 60; Self-defeat and addiction from negative, 59–60, 112; We cannot fix the present when focused on the past, 122, 185; see also: Attention; Pornography

Force: Satan cannot f. us, xx, 56, 87, 90–91, 96–97, 100–02

Formulas, Spiritual: Devotion to or neglect of scriptures, 225–27; How to apply f. for victory, 273–81

Fornication: A persuasive Satanic weapon, 122–25; Second only to murder, 103–04

Forsaking: Repentance requires total abandonment, 167–68

G

Garment, Temple: 245–48; Casual regard diminishes blessings, 247–48; Reminder of temple covenants, 247; Symbolizes the armor of God and armor of righteousness, 245, 247

Godly Sorrow: Contrasted with worldly sorrow, 165–66; Twisted into self-loathing, 186; see also: Guilt

Going: Positive repentance means moving forward, 166–67

Gradual Temptations: Too small to be noticed, 44–45, 84, 109–110, 112

Guidance: A father receives personal revelation in temple, 244-45; The temple is a place to receive personal revelation, 250-53

Guilt: Christ felt our g., 66–67, 68; Not always appropriate, 55–56; Repeated sin can dull the conscience, 106; Unrepentant g. self-destructive, 170, 265; Used as a Satanic weapon, 64, 76, 138–39, 164, 185, 272; see also: Godly Sorrow

H

Habits: Result of improper focus, 54; Satan uses to his advantage, 85–86, 112; see also: Behavior Modification, New Creature, Transformation

Half the Blessings: Our temple blessings reduced because of not doing family history for our own ancestors, 256

Healing, Spiritual: Through temple service, 254–55, 259

Helmet of Salvation: Christ Himself used, 52; Protection against Satanic "whisperings," 38–39, 56–61, 222; see also: Thoughts

Help: H. from ancestors entitled and authorized through temple and family history service, 260–61

Hidden: No sin can be h. or secret, 79–82

Holy Ghost: Companionship dependent upon our relationship with scriptures, 223–34; Driven away by use of pornography, 114; Protection against Satan, 102

Homosexuality: A deceptive Satanic substitute for virtue, 129–38; A spiritual issue more than behavioral, 131, 134; An addictive substitute for love that leads to "spiritual oblivion," 129–30; Causes and origins irrelevant to healing, 130–33, 136; Clean again, 140–41; H. desires never justify acting out, 135–36; Healing possible through Christ and His Atonement,135–38; Satan's false justifications, 133–34; H. are loved by God, 138–40

House: Symbol of separation between spirit and body, 146

Hunger: For spiritual nourishment, 223; To do what is right, 224

I

Imagination: Dangers of, 56–57, 95; Positive power of, 157

Immorality: A form of stealing, 108–09; Desires or predisposition no justification, 134; Satan's favorite weapon, 106

Independence: Only when fully dependent upon Christ, 203

Internalize: How to saturate thought patterns, 278; Key to victory, 273–74; Scriptural promises need to be digested, 228, 273; Wearing a path in the brain cells, 276

It Is Not Worth It: 146–48

J

Janae: Receives miraculous comfort, strengthening and relationship healings through increased temple attendance, 254–55

K

Keeping Score: 158–61

L

Laughter: Satan laughs at our follies and suffering, 22, 31, 47–50, 96, 146, 148

Line: Between God and Satan, 75–76, 142, 162

Lucifer: Became Satan, our enemy, 3, 7

Lust: Satan's counterfeit for virtue and chastity, 107, 125

M

Marriage: Satan's attacks against, 125–26, 128

Masturbation: A powerful, addicting Satanic weapon, 117–22; An attempt to self-medicate, 121–22; Can lead to demon possession, 96; Can produce barriers or a closer relationship with God, 271; Conquering requires honest and broken heart, 271; Importance of honest prayer regarding the habit, 269–70; Satan's angels can tempt us even when we are sleeping, 268; Seven strategies for breaking the cycle, 268–70; This weakness, conquered, can be turned into a strength, 272; Two major battlegrounds are bedroom and bathroom, 268; Unrepented m. will be exposed in judgment, 81–82; see also: Relapses

Matt: Example of healing and sanctification by temple service, 241–43

Memories: Christ has power to change, 115, 187–88; Harmful m. created by immorality, 109, 113; One of Satan's favorite weapons, 128, 185–88, 190; Pornographic m. indelible, 113

Mental Adultery: 112, 167, see: Pornography

Mental Programing: 146–48

Mind: Compared to electromagnet, 59–61; Compared to temple, 57–59; Compared to theatrical stage, 54–56; How to repolarize for victory, 60, 146, 273–81; Inability to eliminate unworthy thoughts and images, 57, 112–16; Most important battles fought within, 52; Polarized like an electromagnet, 59–61

Misery: Our m. is Satan's goal, 47

Missionary: Drowning, an example of subliminal whispering, 26–28

Moving Forward: Positive repentance is more than stopping, 166

Music: How to use m. as a shield, 152–53

N

Nauvoo Temple: Endowment gave pioneers strength to endure, 253–54

Necking and Petting: Forbidden by God outside of marriage, 108; Satan's weapon, 108–11; Similar to adultery, 108

Never Too Late to Change: 180–81, 216

New Birth: Dependent upon Christ, not ourselves, 54, 136, 139; Reprogram and repolarize the mind by repetition of scriptural promises, 273–77; Removes compulsive desires for evil, 147; Transformation better than behavioral control, 176–78, 180–81, 185, 213

Not Worth It: 146–48

O

Only Half the Blessings: Our temple blessings reduced because of not doing family history for our own ancestors, 256

Ordinary Life: Don't feel guilty about imperfections, 250; Temple worship improves, 240, 248–50

P

Partnership with Christ: 137, 149; Combination of our best effort and Christ's grace, 205–07; Draw upon his power by internalizing his promises, 273–81; Family history and temple service a powerful way to partner, even while striving to overcome weaknesses, 240–62

Past: Memories of past a favorite weapon of Satan, 128, 185–86, 190; Must be surrendered to move forward, 185; Rear-View Mirror, symbol of overemphasized emphasis on past, 184; To be learned from, not lived in, 122, 158, 184–88

Perfect, Perfectionism: Confusion between going fast and being valiant, 191; Even Christ had to develop incrementally, 191; Expecting too much of ourselves is self-defeating, 189, 191, 192–94; God's love not dependent upon degree of perfection, 194–97; No scriptural timetable is given, 189; Nobody becomes p. in this life, 192; Requires reasonable process of growth, 191; Satan's three p. lies: 1. "God Cannot Love You Because You Are Imperfect," 194–97; 2. "Nothing Less Than Perfection is Acceptable to God," 192–94; 3. "You Have to be Perfect Right Now," 189–92; Speed not as important as direction, 194; Don't feel guilty about imperfections, 250; Impossible without temple and family history service, 257–59; Okay to be "ordinary" as we pursue p., 250; Our life is improved with each sincere temple attendance, 240, 243

Persistence: Our need for p., 70–71; Satan is compulsively p., 10–11; Ten thousand attempts, 56

Piloted: 250–53; see also Guidance

Pioneers: Strength to endure hardships given through Nauvoo temple endowment, 253–54

Place: Faithful temple service assures a p. at Christ's right hand, 250, 255–56

Plan: God has an individual p. for each person, 251

Playground: This life is not a p., xviii

Polarized Mind: 59–61, 185; How to repolarize for victory, 61, 146, 273–79; see also: Electromagnet

Pornography: Can be overcome through the atonement, 115; Compared to filthy trash, 57; Destroys spirituality, 114; Drives away the Holy Ghost, 114; One of Satan's most addictive weapons, 111–17; The mind's inability to eliminate, 57, 112–16; Unrepentant users will be exposed, 81–82; see also: Mental Adultery, Thoughts

Possession by Demons: 93–97, 106, 169; Controlled like puppets and robots, 96; Evil imaginations and choices invite p. 95–96; Relationship to addictions, 94, 97–100; Satan's goal to possess and control our bodies, 93–94

Power: Family history builds personal spiritual power, 256–61; Keeping covenants endows with divine p., 243–44,248–49, 253; P. to overcome comes through faithful temple and family history service, 240, 243–44, 253–55

Prayer: Asking for help is a form of worship, 207; Example of Christ's p. in Gethsemane, 66–68; How to use p. as a shield, 151–52; Importance of honesty in p., 65–68; In reverse, 54; Need for freqent p., 62–63; Need for persistence and patience in p., 70–71; P. does not "bother God," 65, 70; Perfect worthiness not required, 68–69; Satan tries to prevent p., 63–64; Self-defeating p., 54; Why answers to p. are delayed, 71–74, 235–36

Prevention: P. of temptations better than struggling to overcome, 110, 117, 126, 143–44

Prisoners to Addiction: 97–100; see also: Addictions; Possession by Demons

Procrastination: Diminishes ability to repent, 168–69; One of Satan's strategies, 64, 70, 168–69, 172, 181

Promises: Accumulated power of internalized p., 273–81; Can be blocked by fear and disobedience, 233–34; Example of bicycle and camera, 232–33; "Exceeding and great" p. dependent upon temple service, 240, 243; Half forfeited by neglecting family history work, 256; God wants to confirm his p., 236; How to internalize, 273–81; Our duty and privilege to personalize and internalize, 229–31;

Protection: Family history rewards personal and family p., 243–44, 260; Our personal temple blessings, including p., extend to our families, 244–45, 249, 256–58, 260; Temple and family history work provides divine protection and power, 258–59; Temple and family history work provide "more of a protection" than any other work we can do, 243–44, 258–59; Temple service provides "protection for us in our trials and tribulations," 248–49 Temple worship covers us with a spiritual shield and protection, 243–44

Puppets: 96; see also: Possession by Demons

R

Radiator Hose Miracle: 220–21

Radio: Tuning r. an example of choosing Satan's or God's "whisperings," 39

Rear-View Mirror: Symbol of overemphasized emphasis on past, 184

Relapses: Not the same as deliberate sin, 272; Satan will use as a weapon, 162–63; 175–76; 178–79; 213; A person can live an ordinary life and still be faithful to their covenants, 250; see also: Cycles of Defeat

Repentance: A form of honoring Christ, 165–66; Applies to every person, 163–64; Best motivation for, 165–66; Christ promises acceptance of our r., 173–74; Defined, 163; Does not require self-punishment, 165; Evidence that we are progressing, 164; Requires total abandonment, 167–68; Procrastination can rob our ability to repent, 168–69; Stopping compared to going forward, 166–67; Substitutes of guilt and self-deprecation, 164

Rescue: Both from sin and carnal nature, 213: Christ's great desire to r. us, 214; Drowned girl beneath houseboat illustrates divine r., 264–65; Never against our will, 214; Result of prayer and trust, 215

Robots: 96; see also: Possession by Demons

S

Sacrament: A reminder of temple covenants, 249

Same-sex Attraction: See Homosexuality

Savior: See Christ

Satan: A dirty fighter, xvii, 15–17, 86; Accelerating his efforts, 15, 17; Attack on Moses, 9–10; Awareness of provides protection, xviii–xix, 14, 18, 21, 26, 28, 40–41, 92, 107, 263; Cannot force us, xx, 56, 87, 90–91, 97, 100–02; Drive S. away with scriptures, 153–54; Focuses his efforts on righteous, 19–21; Has over 30 billion followers, 19–20; His eternal doom described, 264; His expertise in deception and manipulation, 41–42, 44–46; "It mattereth not" lies, 42–44; Laughs at our follies and suffering, 22, 31, 47–50, 96, 146, 148; Master of contradictory attacks, 189–90; Master of imitation and illusion, 45–46, 82–84; Motivated by pride and selfishness, 5–6, 7–11; No power over us that we don't permit, xx, 56, 87, 90–91, 96–97, 100-02, 142–44, 147; Originally an angel in high authority, 3–4, 8, 13; Our misery is Satan's goal, 47; Resists our efforts to confess, 172–73; Resists our efforts to repent, 162; Seduction his greatest weapon, 44–46; Seeks the throne and place of God, 5–9; Strategies against repentance, 163; Temptations to Christ, 10–11; Tries to preoccupy us with the past, 184–88; Tries to prevent prayer, 63–64;

Tries to slander scriptural promises, 232, 235; Uses guilt to destroy us, 164; Uses mortal men and influences, 21–24; Uses subtle, gradual temptations, 44, 84, 109–110, 112; We can send him away, 148–49, 153–54; Whispers temptations and discouragements, 28–34, 55–56; His power diminished by temple and family history service, 243–45, 258; see also Protection; Whispering

Score, Keeping: 158–61

Scorpion: Illustrates Satan's lie of no change possible, 175–76

Scriptures: Examples of victory promises, 277; How to drive Satan away with s., 153–54, 273–81; How to use s. as a shield, 153–54; Internalize, "lay hold"," hold fast", "keep the sayings," 273–740; Neglect of s. handicaps our battles, 224; Not all s. of equal value, so find the victory promises, 273–77; Nourishment from a. more important than food, 223; Spiritual formulas for success, 225–27; Sword of the Spirit is word of God, 227–229; Victory or defeat dependent upon our relationship with scriptures, 216, 225–27; see also: Formulas, Spiritual

Scroll: Symbol of judgment revelations, 81–82

Secret: No sin ever hidden or s., 79–82

Seen Realities: Don't allow them to limit your faith, 219–21

Self-Condemnation: Do not confuse with repentance, 185, 190, 196; Just for being tempted, 78–79; Refusing to forgive ourselves, 185–86, 190; Result of preoccupation with past, 186; Tool of Satan, 139, 265, 272

Self-Defeating: Emotions, Satan encourages, 30; Excessive zeal, 192–93; Focus on symptoms, 132–33; Negative thoughts, 59; Reprogram thoughts and emotions, 273–81

Self-Reliance: Contrasted with reliance on Christ, 200–10; Likened to building upon sand, while building upon Christ like unto a rock, 200–01; Substitute plan of Satan, 177, 200–04, 206;

Seminary Student: Example of revelation received by Book of Mormon symbols, 251–52

Sexual Relations: In marriage, a beautiful and divine gift, 103–05, 111, 124; Not given to mankind as an indiscriminate plaything, 106

Shield of Faith: 38, 149–50, 222; How to create powerful s., 273–81; Use shield of faith "above all," 149

Shields, Additional: Christ as our personal shield, 156–57; Commitment as a shield, 154–55; Light as a shield, 150–51; Love of God as a shield, 155–56;

Music as a shield, 152–53; Prayer as a shield, 151–52; Scriptures as a shield, 153–54

Sin: Never hidden nor secret, 79–82; Not a s. to be tempted, 76, 78–79

Sister, Janae: Receives miraculous comfort, strengthening and relationship healings through increased temple attendance, 254–55

Space Suit: Symbol of separation of spirit and body, 146

Spiritual Weapons: Examples of victory promises, 277; How to develop S. W., 273–81

Stopping: Positive repentance means moving forward, 166–67

Strategies of Defense: Decide ahead of time, 144–45; Defend yourself with eight different shields, 149–58; Don't create unnecessary temptations, 142–44; Keep positive scores, 158–61; See temptations separate from yourself, 146; Practice saying "It is not worth it," 146–48; Send Satan away, 148–49, 153–54; Use scripture to develop invincible armor, 273–81; Temple and family history work provide "more of a protection" than any other work we can do, 243–44, 258–59

Subliminal Suggestions: Saturate and program your own brain, 273–81; Whispered by both God and Satan, 26–39; see also: Whispering

Substitutes: World's self-development provides only Terrestrial help at best, 177, 203–05

Sword of the Spirit: 222, 226, An offensive weapon, 222, 227–29; How to create a powerful s., 273–81; Use to drive away Satan and temptations, 153–54, 273–81

Symbols: Lord's use in teaching, 245, 247–48, 251–52

Symptoms: 53–55, 73, 121–22, 176, 181; see also: Behavior Modification, Transformation

T

Temple: A place to remember and receive the Lord's great and precious promises, 240, 243–44; Bestows power over Satan, 243–45; Father receives personal revelation in temple, 244–45; Matt an example of healing and sanctification through temple service, 241–43; Our personal temple blessings extend to our families, 244–45, 249, 256–58, 260; Power and blessings of keeping temple covenants, 243–44,248–49, 253, President Hinckley urges to appreciate and attend the temple frequently "with all of the persuasiveness of which I am capable," 241; T. and family history work provide "more of a protection" than any other work we can do, 243–44, 258–59; T. and family history work provides divine protection and power, 258–59; T. blessings reduced because of not doing family history for our own ancestors, 256; T. service blesses us with power to overcome, 240, 243–44, 253–55; T. service provides "protection for us in our trials and tribulations," 248-49; T. worship covers us with a spiritual shield and protection, 243–44; T. worship should be our "ultimate earthly goal and the supreme mortal experience," 245; The t. a place to receive personal revelation, 250–53

Temptations: Clever and disguised, 82–84; Come from three sources, 142; Customized to our weaknesses, 85–86; Drive Satan away with scriptures, 153–54, 273–81; Don't create unnecessary t., 142–44, 168; Everyone is t., 76–77; Gradual, too small to be noticed, 44–45, 84, 109, 112; Line between right and wrong, 75–76; Major part of Christ's sufferings, 88–90; Never beyond our power to resist, 90–91, 100–02; Not a sin to be t., 76, 78–79; Prevention better than struggle, 110, 117, 126; See t. as separate from yourself, 146; T. serve necessary purpose, 77–78; The Savior understands our t., 88–90; see also: Prevention

Thoughts: Compared to electromagnet, 59–61; Compared to temple, 57–59; Compared to theatrical stage, 54–56; How to create new t. patterns, 273–77; How to drive out failure patterns, 278; Like blueprints of our future reality, 53, 112; Need for Christlike t., 58; Placed directly in our minds by both God and Satan, 26–39; Replace bad t. with good t., 56; Satan's power to manipulate t., 30–31, 37–39, 55–56; Ten thousand attempts to control bad t., 56; The mind's inability to eliminate unworthy thoughts and images, 57, 112–16; Will reward or condemn us in day of judgment, 58; Withstand t. with faith, 149

Tiffany: Bunny's rescue a symbol of God's desire to rescue us, 211–13

Tiredness: Satan uses this vulnerability against us, 64, 268

Transformation: New birth better than behavioral control, 176–78, 180–81, 185, 213; Removes compulsive desires for evil, 147–48; Reprogram and repolarize the mind by repetition of scriptural promises, 273–81

Trials and Tribulations: Strength and protection provided by temple service, 248–49; see also: Protection

V

Veil: Satan retained knowledge, we did not, xvii–xviii; Our ancestors allowed to help us when we do temple and family history work for them, 260–61

Video: Mental replay of past mistakes, 186

Virtue: More important than life, 104

W

War: Most intense battles within the mind, 52–53; Premortal w. continues, xvi, 12–17

Wavering: Not a sin, 66–68; Christ's example in Gethsemane, 66–68

Weaknesses: Temptations customized to our w., 85–86; The Savior understands our w., 88–90

Whispering: Balance between divine and Satanic w. guaranteed, 36–39; Direct communication to our spirits by both God and Satan, 26–39; Examples of divine w., 34–36; Examples of Satanic w. 28–34, 55–56, 133–34, 140–41, 162, 171–72; Illustrated by drowned missionary, 26–28; Satan tries to slander scriptural promises, 232, 235; see also: Delay

Wicked: Deliberate wickedness invites demon possession, 92–97, 99; This world the most w. of all creations, 16

Will Power: Can invite Satan to stay, 148; Christ wants to enhance, 148, 177, 270; Focuses on outward symptoms, not causes or solutions, 53, 121–22, 176–77, 204; We need more than superhuman restraint, 176–77; see also: Behavior Modification

Worthiness: Least of us are "worth worlds," 263; Our w. may change, but worth will not, 263